Childhood
Socialization

Childhood
Socialization

Norman K. Denzin
With a new introduction by the author
Revised Second Edition

Transaction Publishers
New Brunswick (U.S.A.) and London (U.K.)

Library of Congress Catalog Number: 2009044819
ISBN: 978-1-4128-1059-3
Printed in the United States of America

Library of Congress Cataloging-in-Publication Data

Denzin, Norman K.
    Childhood socialization / Norman K. Denzin.
        p. cm.
    Includes bibliographical references and index.
    ISBN 978-1-4128-1059-3 (alk. paper)
        1. Child development. 2. Socialization. I. Title.

HQ767.9.D46 2010
303.3'2--dc22

2009044819

Contents

Contents

For Johanna and Rachel

Preface

The voluminous literature on child development does not contain any serious social psychological account of the childhood socialization process. The essays collected in this volume represent one attempt to fill this void. Students of child development, cognitive growth, language acquisition, and family behavior should find, in these chapters, a new perspective and a new method for the study of the child's world. The topics of language development, social behavior, and identity acquisition are examined in turn, as are the politics of childhood. *Childhood Socialization* offers a social psychological perspective on childhood socialization experiences and proposes new directions for theory and research on this subject.

Acknowledgments

I wish to thank Howard S. Becker and Anselm Strauss for their support of this project. For their patience, I thank my wife, Evelyn, and my daughters, Johanna and Rachel. For her preparation of the manuscript for publication, I thank Catherine Daubard.

I also wish to thank the publishers who graciously have given permission to reprint in this volume some of my previously published works, including:

"The Politics of Childhood," in N. K. Denzin (Ed.), *Children and Their Caretakers* (New York: Dutton, 1973), pp. 1–16; "The Logic of Naturalistic Inquiry," *Social Forces*, 1971, *50*, 166–182; "Interaction and Language Acquisition in Early Childhood," *Word*, 1975, *27*, 445–459; "Childhood as a Conversation of Gestures," *Sociological Symposium*, 1971, *7*, 23–35; "The Genesis of Self in Early Childhood," *Sociological Quarterly*, 1972, *13*, 291–314; "Play, Games, and Interaction: The Contexts of Childhood Socialization," *Sociological Quarterly*, 1975, *16*, 458–478; "Child's Play and the Construction of Social Order," *Quest*, 1976, *26*, 48–55; "The Work of Little Children," *New Society*, 1971, *7*, 12–14; "Children and Their Caretakers," *Society*, 1971, *8*, 62–72.

Urbana, Illinois   NORMAN K. DENZIN
September 1977

Introduction to the Transaction Edition

*T*he opportunity to write a "New Introduction" to *Childhood Socialization* requires location in the contemporary literatures on children, childhood and the processes of socialization (see Bass, 2007; Cook, 2004, 2002; Freeman and Mathison, 2009; Handel; 2005; Handel, Cahill and Elkin, 2007; Thorne, 2003; Vigilant and Williamson, 2007). Much of what is taken for granted today on the global landscape was barely on the horizon in 1977: specialized children's media, home computers, virtual worlds—Webkinz, Club Penguin, kid videos, Pokémon, interactive media, video games, "Toys R Us," post-modern children. In 1977 the field of childhood socialization was in the hands of family sociologists who studied the socializing influences of family, child psychologists who theorized cognitive developmental stages, a few anthropologists of play who catalogued children's games. Children and their worlds were not the topics of inquiry.

A sociology of childhood, also known as the "new social studies of childhood" (Thornwe, 2003) emerged in the 1980s. This interdisciplinary discourse moves in several different directions at the same time. Childhood and its production, rather then children and their values, self concepts or languages, are the object of inquiry. Children are constructed in and through language, the media, and the practices of everyday life.

Shaped in part by feminism, the new social studies of childhood breaks from developmentalism, biosociology, and functionalist theories of the family and socialization. Scholars re-theorize gender and age categories, and age relations. An interactive approach to children's play and games continues to emerge. By 1998 the Sociology of Childhood became a full-fledged research section in the International Sociological Association. Sociological journals focused on children appeared, including: *Childhood: A Global Journal of Child Research*, and *Sociological Studies of Child Development*. The field went global, anthropologists, and sociologists from Latin and South America, Asia, and Europe entered the scene, and soon there were collections on postcolonial children (Cannell and Viruru, 2004), history, geography and symbolic childhoods (Cook, 2002), street children in Brazil, child prostitution, children and violence (Diversi and Moreira, 2009), studies on the social construction of childhood, children's worlds, their lives in schools and preschools (Corsaro, 1997); childhood and public life (Cahill, 1990), children as consumers (Cook, 2004).

The children we know and study today, are not the children that the field was studying in the 1970s.

This Thing Called a Child

We only know things through their representations. Nothing stands outside language. Children are social, cultural and linguistic objects, to be defined as a child is to be a child. There are many different types of children: first and third world, male, female, upper and lower class, battered, hyperactive, slow learners, abused, good and bad, white, Asian, Native American, poor and rich.

If children are social things, they are economic objects as well. In the twenty-first century children have been defined as consumers, given consumer identities, constructed as persons who have agency within a political economy. This political economy involves the representation, design, manufacture, distribution, retailing, advertising, and consumption of children's goods. This system of production incorporates and institutionalizes the child's, not the adult's perspective. This economy extends from children's literature and television to the home, daycare, school, and playground, to hospitals, malls, and other public places.

This apparatus, modifying Stuart Hall can be termed the circuit of childhood (see Hall, 1997). In this circuit objects and experiences are represented in terms of salient cultural categories associated with children and their identities, i.e., the robust baby. These childhood identities embody performative representations of family, race, gender, nation, and class. This political economy connects the sacred, moral side of childhood, with the profane market place. It does this by framing the goods of the market place in positive terms, while contending that children as consumers are persons who have the right to these objects.

Thus are born retail spaces for children in the department store, clothes, toys, games, books, and garments for toddlers, the upright child, the child 18-24 months, the grouping of clothing by age categories, markets aimed solely at children, websites for children, and so on. None of this would work without the media. The circuits of childhood connect parents to the new media. The children's new media complex creates parents who become consumers of advertised products. This allows the parent to engage in consumption practices that conform to the norms of possessive individualism endorsed by the capitalist political system. This media apparatus does everything it can to make parents (and children) think they are free agents solving problems, not commodities produced by a complex ideological apparatus.

But this is only part of the story. The media and the department stores, and the mass circulation magazines needed social science, needed theories of personhood and child development. Here I briefly elaborate a theme only recently considered in the literature, namely the complicity between monopoly, corporate, and transnational capitalism, and the human disciplines, in particular the naturalists (Darwin), the anthropologists (Wolfenstein, Mead), behaviorism (Watson), genetic psychololgy (Baldwin, Hall), the child developmentalists (Piaget, Gesell) psychiatry (Freud), and children's medicine (Spock). The scientists provided the rhetoric and ideology for a naturalized childhood, for a conception of the child as a person with agency and needs.

As I discuss in Chapter One, Darwin's 1877 *Biographical Sketch of an Infant* marks the beginning of modern genetic child psychology. This work emphasized the orderly, evolutionary relationship between the species and its expressions of intelligence and emotion. As a naturalist, Darwin objectively described the chronological stages his son moved through. Darwin argued that the human develops along two distinct levels the mental and the physical. Darwin's work set the stage for future theories linking chronological age with developmental ability and personality growth. The emergence of intelligence tests in the 1900s (Binet) joined mental age with maturational age, and age norms. The new field of child development set age norms, defining specific periods of infancy and childhood. This field was quickly entered by the psychoanalysts, child psychologists, developments, experimentalists, and Watsonian behaviorists. By 1928 every major research university had a child development laboratory.

It is no accident that the scientific study of children emerges in the period between 1870 and the turn of the century, the period between the Civil War and the beginning of World War I. Under the impetus of the industrial revolution, and the end of the Civil War, there was intense migration from the south to northern cities, and immigration from eastern and southern Europe to urban centers. Class differences became more pronounced as wealth was concentrated in the hands of a small ruling class. Demands for women's suffrage, the absence of child labor laws, and the movement of women into the labor force heightened tension in the culture.

The eugenics movement and Social Darwinism aroused fears that non-Aryan immigrants were lowering the genetic strength of the American population. Ghettos in the major urban areas filled with savage, uncivilized, barbaric, non-English speakers. Social Darwinists feared that these people and their children were undermining traditional American values and eroding the integrity of the educational system. These children had to be integrated into the culture, properly trained, properly dressed, properly mannered. The properly trained child was innocent and pure. If immigrant (and migrant) children could be lifted out of their barbarism, society as a whole could hope for redemption.

Without exception, these racist, sexist theories fitted smoothly into the Darwinian developmental theories. These theories, in turn, complimented a capitalist ideology that thrived on the survival of the fittest. The final pieces in this puzzle fell into place with the appearance of the field of advertising and market research, and the development of the modern department store.

And today, in the multiple spaces of cyber-space, we debate this legacy. In a new era of globalization and free trade, we once again find third world children in sweat shops contributing to the production of yet another version of children and their cultures of consumption. This will last as long as we insist on treating children as commodities. On this, I paraphrase Aldo Leopold (1949), who has said of the land, "We abuse the land because we regard it as a commodity belonging to us. When we see land as a community to which we belong, we may begin to use it with love and respect" (p. viii). Substitute the word childhood, for community, in the above lines. We will stop abusing children, when we stop seeing them as commodities belonging to us.

Norman K. Denzin
University of Illinois at Urbana-Champaign

March 31, 2009

References

BASS, LORETTA E. 2007. "The Sociology of Children and Youth." Pp. 140-47 in CLIFTON D. BRYANT AND DENNIS L. PECK (Eds.), *21ˢᵗ Century Sociology: A Reference Handbook*. Thousand Oaks, CA: Sage Publications.

CAHILL, SPENCER, 1990. "Childhood and Public Life: Reaffirming Biographical Divisions." *Social Problems*, 37, 3: 390-402.

CANNELLA, GAILE S., AND RADHIKA VIRURU. 2004. *Childhood and Postcolonization: Power, Education, and Contemporary Practice*. New York: Routledge.

COOK, DANIEL THOMAS. 2004. *The Commodification of Childhood*. Durham, N.C.: Duke University Press.

COOK, DANIEL THOMAS. 2002. "Introduction: Interrogating Symbolic Childhood." Pp. 1-35 in Daniel Thomas Cook (Ed). *Symbolic Childhood*. New York: Peter Lang.

CORSARO, WILLIAM A. 1997. *A Sociology of Childhood*. Thousand Oaks, CA: Sage.

DIVERSI, MARCELLO, AND CLAUDIO MOREIRA. 2009. *Betweener Talk: A Dialogue on Decolonizing Class, Knowledge Production, Praxis and Justice*. Walnut Creek: Left Coast Press.

FREEMAN, MELISSA ANDSANDRA MATHISON. 2009. *Researching Children's Experiences*. New York: Guilford Press.

HALL, STUART. 1997. "The Work of Representation." Pp. 13-64 in S. Hall (Eds.), *Representation: Cultural Representations and Signifying Practices*. London: Sage.

HANDEL, GERALD (Ed.) 2005. *Childhood Socialization*, 2/e. New Brunswick, NJ: Transaction Publishers.

HANDEL, GERALD, SPENCER CAHILL, AND FREDERICK ELKIN. 2007. *The Sociology of Childhood and Childhood Socialization*. New York: Oxford

LEOPOLD, ALDO. 1949. *A Sand County Almanac*. New York: Oxford University Press.

THORNE, BARRIE. 1993. *Gender Play*. New Brunswick, NJ: Rutgers

THORNE, BARRIE. 2003. *Bibliography on the Sociology of Childhood*. Department of Sociology, University of California, Berkeley.

VIGILANT, LEE GARTH, AND JOHN WILLIAMSON. 2007. "The Study of Socialization." Pp. 143-152 in Clifton D. Bryant and Dennis L. Peck (Eds.), *21ˢᵗ Century Sociology: A Reference Handbook*. Thousand Oaks, CA: Sage Publications.

Chapter One

Childhood Socialization: Interactionist, Historical, and Contextual Dimensions

There does not exist, nor has there ever existed, a sociology of childhood. This book represents an attempt to restore respectability and interest to this neglected field of sociological inquiry. Utilizing a symbolic interactionist perspective, the chapters in this volume examine, within a naturalistic context, the languages of children, their socialization experiences, and the emergence of their self-conceptions. These essays contend that children must be approached from the dual viewpoint of the adult caretaker and of the child. A social and socializing relationship binds these two categories of interactants into special and unique worlds of discourse and dialogue. Any account of the socialization process must probe

1

the hidden, secret, and private worlds of the child and the caretaker.

Becoming a Child

Children must be viewed as historical, cultural, political, economic, and social productions. There is nothing intrinsic to the object called "child" that makes that object more or less "childlike." Accordingly, children as they are known in current social and psychological theory may in fact be historical and cultural products of the nineteenth and twentieth centuries (see Ariès, 1962). As different historical and cultural groupings are studied, it may well be the case that current theories of child development will be forced to undergo revision, much as Malinowski's Trobriand Island tests of Freud's theories of the family forced revisions of the effect of the father figure on the socialization process.

All societies must ultimately address the following question concerning socialization: "How are the raw products of that society to be transformed into workable human objects?" On this point, Goffman (1967, pp. 44–45) has observed, "Societies everywhere, if they are to be societies, must mobilize their members as self-regulating participants in social encounters. One way of mobilizing the individual for this purpose is through ritual; he is taught to be perceptive, to have feelings attached to self and a self expressed through face, to have pride, honor and dignity, to have considerateness, to have tact and a certain amount of poise. These are some of the elements of behavior which must be built into the person if practical use is to be made of him as an interactant, and it is these elements that are referred to in part when one speaks of universal human nature."

Perceptiveness, pride, honor, dignity, and poise—those attributes that Goffman attributes to learning—arise out of the socialization process. Socialization, from the standpoint of symbolic interactionism, represents a fluid, shifting relationship between persons attempting to fit their lines of action together into some workable, interactive relationship. It is not a process that ends on the completion of adolescence, as Freud and the neo-Freudians would have it. Nor is it a structurally determined process whereby the values and goals of social systems are instilled in the child's behavior repertoires. Socialization is a never-ending process that is negotiated and potentially problematic in every interactional episode that appears between two or more individuals. It is a process that cannot be separated from the demands of social situations, from the restrictions of language, and from the self-definitions of the persons involved. This ubiquitous social process involves, as George Herbert Mead (1934) suggested, three phases or steps: (1) taking the attitude of the other; (2) arousing a line of action on the part of the other that compliments one's own attitude; (3) thereby producing a joint line of activity that brings two persons together in a common interaction sequence. Should interactants fail to accurately or correctly take one another's attitude, they will be unable to arouse a common response that will join their two separate lines of action. The term *childhood socialization*, which describes those experiences and interactive relationships that build human nature into that object and person called "child," rests on special languages, is located in special kinds of social situations, and is focused around special classes of social objects that range from the child to the caretaker and to those physical objects (including clothing) that endow the child with "human-like" qualities.

Central to the socialization process is the acquisition and use of language. It is language that provides the link between the child and the human primary group (Cooley, 1922; Mead, 1934; Markey, 1928). Unlike such recent linguistic theorists as Chomsky (1968) and unlike such psycholinguists as Slobin (1971)—who regard languages as complex systems of syntax, semantics, and morphemes, the meanings of which are lodged in underlying deep structural processes and whose transformation find expression in the speech sequences of "ideal" typical speakers—the symbolic interactionist studies languages as "conversations of gestures."

As a conversation of gestures, any language can be regarded as a community of symbols, meanings, and utterances, the use of which calls out for speaker and listener "universal" meanings or understandings. These gestures, some spoken and some not, some intended and others accidental, some understood and some misconstrued, permit interactants to take each other's attitude in social situations. The conversation has two sides: one spoken and one internalized in terms of thought. As conversationalists talk to one another, they also talk to themselves, and in this process each enters into the organization of the other's experience.

Language joins the person with the group and links the child with the caretaker. As a "conversation of gesture," language in use mediates and produces the socialization process. As the child acquires the languages of the caretaker, skills at taking the attitude of the other increase, and more complex interactional exchanges result. Children are active participants in this process, and in fact they produce their own languages and conversations of gestures that may be unique to them. Children produce their own worlds of social experience, construct private meanings of themselves, violate their caretakers' sense of morality, and often retreat into their own universes of play, games, and fantasy. By producing their own worlds of experience and discourse, children develop special ways of socializing themselves; that is, they develop their own strategies for producing interactional episodes. In so doing, they may arouse contradictory attitudes on the part of the caretaker, or they may force social "scenes" that embarrass adult onlookers.

An underlying tension exists between the worlds of the child and the worlds of the caretaker. Often viewed as incompetent interactants, children are treated "as if" their views, attitudes, games, and favored self-images were irrelevant, if not childishly irresponsible. Accordingly, the caretaker assumes the moral task of transforming this incompetent person into a properly functioning member of adult society. Daycare centers, kindergartens, and schools, with their assorted educational experts, take on the assignment of instilling proper human nature in this object called "child."

The Significance of Childhood Studies

All sociological theories of society assume, however implicitly, a theory or theories of self or personality, and, conversely, all theories of personality assume a theory of society. The nexus between self and society lies in the socialization process, and any theory of "how society is possible" (Simmel, 1950) must be one that accounts for the social and socializing experiences of the young child. Herein lies the significance of childhood studies for the social psychologist. There will be no coherent sociological theory of self, society, social relationships, and social structure until the sociologist has adequately grasped and understood the symbolic, interactional, and linguistic foundations of the socialization process. The worlds of the child, whether hidden or private, public or open, serious or playful, constitute a set of obdurate realities to which all sociological theories must eventually return. Everyday in character, constant in presence, children are everywhere, yet are seldom taken seriously; nor are they often studied in their natural habitats. The chapters in this volume call for an opening of the child's worlds to the direct scrutiny of the sociologist. It is time that sociologists establish their rightful claim to the field of childhood studies.

Historical Contexts of the Study of Childhood

The scientific study of children and of childhood first emerged in the period between 1870 and the turn of the century, the turbulent times between the Civil War and the beginning of World War I. This period wrought almost overwhelming changes in the character of American life. Under the impetus of the industrial revolution, migration from the South and immigration from abroad crowded large numbers of people in urban centers. Class divisions became more pronounced as industrialization and the growth of big business concentrated great wealth in the hands of a few. Ward politics and the "boss" system took advantage of the poverty and naiveté of many immigrants, great waves of whom began to arrive from southern and eastern Europe.

In the perception of many Americans, these conditions augured overwhelming change. The highly visible phenomena of urban poverty questioned the American folklore of opportunity for all. Traditional government appeared less stable in the face of radical philosophies such as communism and socialism. The doctrine of Darwinism undermined the firm foundations of religious assumptions. Large numbers of southern and eastern European immigrants threatened the former Aryan homogeneity of previous immigrations. The demand for women's suffrage and the movement of women into the labor market seemed to attack the basis of family life. The sanctity of private property was no longer taken for granted in the face of demands for regulation of large corporations.

Immigration became a focus of much of the resulting apprehension, in part because it was such a visible phenomenon and in part because for many Americans it came to symbolize all that threatened "the American way of life." The collective anxiety of the period favored the growth and popularization of reactionary and self-serving social theories, many of which embodied sexist, racist, ethnocentric, and totalitarian themes. Social Darwinism, with its doctrine of survival of the fittest, rationalized class divisions and the concentration of wealth among the upper classes. The eugenics movement distorted Darwin's theories and aroused the fear that non-Aryan immigration would lower the genetic strength of the "native" (that is, northern European) American population. Numerous social evolutionists made the analogy between evolution of species and evolution of cultures, ranked cultures in terms of "savagery, barbarism, and civilization" and implied or explicitly preached that some cultures were incapable of attaining civilized status (Leopold and Link, 1952).

The growth of interest in child development and childhood socialization was also intertwined with reaction to the phenomena of immigration. Two concerns were prevalent. How were native children to be raised so that the traditional values of American life would remain sacrosanct despite social turmoil? And how were immigrant children to be integrated into society?

Social workers, philanthropists, social thinkers, and reformers defined children as vehicles for the transmission of social values and as raw materials for the building of citizenship. Popular attitudes toward children viewed their development as a recapitulation of the social evolutionary stages of civilization. If children could be lifted out of their barbarism, society as a whole could hope for redemption. The innocence and purity of "properly trained" children represented the hope of succeeding generations. Although there were certainly exceptions, most of the related theories of children were implicitly sexist; others were ethnocentric at best and explicitly racist at worst. From the viewpoint of symbolic interactionism, the majority of childhood socialization theories were "adultist," in that they viewed children as passive or resistant participants in the socialization process.

Theories of Childhood Socialization

The publication in 1877 of Charles Darwin's "Biographical Sketch of an Infant" is said to mark the beginning of modern child psychology (see Karpf, 1932; Brett, 1912; Taine, 1877). Naturalistic in method, Darwin's account of his young son's development over the first two years of life defined the field of genetic psychology, which emphasized the orderly evolutionary relationship between the species and its expressions of intelligence and the emotions. Like a true naturalist, Darwin's records were "atheoretical" in nature; they simply described the developmental phases his child passed through. Chronologically ordered, the observations dated each developmental change by year, month, and day. Darwin's method set the stage for subsequent research and theory in the field, which also stressed the relationship between developmental changes and chronological age (for instance, Piaget). It remained for future theorists, most notably Freud and his students, to overlay the "atheoretical" naturalism of Darwin with a substantive theory of personality growth and development. (See Markey, 1928, for a review of these developments in American sociology and Baldwin, 1913, and Hall, 1923, for discussions on the field of psychology at this time.)

The field of *genetic psychology* (Brett, 1912) established the early psychological and sociological foundations for the study of child development, which rested on an eighteenth-century philosophical debate surrounding the dualistic relationship between the "mind" and the "body." Locke, Hume, and

Kant contended that the mind and the body were interrelated parts of a unified whole and that the understanding of one could not proceed without an understanding of the other. Early genetic psychologists (Hall, 1923; Baldwin, 1913), child developmentalists (Gesell, 1923), and sociologists (Spencer, Small, Ross, Giddings, Ellwood, and Bernard), following the evolutionary lead of Darwin, assumed that the human species developed along two distinct planes or levels: the one physical, the other mental. Thus, the maturational growth of the young child (see Hall and Baldwin) could be studied as a process quite distinct from cognitive, mental development. The relationship between the mind and the body was thus severed, and two discrete fields of inquiry within child development appeared. The joining of these two fields awaited the emergence of intelligence tests in the early 1900s. The IQ test, itself a measure of the relationship between mental age and chronological (maturational) age, brought the mind and the body of the child back into a new field of empirical inquiry labeled *child development,* a field that was soon to be captured by psychoanalysts, child psychologists, developmentalists, and Watsonian behaviorists. With this capture emerged the modern child development research laboratory, and by 1928 many major universities in the United States (including Columbia, Yale, Chicago, and Minnesota) had their own research quarters for the study of cognitive and physical development in early childhood (see Whipple, 1929).

The Shape of Developmental Theories: Political Consequences

The field of child development, as the term suggests, is dominated by theories that stress the orderly progression of the child (physically and mentally) through a series of sequentially linked stages or phases. Freud posited five stages, Sullivan eight, Piaget six, Kohlberg six, and Erikson posits eight, although these continue into adulthood. It is assumed that movement from stage to stage can be measured or naturalistically described and often, as for Piaget, that such movements can be captured in the child development laboratory. The end point in development is never clear-cut, although the adult years are typically taken as a cutoff point. The mind of the adult, for Piaget at least, is used as the model against which child development can be measured.

Within the developmental formulations, the concept of socialization often gives way to the term *learning,* and what is learned are cognitive skills involved with reasoning, logic, causality, and morality. As a view of socialization as process gives way to the learning of a discrete set of tasks and skills, an antagonistic picture of the relationship between the child and the human group emerges: It is society's responsibility to mold its children, regardless of their wishes, into properly educated actors who have the cognitive abilities appropriate to their mental and physical ages.

These developmental theories assume a normative complexion that quickly translates into the arenas of education, politics, and morality. That is, American children who are properly educated should cluster somewhere around a set of national normative standards that depict normal growth and development. The educational testers in American society thus operate as the empirically applied arm of the development theorist. Indeed, the rise of developmental theories and IQ tests go hand in hand in American history, as any inspection of the response of American society to the influx of eastern and southern European immigrants reveals (see Lazerson, 1972). As urban locales became glutted with non-English speaking populations, social workers, politicians, and philanthropists became concerned. The solution was to move immigrant children, as quickly as possible, into the school system, where they can hopefully be "Americanized." Lazerson (1972, p. 39) quotes a 1903 publication of the National Education Association: "You cannot catch your citizen too early in order to make him a good citizen. The kindergarten age marks our earliest opportunity to catch a little Russian, the little Italian, the little German, Pole, Syrian, and the rest and begin to make good American citizens of them."

Developmentalism Reconsidered: Symbolic Interactionism

Whether or not the growth and development of the child occurs in an orderly sequence is taken as largely irrelevant for the symbolic interactionist. That change occurs is a given. That self-images appear and become elaborated and more complex is also taken as a given. For the interactionist, there is little interest in development per se. Instead, the concern involves an understanding of how the object called "child" comes to enter into the very processes that produce and shape its own self-consciousness and awareness of others. Cooley, Mead, James, Dewey, and other early interactionists assumed that the human organism possessed the neurological capability to engage in minded, symbolic and self-reflexive behavior; that is, the human, unlike other organisms, could enter into the organization of its own conduct. Accordingly, the child, like the adult, is able to shape, define, and negotiate its relationship to the external world of objects, others, and social situations. Such a self-conscious organism can define its own reality and its own relationship to that reality. In turn, the child, like other actors, can enter into the organization of its own developmental sequence, bypassing certain stages, regressing to others, ignoring still others, and perhaps creating stages or phases that have yet to be imagined. The interactionist, then, eschews a strict developmental approach and prefers instead a naturalistic account of the growth and emergence of self-awareness and self-consciousness in childhood.

The Method of the Interactionist

A naturalistic account of the socialization process should (1) permit entry into the closed worlds of childhood; (2) provide data on attitude and act; (3) be sufficiently reliable and valid so as to permit future investigators to build on such accounts; and (4) be grounded in a theory that purports to explain and organize what has been observed. In addition, these accounts must (5) take children seriously and attempt to understand and comprehend them on their own grounds; (6) be lodged in the natural worlds of childhood—for instance, home, sidewalk, playground, stores, and preschools; and (7) give equal attention to all the relevant participants in the socialization process, such as mothers, fathers, neighbors, peers, siblings, teachers, and store clerks. In short, it should not be a one-sided account that stresses only the child's or mother's or father's point of view.

The empirical observations reported in this volume were collected through the use of the naturalistic method. They are drawn from my field work in preschools, daycare centers, and family homes. The core materials are taken from a study of the socialization experiences of my two daughters and their friends and acquaintances. Overlap between chapters (which has been reduced as much as possible) can, in part, be explained by the fact that I was learning the technical, empirical, and theoretical subject matter of the field while I was engaged in the process of observing young children at play and at work. Each chapter attacks the sociology of child development from a slightly different angle, but always the focus is on children and the caretakers of children. I turn now to a brief discussion of each chapter.

Overview of Book

Chapter Two, "The Politics of Childhood," takes up the assumption that children, rather than embodying some intrinsic character, are historical, cultural, political, and social productions. These varying definitions of children become translated into the politics of education and socialization through the entrenchment of theories of child development. Children confront these definitions of childhood, reflected within their schools and families, on an everyday interactional level. Such definitions directly influence the emergence of the child's self-conceptions. This chapter argues that—because they fail to conceptualize children as being capable of minded, self-reflexive behavior—current theories of childhood socialization distort the potential of socialization experiences for the child. Adults must relinquish theories of socialization that derogate the child, that view children as passive participants in the socialization process. Adults must recognize that current definitions of childhood disparage children at the expense of the status quo.

Chapter Three, "Logic of Naturalistic Inquiry," offers

a plan for approaching the study of children from within a symbolic interactionist framework. If sociological theories of childhood are to avoid the fallacies of previous research, empirical analysis must be grounded in the everyday interactive worlds of childhood. This chapter clarifies the problems of causal analysis, measurement, sampling, validity, and reliability that confront the naturalistic investigator. Introspection and case studies are advocated as major data sources and as guidelines to the naturalistic study of the child's world.

Chapter Four, "Studying Symbolic Interaction in Childhood," identifies childhood as a world that is unique to children and their caretakers. The child is assumed to be a serious, accountable actor who makes the production of routine social order a problematic enterprise. Case studies of socializing encounters between children and adults are analyzed and placed within the context of family negotiation. The chapter addresses five main topics: (1) language acquisition and linguistic uniqueness; (2) candor, openness, and truthfulness; (3) play, work, and situated activity; (4) friendship and shifting group alignments; and (5) deference, demeanor, and tact. These issues are qualitatively different from the taken-for-granted, everyday behaviors of socialized adults and simultaneously constitute factors that impede the sociological study of young children.

Chapter Five, "Interaction and Language Acquisition in Early Childhood," proposes a model of language acquisition and early childhood socialization that is consistent with the work of G. H. Mead and James Markey. The interpersonal relationship between the child and the caretaker is proposed as the nexus of linguistic socialization. The interactional experiences and conversations produced by the adult/child relationship enable the child, as an organism capable of self-reflexive thought, to become a competent speaker of his native language as well as an integrated member of his social group.

Chapter Six, "Childhood as a Conversation of Gestures," asserts that even young children engage in behavior that is as humanly social as those actions routine to normal adults. Analysis of field observations of one-, two-, three-, and four-year-olds in family, preschool, and recreational settings highlights the

function of words and gestures for both children and adults.*
Society, as it is known and experienced, appears in interactions
between children and parents. Such research suggests that socialization is an ongoing process by which persons of any age attempt
to make society real through the process of self-objectification.

Chapter Seven, "Genesis of Self in Early Childhood,"
poses the question, "How do selves develop out of the interaction
process?" The chapter reviews the Mead-Cooley-Piaget perspective, summarizes the literature on developmental linguistics, and
presents field data from observations of children between the
ages of one and three. The acquisition of linguistic skills facili-
tates a simultaneous awareness of self and other, an ability to
take the attitude of the other that is the requisite of socialization.
The naming process and pronoun usage are analyzed as indicators of self-other awareness, as are those interactions between
child and caretaker that reveal self-reflexive behaviors on the
part of the child. Verbal and nonverbal actions are revealed as
attempts by the child to act on his environment in a sensible and
orderly fashion.

Chapter Eight, "Play, Games, and Interaction," focuses
on the import of play and games for early childhood socialization experiences. This chapter extends the Piaget critique and
reviews existing theories of play, games, and socialization, particularly those of Piaget and Caillois. The main criticism is that
existing theories divorce games and play from the interpersonal
contexts that produce them. A typology of play and games is
offered that incorporates the viewpoint of the child and includes
working at play, playing at work, playing at play, playing a
game, and playing at a game. These forms are treated as processes, rather than as static characters. Field data on young children at play illustrate the typology and theories discussed.

Chapter Nine, "Child's Play and the Construction of
Social Order," looks at specific instances of children learning

* I describe one of these research settings in this book. This is a
racially mixed preschool that accommodates approximately 100 three- and
four-year-old children. My observations on two-year-olds also come from
a racially mixed preschool that accommodates 50 children under a parent
cooperative system. My observations on children under the age of two
years came from my daughters.

how to play. Play and games are placed in a historical and interpersonal context through analysis of the careers that children
have through and with games. This chapter proposes that games
introduced into the existing personal networks of children will at
first reflect the relationships within that network. Over time,
games become decreasingly personalized and increasingly impersonalized, eventually transcending the lives and identities of
their players.

Chapter Ten, "The Work of Little Children," stresses
that for children play takes on the seriousness of adults' work.
When left on their own, young children do not play; they work
at constructing social order. Children's work involves such serious matters as developing languages for communicating, for
defining and processing deviance, and for constructing rules of
entry and exit into emerging social groups. In play, children
work out social relationships and self-conceptions. The similarities and discrepancies of childhood conversation to adult speech
and the importance of such conversations for play and games are
analyzed. To understand the conversations and work-play of
young children, it is imperative that one enter into their language
communities and learn about the network of social relationships
that bind children together.

Chapter Eleven, "Children and Their Caretakers," picks
up the theme of Chapter Two and looks again at the production
of children, this time more specifically in the educational arena.
This chapter analyzes the conduct of schools as agencies of fate
or career control. Definitions of childhood that mold school interactions are discussed, and the everyday life of the school is
viewed from the viewpoint of the child. This chapter stresses
that schools need to be redefined to maximize children's self-
development and to permit maximum child-parent participation.
Rather than treating children as passive organisms, schools need
to take children seriously and to treat them with respect.

Chapter Two

The Politics
of Childhood

*E*very society creates a period
between birth and maturity and consigns to that period persons
who have yet to acquire the attributes of adulthood. Such persons may be called *small adults, infants, children, adolescents,
little people, troublemakers,* or simply *incompetents.* The
United States, like other industrialized societies, has constructed
and politically institutionalized a series of age-graded phases
through which its young pass. Associated with each of these
phases are socially approved institutions that are directed to
transform the young into more competent individuals: preschools, daycare centers, Head Start programs, elementary and
secondary schools, colleges, trade schools, finishing schools, summer church camps and institutions for the delinquent and wayward adolescent. These institutions are inextricably interwoven
with the society's political system. Most if not all are legit-

15

imated—accredited—by the political system, and federal funds
support their long-range programs. Thus, the politics of childhood quickly translate into the politics of education and socialization—for to be a child or the caretaker of a child is to be a
political creature, a person who acts in a number of ways that
complement or challenge broader political ideologies and beliefs. Children, then, are political products—they are created,
defined, and acted on in political terms.

Americans, in their sometimes confused attempts to produce better children, have relegated their responsibilities of child
care and education to the political system; and these responsibilities, in turn, have generally been acted out in the schools. But
politicians often undertake to legislate their conceptions of what
a proper child should or should not be with little if any attention
to the interests of children. Educators translate political and legal
directives into educational programs, often in ways that serve
their own best interests, not the child's. Parents, lacking a solid
political base, are seldom able to consensually organize themselves as a counterpower block; they act in ways that reflect their
own self-interest or in ways that will potentially benefit their own
children instead of the children of other parents. Caught between these competing forces, without a clear spokesman for
their collective position, children find themselves talked about,
legislated over, tested, and scrutinized by society's experts: by its
social workers, educational psychologists, probation officials,
judges, courts, teachers, sociologists, anthropologists, politicians,
and psychiatrists.

It is time to call into question America's theories of children and child development. It is my intention to discuss how
a society's theories of childhood and adulthood become en-
trenched in the ways it educates its children. But first it will be
necessary to define what a child is and to show how the perspective of the caretaker is embodied in our definition of the child.

Producing a Child

Children are *social objects*—objects without intrinsic
meaning. To be defined as a child is to be a child. All social

objects, whether ephemeral, like democracy and belief in God, or concrete, like chairs, typewriters, or people, are social products. Their specific meaning arises out of the behaviors people direct toward them. Children are like other social objects in this respect. There are as many different types of children as there are people defining what a child is. The chapters in this volume describe battered children, good children, delinquent children, hyperactive children, slow learners, white children, black children, American Indian children, poor and rich children. But, while diverse definitions are to be encouraged, American parents, educators, and politicians have blithely assumed that if only the right set of experts could be located and trained, right and proper children would be produced. Thus, without malice they legitimate daycare centers for the urban poor, support separate and unequal educational programs in their high schools, discourage interracial dating, and encourage the destruction of distinct ethnic and racial identities.

If children are social products, they are *cultural products* as well. Every social group with a distinct cultural awareness attempts to legislate what to them is a proper concept of children and adulthood. The Amish, for example, eschew dominant American values, balk at compulsory education, and encourage their children to go only as far as the eighth grade, in schools managed by the Amish. By the age of two, the Amish young cease to be children: They are treated like small adults and are encouraged to assume an adult's responsibilities. Similar support for the cultural product assumption can be drawn from the practices of other ethnic groups. Traditional orthodox Jewish families, for instance, attempt to instill in their children a set of values different from those found in Italian, German, Moravian, French, Polish, Spanish-American, or Japanese-American families.

As we have already indicated, children are *political* products, but in a special sense. If politics is broadly construed as a battle over scarce resources and over the allocation of power and authority, then children can be seen as pawns in a larger political arena, which extends beyond the closed havens of the family to the preschool, the grade school, and the high school.

Their caretakers argue and debate over who the child shall be and what he or she shall become. In these political debates, children are collectively bargained over, priced, and sold to the lowest bidder. For example, some metropolitan high schools give contracts to educational resource corporations in exchange for a promise that the corporation can raise the IQ, reading, and mathematics test scores of each child 15 to 20 points over a year's time. Social workers, teachers, and politicians often use children and their welfare as an excuse for gaining more personal and institutional power.

As president, Nixon recognized this fact in his 1971 veto of the national daycare program. He pandered to the silent majority's fears that their traditional family systems would be destroyed if national daycare centers were instituted. To Nixon, this program represented a challenge to the American nuclear family and as such constituted a radical departure from traditional child rearing. It signaled, he feared, a movement to communal modes of child care. That Americans have had some form of extended, extrafamilial child care for at least 150 years went unnoticed in his public statement. Nixon and other critics have overlooked such diverse forms of child care as hired babysitters, summer church camps for children, and expensive boarding and finishing schools for the economic and political elite. And of course they have ignored nineteenth-century forms of child care, such as orphanages, reformatories, and the "putting-out system" (placing children in care centers) in England. Had they not, they might have noticed that some nineteenth-century forms have twentieth-century parallels: *Crèches* in Russia and England functioned much like contemporary daycare centers for the urban poor.

Children are *historical products*. This fact was recognized by Phillipe Ariès in *Centuries of Childhood* (1962), where he argued that children as they are known in the contemporary Western world did not come into existence until the mid sixteenth century. Peter Lasslet and Richard Sennett have criticized certain aspects of Ariès's research, but certainly prior to this time, particularly in France, children were considered small adults.

Every social group asserts through its actions toward

children what a child is, and this assertion reflects the group's particular place in history. Thus, French peasants view children differently from the way their middle-class and aristocratic counterparts do. And ghetto blacks of a Muslim persuasion hold views of their children that are quite unlike those held by upper-class blacks or middle-class Italians. Furthermore, each group attempts to mold the school setting to fit its concepts of child and adult. Recent challenges to the present school system from "free-school" proponents display an inclination to redefine currently held concepts. John Holt (1970) and Paul Goodman, for example, argue that today's child will not be like children of the past. To challenge the idea that what a child is today is what children have always been and will always be is to challenge long-standing institutional arrangements.

If children are social, cultural, political, and historical products, it can also be argued that they are *economic products*. For Americans, membership in the extended developmental period called *childhood* is an economic luxury, a luxury that is denied the urban poor and nearly all nonwhite racial and ethnic groups. (Ariès's research also supports this proposition: Aristocratic or elitist concepts of childhood emerge in societies before lower-class or ethnic minority views.)

Groups that lack regular access to a stable set of economic resources simply cannot afford to send their children to expensive preschools, to hire babysitters, and to give their sons and daughters large allowances. In the typical pattern of child caretaking in the black lower class, for example, a daughter ceases to be a child at the approximate age of seven and becomes a woman at the onset of menstruation. Joyce Ladner (1971), in her sensitive study of the black adolescent female (*Tomorrow's Tomorrow: The Black Woman*), reveals that the eldest daughter in the black family automatically becomes the chief caretaker for the younger brother or sister. Similarly, the young black male, as David Schultz (1969) and Lee Rainwater (1971) have shown, is expected at the onset of adolescence to make his own money and earn his keep in the family. Thus, for many black males living in the ghetto, schools are dysfunctional in the attainment of manhood.

Members of the white middle class, on the other hand,

have exploited their economic advantages. They encourage education at an early age, systematically deny their young access to adult rights and obligations, and prolong childhood through the period of high school and usually college. For them, a child becomes a man or a woman only after regular entry into the economic marketplace and only after marriage. For the woman, adulthood may not be gained until the birth of a legitimate child.

It can be argued, finally, that children are *scientific products*. Here we have only to compare the children studied by Pavlov and Watson with the offspring examined by Freud, Hull, Skinner, Piaget, Bruner, Gessell, Spock, and the modern behaviorists. Each of these scientists views children differently. Each proposes different developmental sequences; each shortens or prolongs the period of childhood; each offers a different explanation for good and bad children. Their theories have been debated in political arenas, differentially incorporated into textbooks for grade school and high school teachers, and each has found its way into preschool and daycare centers. Fads and fashions in the social and psychological sciences quickly appear in schools, in popular magazines, and eventually find their place on the bookshelves of concerned parents.

If there is one quality shared by all of these theories of children and human behavior, it is that they fail to see the human being in active, interactionist terms. They pay little attention to the fact that humans are symbol-manipulating organisms and as such are capable of engaging in *mindful, self-conscious activity*. By proposing that the child is responsive to fixed innate needs or drives or by suggesting that the personality is firmly established in the first five years of life, these theories fail to grasp the shifting, unfolding, creative aspects of all human behavior, from birth to death. These theories of learning, which view the child in passive terms, have been systematically translated into theories of education. Teachers, not children, are seen as experts on all matters. Children are thought to be unreliable objects, who must be actively controlled, tested repeatedly, never given a say in what they are taught, and rewarded for passive acceptance of the teacher's and the school's point of view. These theories of learning, then, complement and support the broader position that children are incompetent social beings.

Alternative views, such as the progressive education movement led by Dewey, James, Mead, and others, have seldom been given a chance to prove themselves. More often than not, the central thesis of the progressive education movement—that children can engage in self-conscious behaviors if stimulated to do so—has been exploited to the educator's advantage. Consequently, while experimental laboratories for children from preschool on were established at many nationally prominent universities, these settings were quickly transformed into laboratories where the psychologist and social psychologist could exploit his or her captive audience for research purposes. Their original intent—to present the child with a stimulating learning environment—was subverted for "scientific" purposes.

A Brief Digression on Theories of Child Development

In general, it can be said that theories of child development fall into one of three broad categories: structural, psychological, or interactional. Psychosocial developmental schemes (Piaget's [1926] is the most well elaborated) propose that age per se is associated with and calls out certain fixed responses on the part of children. Thus, children pass through a variety of age-graded developmental phases: autistic, egocentric, sociocentric. Children may not act as accountable social interactants until after the age of seven. Until that age, Piaget suggests, they engage in egocentric conversations and parallel, not conjoint, play; in short, they do not take account of one another in reciprocal terms. Evidence presented later in this volume calls these psychosocial schemes into doubt. It is proposed, instead, that by the age of three children are able systematically to take one another's roles, present definitions of self, construct elaborate games, and manipulate adults in desired directions. The interactionist view of child development, which is my position, argues that neither age nor sociostructural variables such as race, religion, and ethnicity will directly call out fixed responses or developmental skills in childhood. Rather, it is the nature of the interactive experiences children are exposed to that shapes their behavioral styles and abilities. Children, then, must be approached seriously and taken seriously. Translating this proposi-

tion into research and into the educational arena suggests that
schools should be constructed so as to allow children to actively
construct and take part in their own learning experiences. It
demands that the researcher actively attempt to enter the child's
world of behavior and thought. Experimental paradigms, fixed
interview questions, and standardized IQ tests do not enter that
world. Schools as presently constructed reflect mixes between
the structural and the psychosocial view of childhood. The read-
ings in this volume call for a new perspective, here labeled
interactionist.

Clarifying the Status of Children and Youth

The view one holds of any object generally reflects the
relationship one has with that object. Politicians view children
politically. Parents see them in moral dimensions. Social scientists value children as sources of data for their theories of human
behavior. Children are thus confronted with competing definitions of who they are. The fact that there are no consistent definitions of children and childhood accounts, in part, for the
enormous variations in "childlike" behavior among children.
And it can be argued that bad children—delinquents—are
simply acting out their rejections of the usual concepts of who
they are.

Children are complex beings. They are continually confronted with competing and conflicting definitions that span
cultural, historical, political, economic, social, and scientific
dimensions. The sheer complexity of these definitions increases
the probability that *no* clear-cut image of children and childhood will emerge. While Americans make social and legal distinctions between infants and children (birth to five years),
children and adults (five years to sixteen, eighteen, or twenty-
one) and adults (married and stably employed), they have no
clear image of what kind of person one should be at six, eight,
ten, fifteen, eighteen, or twenty-one. Nor do they make any
systematic sexual and racial differentiations. Accordingly, the
child's self-definition directly reflects the definitions of childhood
he or she confronts on a daily basis, from conversations with

peers, siblings, parents, and teachers. Images of youth, children, and childish behavior presented in the press and mass media, on records, in movies or television programs to a considerable degree also shape his self-definition. To be a child in America today is to be in an ambiguously defined status category. In some respects, however, these diverse definitions of children and childhood are functional and useful. Those who occupy positions that are ill defined have greater latitude in defining who they are and who they wish to be. The problem is that the current situation neither systematically rewards nor sanctions children for selecting one set of definitions over any other.

Despite their attempts to give massive attention to their young, American adults have only complicated the growing up of their children. Adults quarrel and debate over which scientific theory of childhood is correct. They challenge and disparage the social organization of schools. They ridicule the fads and fashions of the young, yet incorporate into their own wardrobes long hair, bell-bottom and flare pants, miniskirts, and see-through blouses. They mock the symbolic leaders of youth, yet they buy the records of Dylan, the Beatles, and the Rolling Stones. They recoil at the thought of their children smoking marijuana, yet they drink to excess themselves and perhaps on occasion smoke a joint if it is passed to them. They deplore sexual intercourse before marriage, yet they forget their own sexual experiences as youths and perhaps overlook their own sexual promiscuity after marriage. Adults ridicule the position of children and youth, yet they take from children that which pleases and withhold from youth those prizes that would confer the sacred status and rights of adulthood—the right of self-control, the right to give and take at will, the right to make contracts, and so forth.

The status of children could be clarified legally and has been in some instances, as when the state defines what a child is. But legal definitions alone will not resolve the meaning of children and childhood, because these meanings must be established and reestablished every time children confront adults. Legal definitions must be acted on by individuals in their daily encounters and confrontations with one another, encounters that will be different for each participant. The meaning of any object, then, must be established every time one confronts it, and modifications of the legal code alone will not solve the problem.

Economic solutions are often sought: "If we only had more money for our schools, the problem would be cleared up." But economic measures work only insofar as people commit themselves to such measures. New schools, more teachers, higher salaries, and better buses will not in themselves clarify the status of children, nor will these expenditures give children new role models or better educations. They only cost money and obfuscate the real issue, which is: *What stance do Americans want to take toward their children and their schools?*

Recently a romantic solution has been proposed. Like most romantic solutions, it is quite simple: Return to a less complex, more rural society—take our children out of the urban rat race. Like the economic proposals, this solution ignores what adults want children to be and simply states a new definition of what an adult is.

Some Proposals

It appears that some headway might be gained in the educational arena if those persons most central to education—children and youth—were given more say in their daily programs. Legal and economic proposals represent attempts to legislate and act on behalf of children but give no credence to the child's position and point of view. We are conducting a crusade *against,* not for, children.

If Americans are to successfully change the status of the young, if they are to improve the character of mass education, they must systematically seek out the thoughts of youth, take them seriously, and give youth an active hand in the determination of their own fate. They must recognize that current definitions of youth and childhood are largely derogatory and contradictory in nature. "Good" children have always known this and have usually exploited it to their best advantage.

Massive federal expenditures for new and better schools might better be used in the economic marketplace so that children could be given economically respectable jobs, not make-work, during summer vacations. The Philadelphia Plan, for example, attempts to place high school students in work organizations during the academic year so that they may gain on-the-spot experience in a variety of occupational pursuits. Here students serve in a capacity similar to the traditional apprentice role in labor unions and are paid for their work commensurate with their output.

Regular electoral procedures should be developed for hearing the opinions of children and youth. Schools and local communities could hold regular elections for youth in which a fixed number of persons would be elected as minority and majority representatives of the under-eighteen constituency.

Conventions at the local, state, and national level (similar to the annual White House Conference on Children) could be held, attended by elected political figures, educators, and perhaps representatives from parent groups and the social sciences. This proposal would bring together on a regular, face-to-face basis the chief actors in the educational arena: children, parents, educators, politicians, social scientists, and social workers. It would have the main function of at least publicly airing the perspectives of those most intimately involved in the politics of childhood.

Proposals such as these presume that social change starts and ends in the immediate world of everyday social experience: in the worlds of childhood and adulthood; in schools, on playgrounds and street corners; in homes, families, and neighborhoods. But alteration in the relative situations of children and their caretakers must begin in the closed interactive worlds of the family—in the home. Here parents directly confront, reward, and sanction their children for approved and disapproved behaviors. Here, initially at least, children try out alternative views of themselves, their peers, and their parents. Here children report back on their experiences with teachers, principals, social workers, and counselors.

Each family can be viewed as a distinct social unit that values things not valued by other families and sanctions behaviors not rewarded elsewhere. Each family is a distinct political, cultural, and historical entity, whose distinctiveness should be

respected, encouraged, and cultivated in schools and neighborhoods. Parents, as the most immediate caretakers of children,
must assert their obligations in this regard and must not give up
easily those values and definitions they cherish and reward. The
immediate world of the family must be taken seriously by those
in education and politics.

More direct lines of accountability between families and
schools must be established, such as direct parental observation
of classroom activities, parental consultation in program revisions, and student evaluations of teachers and curricula. Regular
forums for involving students and Parent-Teacher Associations
in the operation of schools must be developed.

Ways of expanding and confirming the competence of
children and youth must be developed. While most theories of
education rest on the assumption that children are incompetent
(as indicated earlier in this and in several other chapters in this
collection), this proposal assumes that any person will be as
competent as he or she is permitted to be. Barring massive mental retardation or physical disabilities, most persons can function
at highly complex levels—if they are motivated, encouraged, and
permitted to do so. I am not calling here for a lionization of children (a stance that is romantically motivated and only encourages more childlike behaviors on the part of children). Rather,
I am proposing that children be accorded the rights to act like
adults, be given the responsibility that comes with those rights,
and be given access to the resources to organize and act out such
rights. This suggests a need to reevaluate the current age-IQ
structure of schools. If, as some suggest, preschools are now
functioning as kindergartens, then perhaps children who attend
preschool should be moved directly to the first grade. Furthermore, children should be encouraged to struggle against the age-
structured basis of classroom learning. The assumption that
fourth-graders know more than third-graders works only as long
as teachers, parents, and third- and fourth-graders believe it
works. There is nothing about the age of a child, again barring
mental deficiency, that prohibits that child learning at a higher
level. Society, not age per se, requires such distinction.

Perhaps the entire educational process could be defined

as a creative, exciting experience rather than obligatory drudgery. Smaller, decentralized schools and classrooms would encourage more open interaction between students and teachers and would permit teachers to break out of their formal role. Competition in classrooms over grades might be replaced with a more open appreciation for the learning experience with awareness that an emphasis on grades leads, as Howard Becker (1970b) has observed, to a commitment to *making the grade* rather than learning. The progressive education movement, for example, encouraged students to set their own pace, to pursue their own special interests and abilities, and to join together in a sociable fashion in the pursuit of learning. More recent movements toward the so-called open classroom represent other modest steps in this direction.

The last proposal assumes that schools might best be viewed as complex organizations with multiple paths or tracks to the top. Classes could be organized with children from diverse age groups, and presence in the class could be based on special interest or competence, not IQ score or grade average. The usual model of tracking rests on a two-track model: bright white kids in the best track, dull nonwhite kids in the worst track. The tracking system thus mirrors and perpetuates broader lines of stratification in the outside society. The form of tracking proposed here would disregard age, sex, and racial attributes and simply place children of whatever age or sex in classes that most interest them and in which they have special skills. Student skills in this regard could be assessed through several procedures. Students could be asked to designate those study topics they find most stimulating. Classroom instructors and counselors could be encouraged to develop alternative measures of study ability (for example, self-report, scores on new types of objective tests, teacher reports, parental input, and so forth). In general, I am proposing a more open and flexible system of placing students in those courses and settings where they would be most stimulated. Schools, among other institutions in our society, teach children to fail and to accept their place in society.

Chapter Three

Logic of
Naturalistic Inquiry

*E*xisting formulations of naturalism as a distinct approach to empirical inquiry in the social sciences suffer from several overriding flaws. On the one hand, naturalistic theorists and practitioners have seldom been in agreement on what they mean by the method. Some (Catton, 1966) see it as rigorous positivism. Others (Matza, 1969) view it as humanism in disguise. Still others (Barker, 1968; Hutt and Hutt, 1970; Willems and Rausch, 1969; Wright, 1962) compare it to eco-behavioral science—a bare kind of behaviorism that studies people in their natural habitats. Here the naturalist, like the ethologist, makes little effort to record, probe, and study such socio-psychological processes as attitudes and definitions of the situation. There are those (Lofland, 1971) who view naturalism as a deep commitment to collect rich, often atheoretical ethnographic specimens of human behavior.

These statements also suffer from a failure to specify the empirical phenomena to which the method is directed (for instance, if one observes behavior, what kinds of behavior?). Little systematic attention has been given such traditional and perduring methodological problems as measurement, sampling, validity, reliability, and causal analysis. The basic unit of naturalistic analysis has never been clarified, and the role of the naturalistic observer in his studies remains clouded. This conceptual diversity has led many to take a skeptical, if not irreverent, view of the naturalistic approach, viewing it as soft science or journalism.

Perhaps the basic deficiency of prior naturalistic formulations has been the absence of a more general theoretical perspective that would integrate all phases of the sociological act. With few exceptions, the dominant scientific paradigm has been imported from physics, chemistry, or biology. (The major exceptions here are Becker, 1970a; Lofland, 1971; and Schatzman and Strauss, 1973.)

In this chapter, I offer a view of naturalism that takes as its point of departure the social behaviorism of Mead (1934, 1938) and the symbolic interactionism of Blumer (1969). I call this version of the research act *naturalistic behaviorism* and mean by the term the studied commitment to actively enter the worlds of native people and to render those worlds understandable from the standpoint of a theory that is grounded in the *behaviors, languages, definitions, attitudes,* and *feelings* of those studied. Naturalistic behaviorism attempts a wedding of the covert, private features of the social act with its public, behaviorally observable counterparts. It thus works back and forth between word and deed, definition and act. Naturalistic behaviorism aims for viable social theory; it takes rich ethnographic descriptions only as a point of departure. This version of behaviorism recognizes that humans have social selves and as such act in ways that reflect their unfolding definitions of the situation. The naturalist is thus obliged to enter people's minds, if only through retrospective accounts of past actions (see Campbell's 1969 suggestions for such studies).

The basic unit of analysis for naturalistic behaviorism

becomes the *joint act,* whether this is a dinner party, a socializing relationship, crowd behavior, nations at war, or conduct in small groups. Naturalistic behaviorism places the sociological observer squarely in the center of the research act. It recognizes the observer for what he or she is and takes note of the fact that all sociological work somehow reflects the unique stance of the investigator. It assumes that all studies begin in some fashion from a problem, or set of problems, deeply troubling to the sociologist, whether this be the character of alienation, the socialization of one's own children, or an attempt to understand how mental hospitals create mental illness. Sound, viable, and exciting sociology begins with biographically troubling issues and culminates in an attempt to offer public answers to what was initially personal and private (see Mills, 1959). The naturalistic behaviorist thus stands over and against the broader sociological community and takes himself or herself seriously. In this sense, the sociologist becomes both object and subject in his studies. His reflections on self and other and his conduct in interactive sequences become central pieces of data. Introspection, then, is basic to naturalism (see Cooley, 1926). The naturalist employs any and all sociological methods, whether these be secondary analyses of quantitative data, limited surveys, unobtrusive measures, participant observation, document analysis, or life history constructions. He will admit into his analyses any and all data that are ethically allowable. He works with statistical, quantitative accounts of people and their actions, if such accounts render more understandable the behavior in question. While taking a skeptical stance toward those research protocols that dictate how one approaches the empirical world, the naturalist is committed to *sophisticated rigor:* He is committed to making his data and explanatory schemes as public and replicable as possible. Thus he details in careful fashion the nature of his sampling framework, triangulates his observations, and continually assesses the empirical grounding of his causal propositions. Naturalism is grounded in the study of behavioral acts. It focuses on the timing, sequencing, and consequences of such acts, whether these are symbolic utterances, covert conversations with self, or overt behaviors.

A programmatic statement of the naturalist method is in order if sociologists of the interactionist and microbehaviorist persuasion are to bring their theories in closer touch with the empirical social world. Accordingly, special attention will be given to how the naturalistic observer: (1) samples from ongoing social organizations; (2) employs naturalistic indicators; (3) assesses these indicators by the usual canons of reliability, repeatability, and validity; (4) selects and distinguishes for careful analysis representative, illustrative, and negative cases; (5) develops process-oriented, explanatory models of the unfolding joint act; and (6) records and analyzes his own behavior. A loose, sensitizing scheme for organizing naturalistic studies will be offered. Strategies for implementing such a methodology will be taken from an ongoing study of early childhood socialization.

The Thrust of Naturalism

As a field strategy, nationalism implies a profound respect for the character of the empirical world. It demands that the investigator take his theories and methods to that world. He collects *behavior specimens* (Barker, 1968); that is, he attempts to reproduce in a rich and detailed fashion the experiences, thoughts, and languages of those he studies. Such specimens will reflect the actual temporal sequence of the behavior under analysis, and they will show how each interactant influenced and was influenced by all others in the behavioral situation. These specimens are then examined by the analyst from multiple perspectives. He compares how the persons in question organized and justified their actions and places these explanations over and against his emergent sociological scheme (see Campbell, 1969; Strauss and Glaser, 1970), which is to say he grounds his theory in the behaviors of those studied. The naturalist resists schemes and models that oversimplify the complexity of everyday life. He asks whether such conventional sociological variables as age, sex, race, education, and religion are seen as relevant by those he studies. He attempts to penetrate their worlds of experience to determine what forces they see shaping and influencing their behavior. Yet he understands that there will be an inevitable ten-

sion between his analytic schemes and the interpretative models
of those studied (see Becker, 1970a). The sociological model is
general, abstract, and relativistic. The everyday model is personal and nongeneralizing. He attempts, then, to impose order
on the social world and to reduce as much as possible the distance between his *outsider-imposed* concepts and those employed by the native person.* As a consequence, sampling
strategies are fitted to the temporal, ritual, moral, and sentimen-
tal features of the social worlds under examination. Measurement strategies are couched around naturalistic indicators. While
he may have occasion to use more formalized interview techniques, the observer prefers to take as central indicators behaviors routinely engaged in by his subjects. He moves from
sensitizing concepts to the immediate world of social experience
and permits that world to shape and modify his conceptual
framework. In this way, he moves continually between the
realm of more general social theory and the worlds of native
people. Such an approach recognizes that social phenomena,
while displaying regularities, vary by time, place, and circum-
stance. The observer, then, looks for repeatable regularities (see
Kaplan, 1964). He uses ritual patterns of dress and body-spacing
as indicators of self-image. He takes special languages, codes,
and dialects as indicators of group boundaries. He studies his
subject's prized social objects as indicators of prestige, dignity,
and esteem hierarchies. He studies moments of interrogation and
derogation as indicators of socialization strategies. He attempts
to enter his subject's closed worlds of interaction so as to examine the character of private versus public acts and attitudes.

His theories are constructed on the basis of such observations. In building up a theory, the naturalistic observer respects
and takes seriously those he studies. Indeed, he cultivates close
relationships. Hoping to be taken seriously by the subject, he
recognizes that alert, observant participants know more than he
ever will about the realities under investigation (see Blumer,
1969). Such persons serve as natural resources and checks on

---

* *Native person* is introduced here as a generic term that covers
all people studied by the sociologist. These may be experimental subjects,
interviewees, friends, colleagues, or neighbors.

the emerging theory. Acting as a panel of judges, they collectively and singly evaluate and help reconstruct valid and viable theories of their social worlds (see, for example, the work of Alan G. Sutter, 1966, on righteous dope fiends). Native persons serve, too, as methodological consultants and field guides. While this feature of the informant has been repeatedly noted in the field-work literature (see, for example, Back, 1960; Becker and others, 1961; Dalton, 1964; Lofland, 1971; Strauss and Glaser, 1970; Whyte, 1955), it must be stressed again. Often the observer finds himself in a situation where the phenomena he wishes to observe (1) occur at a low frequency or (2) are not amenable to investigative procedures used in the past. In such situations, the native person can often produce records of past occurrences of the phenomena in question, thus broadening the sociologist's data base. The observer can then check his hunches against the "native's" interpretations.

On other occasions, the native can coach the observer on new field techniques, suggesting important modifications in existing research strategy. In the early phases of my field study on two-, three-, and four-year-old children, I wished to gather data on the self-concept and intended to employ a version of the "Who Am I?" Twenty Statements Test (McPhail and Tucker, 1972). Such data, if gathered, would have permitted comparisons with previous studies on older age groups. I subsequently approached the head preschool instructor in the setting where I was working and sought her counsel. She suggested that I modify the question by telling the children that I was writing a book about the school, wanted a page about each of them, and ask what they would like to write on their page. I then asked the children, "What should I say about you? If someone asked me who you were, what would you want me to say?" This modification of the standard research procedure proved highly successful and permitted me to approach the children on a more familiar footing.

It is important to stress that equal weight cannot be given all native informants. Their perspectives and ability to aid the observer vary by their position in the social organization under study (for example, isolate, leader, old hand, or mar-

ginal). Their motives for aiding the observer shape the character
of their information (for example, attempts to win his favor and
so on). There exists, then, a hierarchy of credibility among informants (see Becker, 1967). The naturalist seeks to employ
multiple native informants. His task is one of threading and
weaving their diverse and often contradictory reports into an
accurate picture, which means that he may eventually have to
discredit or drop one or more of his informants because their information fails to stand up under close scrutiny.

Naturalism places severe strain on the observer—emotional, physical, and ethical. It obligates him or her to take seriously his or her own introspections and reflections on the social
process, as that process is recorded, perceived, and acted toward.
This methodology immediately opens for sociological analysis all
of one's daily actions and conversations as sources of data on
the self and the joint act. Recording one's behavior permits the
observer to be both objective and subjective. He can note that he
made a specific act at a specific time and place in the company
of a certain set of others. But he can simultaneously probe the
subjective features of the act by noting what his thoughts were at
the time he acted. In such observations, the sociologist is forced
to stand outside his own conduct and view it as a third party. He
treats himself as an object, like any other object in the interaction process. But by probing his own motives and inclinations
and by discussing them with his fellows he can reconstruct the
covert dialogues with self that produced the behavior just observed. In this way, the sociologist uses himself and his interactive others as native audiences in the construction of social
theory.

The following interactional episode, a ten-minute interaction between myself (Nick) and my two daughters (Ramona
and Jody) illustrates one attempt to move from *interactional
participant* to *interactional analyst*. The episode involves Nick
fixing breakfast for Ramona and Jody. The behavior settings are
the family kitchen, Ramona's bedroom, and the living room. The
central objects are the three persons in question, the food that
went into the breakfast, a highchair, small table, and a television
program. The episode was recorded thirty minutes after it oc-

curred. I have selectively excerpted from the running account, as it totals nearly twenty pages of dialogue and analysis. Actions of Ramona, Jody, and Nick are left unbracketed, conversations are bracketed in quotations. Utterances that were peculiar to Ramona and Jody are followed by bracketed translations given by Nick. If an utterance is repeated, the number of repetitions is given in parentheses. Joint conversations are designated by the initiating speaker (for example, Ramona) with a direct line to the audience (for example, Ramona—Nick). Ramona was two years old at the time of this recording, and Jody was three.

7:30: Nick gets up, Emily (wife and mother) is still in bed. Nick gets paper, fixes coffee.

7:35: Ramona wakes up: "Mommy(2), Daddy(2)."

7:38: Nick gets Ramona up. Nick enters Ramona's room, Ramona is still lying down in bed with blanket over head.

Ramona—Nick: "Bear, bow-wow, Dody." (Translation: Ramona had thrown her bear out of bed, her dog has fallen out, and she asks if Jody is up yet.)

Nick and Ramona go to kitchen.

Ramona—Nick: "Eat, eat."

Nick crosses kitchen and begins fixing a poached egg for Ramona and thinks about fixing juice but remembers he had promised Jody the night before that she could fix it. Nick decides to wait on juice.

7:40: Jody comes running into kitchen, gives Nick a big hug: "Hi, Daddy."

Jody—Nick: "Dody, Mommy room, eggs, no Daddy, cornflakes." (Translation: "I was in Mommy's room, I don't want eggs for breakfast, I want cornflakes.") Jody climbs up on chair to cupboard where the cornflakes are and starts to take her Pampers off.

Jody—Nick: "Daddy, Dody make juice."

Nick—Jody: "Well, you take your Pampers down to your room first."

Jody returns to kitchen. Nick is trying to keep

the poached eggs from boiling over. Ramona has
climbed up on a chair with Jody, and Jody has pulled
the strip off the juice can.

Jody—Nick: "Daddy, help, juice."

Nick moves to sink.

Nick—Jody: "Well, you've taken the strip
off."

Nick takes lid off juice can and starts to pour
it into the blender. Jody takes hold of the can, and
Nick and Jody together pour juice into the blender.
Nick turns on the water, Ramona watching all the
time and trying to get hold of the juice can. Nick fills
the can with water. Nick and Jody pour water into the
blender.

Ramona—Nick and Jody: "Baby help, baby
help."

Jody—Nick and Ramona: "No, Dody fix
juice."

Nick—Jody and Ramona: "Ramona can help;
you pour the last one."

Nick fills the can and Jody helps pour in the
last can. Jody leaves room, returns from living room.

Jody—Nick: "Daddy, Daddy, move, table."*

Space prohibits any detailed analysis of this episode. I
offer it as an example of how the observer can stand outside his
own actions and record them much as he would any other person's behavior. In this case, Nick could have been anyone making breakfast, and any similarly situated observer could have
made note of how Nick went about negotiating the demands of
Ramona and Jody. But this episode differs in one significant
respect. Nick was able to penetrate his covert conversations as he

---

* I suggest that while such actions as this appear trivial to an
outsider they lie at the core of what socialization means inside the family
unit—that is, parents are continually negotiating plans, demands, and
expectations with their children. And these demands flow out of the
dominant ritual features of the family's social organization. On another
level, observations such as this give data on the minute features of the
joint act and offer some insight into the problem of interactional emergence noted here. Barker (1968) and Wright (1962) offer similar kinds
of behavioral specimens in their research on schools and family life.

organized his responses to Ramona and Jody. In analyzing the data, I selected two subphases of this episode for special attention. When Jody climbed on the chair and went after the cornflakes, Nick makes a countermove that put off her request to make juice: He asked her to take her Pampers to the bedroom. At this point, Nick was running a holding company, having committed himself the night before to allowing Jody to fix juice, having told Ramona he would fix her breakfast, and finding that the poached eggs were boiling over. The tactic failed, as Jody returned in fifteen seconds, the eggs boiled over, and both Ramona and Jody now wanted to fix the juice. When Jody challenged Ramona's right to fix the juice, she brought into the act an agreement made the night before that Nick was obliged to meet if he did not want a fight on his hands.

Thus, unlike the naturalist who stands outside his subject's behavior and merely records sequences of actions (see Hutt and Hutt, 1970), the naturalistic behaviorist attempts to take the role of his subject and fit his unfolding definitions into the joint act that is being analyzed. By making himself both object and subject, the naturalist is able to render public at least one side of the covert dialogues with self that shaped the behavior in question. That is, he can publicly record what he was thinking at the time he acted.

An Interactionist Framework for Naturalistic Studies

In implementing naturalistic studies, it is necessary for the observer to have some consistent, if only loosely sensitizing image of the interaction process. While space prohibits a detailed treatment of this problem (see Denzin, 1971), for present purposes I suggest that the following concepts, when combined, give the naturalist an empirically workable perspective for the behavioral study of joint acts. It must be repeated that there will be inevitable conflicts (in any study) between this, or any other framework, and the ideologies and rhetorics people develop to explain and account for their behaviors. I offer the following framework for sensitizing purposes only and propose that naturalists focus on the interrelationships between (1) selves, (2) languages, (3) social settings, (4) social objects, and (5) the joint act.

Combining these concepts suggests that all instances of observable social conduct involve persons, possessing social selves and communicating via a language, in a concrete situation that is transformed into an interactional arena wherein a special class of social objects are acted on. The conduct of selves will be joined through a variety of differing social relationships, whether these be hostile, friendly, cooperative, antagonistic, loving, socializing, or interrogating. Each self will possess differential knowledge about the other and will be confronted with the three-fold problem of defining the situation, identifying the other, and assessing the responses of "other" to the unfolding action sequence (see Strauss, 1969).

Emergence and the Joint Act: Interactional Orderliness versus Predictability. The interaction process must be seen as having a variable, shifting, and emergent career. To grasp the character of the joint act (as in the foregoing example of making breakfast), observers must follow its trajectory over time. To say that interaction is emergent is not to ascribe to it some kind of mystical quality. It merely suggests that when humans coordinate behavior neither they nor any outside observer can say with absolute certainty what the specific contours of the ensuing interaction will be. As each person makes indications to himself, makes note of what others are saying, and attempts to fit his next response to what has just occurred, he can in no precise sense know what the other interactant will say or do. But, with some certainty, all interactants can assume that the next response of alter will fit into the character of the acts that have just occurred. Thus Nick could predict that Jody would return and ask to make juice. When she would return, how she would couch her request, and how Ramona would respond were problematic. Thus interactants can join behaviors in *orderly*, but not *predictable*, ways. It is often only after the act has occurred that sense is made of it. In retrospective ways, then, persons explain their behaviors. That is, they bring their pasts in line with the future, hoping that the future will unfold as the past has.

This suggests that most interactional studies must aim for

the development of explanatory accounts of behavior sequences. And these accounts must be grounded in the retrospective explanations people give for their behaviors. The naturalist, because of his stance toward interactional emergence, sees explanation as his immediate, if most difficult, scientific goal.

Snapshots of opening interactional sequences, videotapes of experimental exchanges and postexperimental inquiry sessions represent useful, but limited research strategies, because they too often leave the covert, private side of the public act unexamined.

Language is the basic medium through which selves are presented, defined, and joined together. Yet linguistic accounts that focus only on word dictionaries, or semantical and syntactical systems, or speech sequencing, or inflection and intonation, or which correlate speech utterances with variables (class, age, sex, race, education, income, and so on) fail to grasp the fact that language itself is a symbolic production (see Goffman, 1964). Thus, while naturalists must make the linguistic or speech act a fundamental unit of analysis, they must record the ways in which their subjects use and create language (see Becker, 1970b).

This suggests a research principle. Observers must totally submerge themselves in the native's speech community. Until the languages of that community are understood, viable studies of social process will be severely limited. Viewing language as a situated production suggests that all joint actions display mixes of many different language systems. Thus there are behavioral and body languages, languages of polite discourse, languages of love, praise, and abuse, languages that are written, languages that are sacred or profane. Languages, then, both bring people together and keep them apart. In studying the joint act, observers must attempt a complete rendering of all their subject's speech acts. Only in this way can the several phases of the act be examined. By making note of the speech act, especially as this act is woven into a joint production, the analyst is able to ground his observations in *overt behavior*. That is, he studies public behavior; behavior that any other observer could record.

Selves forge joint actions through their linguistic acts. To study the joint act, naturalists must gather data on the self as a social production. A paradox exists. With the exception of such ritual occasions as the job interview and sessions with the analyst, few persons announce who they are. Students of the self must go beyond written responses to "Who Am I?" questions, or to checklist indications of self-inventories. They must view the self as a social object that is acted on in the joint act. As a public production, the self is inferable through the subject's speech and behavioral acts, his manners of dress and address, his body-spacing rituals, his self-possessions, and his declarations of intent. No sense can be made of the joint act until the observer uncovers the self's place in the interaction process. The subject's perspective must be penetrated. As the observer makes note of the subject's behavior during specific interaction sequences, he can record the links between verbal and behavioral acts and the unfolding career of the joint act. Each person, then, contributes bits and pieces to every interaction sequence. These bits and pieces must be dissected for what they reveal about the self. And they then must be reassembled so as to give a complete picture of the act under analysis (see the account of making breakfast).

Naturalists begin, then, with public, observable behavior. Their studies are incomplete, however, until they work back to the covert features of the self-act. Naturalists must attempt entry into the private worlds of self-conversations, for here is where the early phases of all joint acts are constructed. Such studies will, of course, reveal that there is never a direct link between self-conversations and ensuing joint actions. To repeat, interaction is an emergent affair. Because the covert act is so difficult to penetrate, I have advocated the use of introspective investigator accounts of the self in process. Such accounts provide the basic source of data on the covert features of the public act.

Social objects must occupy a basic position in all naturalistic investigations. The interactionist assumes that objects carry no intrinsic meaning. Whether they are selves or chairs, houses or cars, social objects are social productions. Their meaning is found in the behaviors directed toward them. To conduct a study of social objects, investigators must examine how their subjects act on, toward, to, and with the objects they routinely confront. Joint acts are built up around social objects, most

centrally the self. Such behaviors are a matter of public record
(for instance, students can record how a man acts toward a chair
or an auto; less easily toward his wife). While difficult, such
accounts are crucial if naturalistic studies are to be behaviorally
grounded. Object analysis suggests that sociologists cannot assume that their definitions of an object are correct, nor can they
assume that their subjects will agree on the meaning of a given
object. Observers must cast aside their own ethnocentrisms and
learn their subject's view of the world and the objects found
therein.

   Setting, scene, and interactional arena provide the behavioral locus of all joint acts—which is to say that all behavior
is situated by time and place. But situations carry no intrinsic
meaning. While behavior is situated, it occurs only in *interactional arenas,* in situations that have been transformed into
scenes. Accordingly, observers must study how subjects transform simple situations into places for interaction. This simple
principle has been grossly ignored in experimental laboratory
studies where investigators apparently assume that their definition of the situation will be the subjects'. Depriving laboratories
of color, dimming the lights, and padding the floors can scarcely
be taken as justification for arguing that the situation was devoid
of external stimuli. Subjects bring to and thrash out in situations,
definitions of the scene. Until such definitions are studied,
naturalistic or any other types of investigation are incomplete.

   Joint actions represent the behavioral merger of the foregoing concepts. Such productions are situationally grounded,
created, and defined through language manipulation, and focused
around the self and its attendant objects. Joint actions have
temporal careers, are differentially embedded in other acts, have
shifting foci of interest, carry varying degrees of biographical
consequentiality, and differ in the extent to which they are self-
consciously, or ritualistically organized. Piecing together these
features of the act gives the student a data base from which his
naturalistic theory of social interaction can be built. In making
such observations, to repeat, the linguistic act must take central
focus. These observations must be grounded in the act's tempo-

ral career, in the sense that each behavioral act and utterance must be placed in precise temporal sequence.

The naturalistic behaviorism that I am advocating partially challenges the "ahistoric" bias of many sociological schemes. By examining the unfolding trajectory of joint actions, naturalists inevitably become microhistorians, at least in the sense that they become concerned with how a previous act or utterance fits into and affects subsequent conduct. Thus, on a small scale naturalists are interested in how selves rewrite the past so as to bring their futures in line with past commitments, intentions, and goals. Every joint action has a history (often many histories), whether this be a ten-minute conversation, a family dinner, a marriage, a social group, or a trip to the grocery store. This history is embedded in a social structure, is variously timed and scheduled, and carries different levels of consequentiality for the implicated selves. Naturalistic behaviorists, then, are microhistorians of social process.

Summary. Thus far I have proposed that five concepts be given basic attention in naturalistic studies. I have indicated how these concepts may be behaviorally observed and have proposed that the basic unit of naturalistic analysis become the joint act. In studying social acts that are forged into joint actions, the observer records interactive conduct that is linguistically produced, spatially situated, and temporally organized. He studies the links between selves as social objects and their attendant interactive productions, here called *joint acts.* The naturalistic behaviorist employs Mead's *social behaviorism* by continuously working from overt behavioral acts to their covert, private counterparts. By examining the emergent features of all social acts, he also utilizes the symbolic interactionist's conception of social process.

He is a behaviorist in the sense that he studies and records public behavior—overt acts. But he is a peculiar behaviorist, because of his attempts to probe the subjective features of organized social life. In his endeavors, the naturalist becomes, by necessity, an introspectionist. But, again, a special kind of introspectionist, for unlike his literary counterparts (for instance, Norman Mailer) he is troubled over the validity and reliability of his observations. It is for this reason that he takes so seriously the people he studies. It is they who provide the basic checks on his accounts of social behavior.

Implementing Naturalistic Studies

Participant observation, however loosely defined, has traditionally been the major method of naturalistic studies. My concern here is not with expanding or criticizing prior formulations of this methodology. I take it as basic that all naturalists are committed to (1) developing interactive, causal explanations of social process; (2) building theory embedded in the worlds studied and to employing theoretically informed sampling schemes that are flexible enough to include simple, random, stratified, cluster, and even interactive sampling procedures; (3) linking a subject's acts with his covert self-conversations and tying those acts and thoughts to the subject's world of significant interactive others; (4) employing some version of the sensitizing concept; (5) utilizing a triangulated methodology or multiple observational approach that enables them to use any and all research strategies that reflect on the problems at hand; (6) situating their observations as precisely as possible in the subject's temporal and social worlds of experience. The naturalist, like the participant observer, is committed to embedding himself in the subject's perspective. But at the same time he is committed to moving out of that world to the reality of sociological theory (see Denzin, 1970b, 1978, for a more systematic treatment of these assumptions).

My concerns at this point are more theoretical than practical, and I shall give little treatment to such issues as (1) getting into social situations; (2) learning a native's languages; (3) standing around and listening; (4) making and writing field notes; (5) presenting self to diverse others; (6) securing permission to examine special files or to openly observe special classes of subjects; (7) becoming emotionally involved with the subject; (8) being rebuffed or rebuked by persons in authority; (9) deciding what to tell a "native" about one's study (see the essays in Habenstein, 1970). These practical concerns are endless in their variations and cannot be minimized. The fact remains, however, that most successful observers develop their own special ways of handling them (see Schatzman and Strauss, 1973). What remains in question, for the naturalist, is how she or he can emerge from the field experience with sociologically reliable observations that can somehow be rendered theoretically understandable. The naturalist is committed to making every phase of the research as public as possible. He must repeatedly address the question of replication and of whether or not his findings can be built on by others. He must, then, take some working stance toward the problems of sampling, measurement, and causal analysis (see Glaser and Strauss, 1967).

Sampling Strategies. The naturalist samples the interactions between people as these interactions are forged into joint acts. Depending on his theoretical interests, he may examine encounters, social relationships, or the webs of affiliation that bind people into social groups. Sampling resolves primarily into a set of procedures that take the analyst into social situations where he makes his observations. As such, a variety of interrelated questions must be addressed. First, what empirical unit is going to be observed, and what behaviors of that unit will be given special attention? Second, can access be gained into the situations where the behavior in question occurs? Third, the analyst must show how representative or typical his observed cases are. That is, can he generalize to unobserved interactive units?

The naturalist begins by identifying the class of joint acts he wishes to study. If he is examining the family as an interactive unit, he may select from a family's total set of behavioral repertoires only those actions that reflect socializing activities, entertainment rituals, ceremonial productions, or work-related behaviors. He then determines which members of the interactive unit routinely engage in the specified behaviors and stations himself in situations where those actions can be recorded and detailed. He must make contact with the world he wishes to study, penetrate its symbolic and physical boundaries, learn its languages, grasp the range and meanings given the social object typically acted on, and carefully note the critical interactional arenas where the specified behavior *most frequently* occurs. In this respect, the naturalistic sampler stratifies the behaviors of greatest theoretical and behavioral relevance. And he makes his observations in the situations where the specified behavior routinely occurs. In studying ritual and ceremony in everyday family life, I have timed and paced my observations to fit those moments when the family as a collectivity comes together for special meals, anniversaries, and national holidays. In my observations of female sex role socialization, I have given primary focus to the mother-daughter interactive relationship and situated those observations in the situations where this form of socialization was most predominant (for instance, bedrooms, dressing tables, bathrooms, kitchens, sewing rooms, grocery stores, and so on).

Before the naturalist can begin to collect his behavioral specimens, he must gain a working knowledge of the settings that constitute his subject's world, noting what situations are routinely entered, with whom, for what purposes, and at what times. He then links his subject's behaviors to those situations, to construct a *representational map* of the subject's interactional world. In my family case studies, I have recorded the frequency of interactions in each room of the house and noted what combination of the family members typically enter each room. It quickly becomes clear where oversampling must be directed. In one family, the parents and children primarily came together as a complete unit in the kitchen and living room. Observations of husband-wife negotiations over socialization strategies were made in these two situations. The presence of the children permitted the collection of data on coalitions and clique formation in the negotiations of proper table conduct and so on. On the other hand, observations were gathered during those times when the husband and wife, in private, discussed their socialization procedures. In this way I was able to examine the behaviors, thoughts, and utterances of one subunit of the interactive unit and to compare these declarations with those occasions when the children were present.

If the analyst wants to compare moments of sharing and polite behavior or etiquette in the preschool with those situations where conflict and hostility are present, he first charts all the objects and situations in the school where these behaviors are

most likely to occur. Working from his representational map of
the field, he may then confine his observations to juice and cracker
time and compare those behaviors to conduct in the sandbox,
the tree house, or the carpenter shed.

The foregoing suggests that the naturalist pays careful
attention to the ritual and temporal features of the social organizations he wishes to study. He samples at "peak" times and justifies his decisions by the working knowledge of the unit in
question. He stratifies and cuts up his subject's behavior into
theoretically informed, empirically grounded subunits. If he has
successfully entered the subject's worlds, he should know the
salient temporal features, and he can make his sampling and
observational decisions on that basis. But, to repeat, he *must* inform the broader scientific community of the steps he went
through when his sampling decisions were made. This is why the
quasi-statistical representational map of the subject's interactional world becomes so crucial. It lays bare the extent to which
the analyst is familiar with and has penetrated the worlds in question. It also serves as an observational aid, for the investigator
may find that he has overlooked a particularly crucial behavioral
area or that he has oversampled an area that is less representative.

The naturalist must be sensitive to the fact that many of
the behaviors he wishes to study occur at a low frequency because they are rigidly timed. Such behaviors cannot be experi-
mentally produced. Students of preschool life cannot replicate
the range of panic and crisis behavior that ensues every fall
when a new batch of three-year-olds are left by their mothers for
the first time. If he wishes to examine the strength of parental
identification in early childhood, one strategic moment becomes
the early weeks in the preschool year; he must be present at
that time.

Generalizing. To the best of his ability, the investigator
must offer evidence on the degree to which his samples of behavior are representative of the class of joint acts he wishes to
generalize to. Unfortunately, the population from which the acts
are sampled may be unknown. This is acutely the case in the
study of deviant behavior that remains unofficially recorded (see
Becker, 1970a). More importantly, while investigators may have

evidence on how classes or types of persons (for instance, college-educated or white-collar) are distributed across a geographical space, there are few, if any, records of how such persons come together in interactive relationships (for example, clubs, parties, and encounters). As a consequence, the naturalistic observer seldom can specify with precise detail the universe of interactive relationships to which he wishes to generalize. He takes several approaches to the problem. He may, as Becker (1970a, pp. 35–36) suggests, locate himself in a situation where the joint act occurs and argue that his sample is drawn from the behaviors of all persons who pass through that situation (see Cavan, 1966). He then attempts to generalize on the basis of how representative that situation is. He may sample by time of year, for example, in a study of national holidays and may argue that his findings hold for all persons who celebrate Christmas, Easter, and so on (see Lueschen and others, 1971, for a cross-national study of families celebrating Christmas). He may select incarcerated populations—for example, preschoolers—and then generalize, not to preschoolers as such but to preschools as a class of social organization, here noting theoretically relevant differences in schools—for example, parents present or absent, number of staff, racial composition, dominant ideology, and income level of parents (see the informative suggestions of Schatzman and Strauss, 1973, on time, person, and situational sampling strategies). He may identify a recurring type of encounter, as Brede (1971) did in his analysis of police-juvenile interactions, and may distinguish types of encounters (proactive, reactive, familial, "shit pinching," "good pinches," and so on). Here the encounter is temporally specified (for example, during a specific month) and is located situationally in police precincts. The population thus becomes all police-juvenile encounters for a specified period of time in a class of precincts, and the sample is drawn from that universe. Here the analyst is aided by formal records. Most encounters are not so conveniently recorded (for example, mothers confronting other mothers with their children in public places). Here the investigator has no other recourse than to specify as rigorously as possible his temporal and spatial sampling frames.

Selecting Cases. The representational question is answered, in part, through the selection of cases for intensive study. Here the analyst distinguishes *representative cases* that appear at a frequency sufficient to accurately cover the range of explained behaviors and *anecdotal cases* that appear at a lower frequency and that depict a small range of behaviors (see, for example, the analysis of medical students in Becker and others, 1961, which compares those who did and did not share the dominant perspective toward studying for exams). The distinction between these two case types is highlighted by the discovery of *negative cases*—those behavior episodes that clearly refute an emerging theory or proposition. Negative and anecdotal cases serve to clarify additional causal properties that influence the behaviors under study (see Lindesmith's classic 1947 analysis of opiate addiction).

In my observations of "becoming a member" of the preschool, I noted five students who remained outside the school's friendship circles. One was under drug sedation, another was autistic, another was a latecomer, one was periodically ill and absent from the school, and the last was suffering from separation problems. Each of these cases suggested a set of variables that could modify a child's social experiences in the school, and each child's isolation required a slightly different explanatory scheme. By contrasting these five cases and comparing them to the representative cases, I was able to lay bare the contours of the typical moral career of a three-year-old preschooler.

Representative cases describe behaviors of acting units, not acting units as such. As already indicated, analysts can select from any acting unit's total repertoire of joint acts a small subset for special analysis. This in effect is what I did when I selected etiquette behaviors in the preschool for separate analysis. Students of family life, as indicated, can select from a family's network of interactions those behaviors that reveal (1) intimacy; (2) socialization; (3) entertainment; (4) work; (5) trip taking; and so on. In short, every interactive unit has associated with it a wide range of differing behaviors. Each of these behaviors carries differential weight for one's emerging theory. Complete familiarity with an acting unit's behavioral repertoires is in order before (1) systematic sampling can occur and (2) representative cases can be distinguished from anecdotal and negative cases.

Naturalistic Indicators. I have attempted to indicate how the naturalist goes about linking his concepts to the empirical world. Starting with loose, sensitizing definitions of his critical concepts, he operationalizes those concepts only after he has entered and understood the world under inspection. In so doing, he attempts to multiply around his conceptual indicators. He includes as many behaviors as possible as indicators of the concept under analysis. Studies of the self in preschool, while enhanced by verbal reports, are severely limited if the observer does not link his conception of self with "selfing behavior" (see McPhail and Tucker, 1972). He studies those actions by the children that display definitions of self, situation, and others. He searches out children who act as play directors, assigning roles and positions to others. He examines those times when children write their names on paintings and place special objects in their lockers to take home. He records those instances when they make declarations of mood, and he makes note of their attempts to stake out special territorial locales. He watches which costumes are routinely worn by which children, and he examines favorite games. Each of these observations represents attempts to link the self as "object" and "process" to the conduct of acting units. The analyst becomes a microbehaviorist, taking his subject's perspective on the concept in question as his own and attempting to record the range of actions that depict the concept.

Triangulation. Triangulation forces the observer to combine multiple data sources, research methods, and theoretical schemes in the inspection and analysis of behavioral specimens. It forces him to *situationally* check the validity of his causal propositions (for example, comparing a family's socialization strategies at home and in public places). It forces him to *temporally* specify the character of his hypothesis (for example, comparing a mother's openness toward her child early in the morning versus her actions late in the afternoon when a meal is being prepared).

It directs the observer to compare his native's theories of behavior (for instance, the rhetoric of any liberation group—

Weathermen, Women's Lib) with his emerging sociological scheme (for example, see Micossi, 1970). Here the analyst endeavors to work back and forth between multiple sociological approaches and native reconstructions. His hope is to construct a theory that rings true at both levels (that is, it is sociologically sound and behaviorally realistic to the native). It is inevitable that contradictions will emerge as the observer combines his triangulated data sources. In part this arises because of the low credibility of some of his sources (for example, many public relations documents put forth by liberation groups are proselytizing public announcements aimed at recruiting new members; they seldom reflect accurately the private interpretations held by all of the group's members, even of their leaders). The naturalist must have an intimate familiarity with all of his data sources so he can judge which ones to discount, which ones to treat as negative cases, which ones to build into his representative cases.

Asking the Right Question. The naturalist organizes and inspects his behavioral specimens in ways that will hopefully lead him to progressively reveal the *underlying problematic features* of the social organization in question. He seeks to ask the right question or questions that will make that organization understandable. This is quite different from approaching the empirical world with a preconceived set of hypotheses. He is directed, initially, toward an interest in the routine, nonproblematic features of the persons in question. He may ask how preschool teachers greet mothers and children every morning; he may ask what dominant activities occur at what times in an average day at the preschool. By noting these repeatable acts, he now has a handle on the more perduring questions confronted by his native actors. It is the character of these questions—the problematic acts confronted by native peoples—that must become his focus of attention. Here new theory is written, past sociological schemes are challenged, and new understandings are gained.

In my own observations of preschools, I was struck by the remarkable differences in interactional style displayed by two-year-olds and three- and four-year-olds. The two-year-old children openly stared at me, seldom talked, and seldom initiated interactions with other children. The three- and four-year-olds, on the other hand, *would not* initiate visual eye interactions with me; did talk, shout, laugh, and cry; and did form friendships and small groups. The difference between these two age groups provoked an intensive analysis of language at these two ages and revealed that two-year-olds spoke a language that was more private and nonconsensual than that found among three- and four-year-olds. In short, the language of two-year-olds is often unique to each child, and when a group of two-year-olds are thrown together they fail to share anything approaching a consensual language. But three- and four-year-olds do share such a language, and they also share a working model of polite behavior, and so on. By comparing these two groups, I was able to develop some working hypotheses concerning the role of language and consensuality in everyday interactions. And I was able to specify the differential impact of language by age level and situational context. That is, I compared two-year-olds in their homes, where their languages were understood, with two-year-olds in preschools, where their speech was more problematic. The naturalist, then, searches for significant questions that can then be cast in terms of behaviorally specifiable propositions and causal arguments. The hypothesis follows, not precedes, the search for significant questions.

Reliability, Repeatability, and Validity. To repeat, naturalistic indicators represent any segment of a subject's behavior that reflect on or describe a sociological concept. They are naturalistic in the sense that they derive from the subject's world of meaning and action. They are not imposed on that world by the sociologist, although they are sociologically interpreted. For example, I contrast here behavioral measures of alcoholism (how much and how often a man drinks) with investigator-imposed attitude scales measuring propensities to drink. To take another example, at one level one can assess a socializing agent's actions toward a child by *counting* the number of times that the agent interacts with the child (see Wright, 1962). Having established that the agent does interact with the child, the next question becomes one of detailing the ways in which the agent carries out his or her interactions. Does he or she challenge, physically coerce, hug, negotiate with, and so on? Additionally, in what situations and at what times do the interactions occur? Proceeding in this fashion, the naturalist is able to build up a set of

behavioral specimens that depict how the agent and child interact. He then inspects these specimens for what they tell him
about socialization in general and in specific about the actors
in question.

The first criterion for assessing a naturalistic indicator is
its degree of behavioral validity. Does it appear in the acting
unit's behavioral repertory? At what frequency, in what situations, at what times? The greater its frequency across time and
situation, the greater its behavioral validity. Thus, if one wanted
to hypothesize that Jody (in the case of making breakfast discussed earlier) defined the act of making breakfast as one where
she *had* and *made* the orange juice, then to test that hypothesis
it would be necessary to observe Jody's behavior in the breakfast-
making situation for a sufficient period of time to determine
whether that definition of the situation routinely appeared or
was an episodic occurrence unique to the morning in question. In
this case, a component of the definition of the situation (one
actor's utterances and actions toward a particular object) is
recorded and extracted for specific analysis. The concept (definition of situation) has been grounded in one actor's behaviors and
is observed naturalistically as it occurs morning after morning.

A second criterion for assessing naturalistic indicators is
whether it occurs at a frequency sufficient to permit repeated observations: While the "separation crisis" in preschools typically
terminates by the second week of each new year, such crises
appear and can be observed every fall. Here the analyst distinguishes between repeatable episodic acts and those which
occur only once, or a few times. He hopes to be present when
such acts occur, thus saving observational time. Of greater importance, many acts only appear once in an acting unit's behavioral biography (those who make only one marriage proposal,
have it accepted, and remain married to the same person for a
lifetime). Such acts can only be retrospectively reconstructed.
The analyst must separate those episodic acts that do not carry
much long-term biographical effect, from those that do.

Third, is the indicator based on public acts? Pronoun
utterances by three-year-olds, for example, represent one class
of linguistic indicators in the study of the self. Such utterances
are public; they are audible productions. Indicators based on

private acts must be employed, but they should never take precedence in naturalistic studies. They must be balanced against the proportion of public indicator acts and must be used as complements to the investigator's data base. Thus, when a man ruminates about a proposed future act, such ruminations are important and must be collected, but they are of little use until the future act is observed. The observer cannot confine his observations of the social act to its covert phases—he must move from attitude to public act. Only in this way can he link the subjective world of social experience to the public world of behavioral acts.

The naturalistic observer recognizes, as Deutscher (1966, p. 241) argues, that human interaction is always changing and shifting as persons confront new and different situations. Reliability, then, becomes more a question of interaction than test variation. It is appropriately replaced by the criterion of repeatability. The naturalist asks two questions when he concerns himself with repeatability and reliability. Will repeated observations of the behavior in question (1) clarify an emergent theory and (2) improve the quality of observation? Some acts, especially those which occur at low frequencies, need not be observed repeatedly (if the observer has carefully recorded the character of the phenomenon during its moment of occurrence). If he has reason to believe that his earlier observations are faulty (lacking in detail or naturalistic indicators), then he is justified in returning to the field. If not, such records quickly decrease in theoretical payoff.

Measurement. The preceding discussion has repeatedly touched on the measurement problem. The naturalist seldom confines himself to one measuring instrument or to one measurement class (for example, attitude scales or direct observation). He works with multiple indicators and data classes. In one sense, the naturalist does not measure behavior—he records behavior specimens and then subjects those specimens to complex and detailed causal inspections. He does not treat measurement as a separate phase of the research act. His aim is to leave the field with records of behavior that have occurred. By continually sifting through those records, he progressively develops analytic models that may combine several types of data (for example, nominal, ordinal, interval, and ratio). He may relate age to

verbal ability, size of friendship network, sex, and class background—all in an attempt to understand the character of the self
in early childhood. He attempts to take processes meaningful to
his subject and to classify and cross classify these processes in
ways that reveal underlying causal relationships. He is obliged,
for both sampling and causal purposes, to show the distribution
of his analytic variables and concepts in the social worlds under
study. These demonstrations more clearly specify the unique
features of those studied, but they also indicate empirical deficiencies in his central indicators. That is, he may treat sex as an
independent variable in the analysis of friendships among two-
year-olds and find that sex has no meaning for his subjects. Or
he may find that his critical causal variables lack naturalistic
grounding or that he has biased observations of them. (IQ scores
given by a particular teacher may reflect her special way of giving the test or of analyzing the child in question.)

    The naturalist assesses the quality of his observations by
their degree of stability across measurement classes. For example, is there observer agreement on which preschoolers are
friends? Do IQ scores vary by the race of test taker and test
giver? Do children agree with an observer's designation of who
their best friends are? As contradictions are located, the observer must return to the problem of data credibility, while at
the same time checking whether temporal or situational factors
are producing the observed differences.

    In brief, the naturalist's stance toward measurement is to
adapt a triangulated observational approach that permits him
to gather behavior specimens and that gives special attention to
naturalistic indicators.

    Causal Analysis. The naturalist forms and tests his prop-
ositions while in the field. He employs native observers as tests
of his explanations. He assesses the quality of his observations by
their degree of behavioral validity. (That is, has he used naturalistic indicators, and do his hypotheses reflect behaviors engaged
in by the subject?) Second, he gives greatest credence to those
hypotheses that have withstood the impact of triangulated observations. Do multiple observers, data sources, or theories lead
to the same analytic conclusions? (See Webb and others, 1964.)
Third, he assesses the repeatability ratio of the acts he has ob-

served and the indicators he has gathered on those acts. Here he must have multiple instances of the concept, and he must have specified its occurrence by time and place. If he locates a critical act that has occurred in the past, he must gather multiple reconstructions of the act so as to determine the range of possible meanings that have been brought to it. For example, what does a separation crisis mean for a particular child? For the child's parents? For the head preschool instructor? Fourth, causal propositions are examined from multiple theoretical stances. Here the sociologist separates his outsider theories from the rhetorics and explanations developed by the natives in question. He places these several theories side by side to see which ones alone and in combination explain the greatest amount of behavior. Last, causal propositions are examined to determine which variables and processes are based on public, and/or only private utterances or actions. The final theory must account for publicly observable behavioral acts.

Naturalistic theorists attempt to develop sequential, phaselike theories; they assume that no event is the product of one variable or process. Children do not just become members of a preschool. They pass through a series of interconnected phases or turning point moments. It is the analyst's assignment to identify these phases and to show how each phase shapes behavior in the next phase or stage of development. (For example, see Becker's classic studies [1970b] of marijuana use, which detailed the interlinked acts one must pass through to become a member of a group that use the drug. And see Lofland, 1971, for a more general treatment of phase analysis.)

To identify the phases persons pass through (that is, the search for necessary, not sufficient, conditions), the observer must have knowledge of what the outcome or final phase is. It may be smoking marijuana, being a member of the preschool, or getting married. He must empirically specify that outcome and gather multiple observations of how it may vary (for example, being a member of a preschool may mean simply having one friend, or it may mean being a leader of the boys' group). He then works back in time, to uncover what actions his focal subjects undertook to get where they now are. At the same time, the naturalist attempts to follow new members into the situation, to gather on-the-spot records of their behaviors. This problem of moving back and forth between the past and the present establishes the cardinal importance of the behavioral specimens. They should be like films that can be replayed and reanalyzed as new questions are asked and as new negative cases emerge.

Introspection and the Observer. I have suggested what role the observer should play in his studies. He (or she) is central to the entire naturalistic enterprise. It is he who provides the basic data on the covert features of the social act. In taking oneself seriously, it is relevant to distinguish first-, second-, and third-person introspective accounts of social process. The observer can treat himself as a third-person object, placing himself in a collective group and noting how "they" acted. He or she can introspectively take the role of a second party, imputing motive to a wife, daughter, or colleague. And finally, he or she can treat self in the first-person sense. Each of these stances reflect observations of self and other from the standpoint of the observing sociologist. A fully grounded introspectionist account would include all three perspectives. But to repeat, even as he or she acts as an introspectionist, the analyst is obliged to move from his or her "private" covert versions of the act in question to its public, interactional features. He or she attempts to forge the several competing "definitions of the situation" into a theoretically valid, behaviorally grounded analysis.

Summary

The foregoing offers a view of naturalistic inquiry that is derived from the symbolic interactionist perspective. A framework for conducting naturalistic studies has been offered, and I have suggested how the naturalist confronts the perduring problems as causal analysis, measurement, and sampling. I have advocated the use of introspection as a major data source. And I have argued that significant sociological studies begin from an attempt to understand personal problems. The naturalistic behaviorist attempts to transform these problems into significant questions that can be publicly addressed. He takes himself seriously and asks that the sociological community do likewise.

Chapter Four

Studying
Symbolic Interaction
in Childhood

*T*he early childhood socialization process has seldom admitted of or been exposed to a thorough-going sociological or social psychological analysis. (Piaget's extensive research is a major exception.) Due to the relative lack of attention to early childhood socialization, a full-fledged sociological theory of self and society has yet to be developed. The links between self and other, between organism and environment, between significant other and socialized other have yet to emerge, although the works of Cooley (1922), Mead (1934), and Markey (1928) clearly indicate the essential features of the socialization process.

It is not my intent to offer a theory of the socialization process, nor can I offer a theory of self and society. Such an

57

offering would rest on speculation and only fragmentary data. (My observations are drawn from the naturalistic study of young children and their caretakers in a midwestern city. As such, these observations may be regionally as well as nationally specific.) My concerns are more restricted and are twofold: first, to address the factors that impede the study of the early socialization process and, second, to suggest five sociological issues of a symbolic interactionist nature that might be advanced through the study of young children and their caretakers. My intentions are to reverse the usual scheme of sociological analysis, which typically asks how young children become adultlike. Rather, I shall ask how it is that children do not act adultlike. Such a reversal will hopefully make more apparent the "taken-for-granted" realities of everyday life that such spokesmen as Garfinkel (1967) and Goffman (1974) have suggested constitute the proper study of social order.

Substantive Interactional Issues Derived from the Study of Young Children

The following five topics derived from the study of young children are not exhaustive, but they share one common feature: They are taken from the study of focused interactional processes and as such reflect on a symbolic interactionist account of human group life. These topics are briefly stated as follows: (1) language acquisition and linguistic uniqueness; (2) candor, openness, and truthfulness; (3) play, work, and situated activity; (4) friendship and shifting group alignments; (5) deference, demeanor, tact, and taste. In short, each of these issues—as observed in early childhood—are qualitatively different from the behaviors of the "socialized" adult. These differences thus (1) make the study of early childhood a differentially difficult enterprise and (2) point directly to what it is that adults take for granted on an everyday basis. The young child is a problematic actor who makes the production of routine social order a problematic enterprise. The implications are hopefully clear. The study of the young child should furnish insights into adult interaction patterns. (The obverse is also clearly the case.) These five topics constitute problematic elements in the study of the socialization process. They

simultaneously become reasons, or causes, that impede a sociological understanding of early childhood and point directly to
those aspects of childhood that adults (and sociological investigators) find most problematic.

Why Children Are Bad Sociological Subjects

Most sociological methods work best in the study of persons most like the sociologist. These methods typically assume
articulate respondents. They work least well with those persons
who do not share the sociologist's perspective, and sociologists
confront real problems when those studied are inarticulate. Children do not make good sociological subjects. Their speech patterns are often slurred and idiosyncratic. They may speak a
private language that only a few other persons can understand.
They often refuse to show proper deference to self or other. They
are subject to the control of their caretakers, and they reside
behind the closed walls of school and home. They are not ready
subjects for naturalistic investigations. If adults have difficulty
articulating their thoughts and introspections, children may not
be aware that they have thoughts. The child's conception of truthfulness is less than candid, and he may not be a willing respon-
dent to the sociologist's interrogations. Brown (1970, p. 79)
makes the following observation on Adam, a two-year-old subject: "We noticed that Adam would sometimes pluralize nouns
when they should have been pluralized and sometimes would not.
We wondered if he could make grammatical judgments about
the plural, if he could distinguish a correct form from an incor-
rect form. 'Adam,' we asked, 'which is right, two shoes or two
shoe?' His answer on that occasion, produced with explosive
enthusiasm, was 'Pop goes the weasel!' The two-year-old child
does not make a perfectly docile experimental subject."

If children vary on these dimensions, it can also be argued that what adults take for work children often attempt to
transform into play. They act as disruptive and irregular per-
formers in the regularized routines of the adult. Their friendships
and conceptions of friendship are often short-lived and are based
on the most fleeting of grounds.

Childhood, then, is a unique social world. An analysis of

each of the dimensions listed earlier should establish the following conclusion: The world of young children is a distinct world that furnishes fertile data for the symbolic interactionist. A study of this world should tell us more about the socialization process and may eventually contribute to a sociological theory of self and society. I turn to each topic in order.

Language Acquisition and Linguistic Uniqueness

Language must be viewed in part as a situated production, the use of which involves speakers talking in three distinct modes. The first form is termed *thought* and involves silent vocal speech that the speaker directs toward himself. The second form is talk of a verbal nature that interactants vocally direct toward one another. The third form involves paralinguistic speech and includes the gestures the speaker gives off through facial movements, smiles, nods, frowns, and other movements of the body. Language consists of a set of more or less significant gestures, the meanings of which are lodged in the concrete moment of the speech act. These meanings need not be consensual, but these gestures must call out a range of possible responses that could and can be made when they are received and interpreted by each interactant. Interactants assume that the utterances and gestures they produce and direct toward another are in some fashion responded to, and this assumption rests on alter's formulating to himself, through silent inner speech, alternative plans of action.
Normalized, everyday interaction between persons who have mastered a common language rests on some version of the speech act as outlined. Interaction between persons who have not mastered a common language produces problematic interactional sequences. Furthermore, if an interactant in a sequence or social relationship has no conception of inner speech, of the concept of work, of the meaning of a sentence, or does not know how to interpret a clap of the hand or a nod or a smile, then interaction becomes even more problematic. Young children constitute one class of speakers who may be termed *problematic*. Mental patients and the elderly perhaps describe another group of actors who could be so classified. (Robert Walsh suggests in

a conversation that unlike the elderly and the mentally ill, it is much more difficult to relegate children to a place where they are "out of sight and out of mind.")

If children and adults do not share the same version of the speech act, what are the peculiar features of childhood speech? The following characteristics have been identified. A discussion of each feature should highlight what adult speakers of a common language take for granted. First, it is often the case that the same word is used in an apparently indiscriminate fashion to identify objects or events that to the adult obviously exist in different categories. As noted elsewhere in this book, my eldest daughter at the age of twenty-five months employed the word *baby* to refer to her younger sister, to her doll, to any small child she observed on the street, and to herself when she was once a baby. To an outsider, her utterances lacked meaning, and they were taken as indicative of her inability to use language correctly. Yet each use of the word *baby* had a contextualized or situated meaning. When accompanied by a nonverbal gesture, as when she would point to her "baby" doll, the word's meaning became quite apparent.

More than the speech of the adult, the child's talk is more likely to be situation specific, to rely on nonverbal gestures, and to depend on previously "contextualized" understandings. An outsider to the child's speech community, lacking these understandings, is often led to regard the young speaker as linguistically incompetent. This judgment further increases the likelihood that any interactions with the young speaker are liable to be problematic and short-lived in nature.

Second, the speech community of the young child, which is grounded in the intimate interactions of the family or primary group, is likely to be a person-specific, situation-specific language. Unlike the language of polite discourse or scientific exchange, this language is unique to the family and to the speakers that make up the family. Furthermore, the speech of the young child is unique to that child, as he or she struggles to learn the meanings (and names) of objects, events, others, self, and caretaker. At early points in the child's linguistic development, not even the caretaker can understand particular strings of utterances or what appear to be pure babblings. This person-specific language produces problematic interactions for the caretaker. He struggles to give meaning to the unwritten language the child speaks. While the child is a potential speaker born into a universe of other speakers, at the outset neither class of speakers can understand the other. That social transactions between these two classes of interactants are somehow managed attests to the strength of the interpersonal relationship that is the nexus of linguistic socialization. Further research into the linguistic transactions that occur between the very young child and the caretaker is needed if we are to understand how an "incompetent" speaker can somehow be incorporated into normalized interaction sequences.

M. M. Lewis (1963, p. 59) offers an example of such research. The specimen is taken from observations of his own son. Since the tenth month, the child has frequently said "a . . . a . . . a" in a tone of delight in a variety of situations.

One year, four months, twelve days:	His mother brings him near some jonquils growing in a bowl. She says, "Smell the pretty flowers." He bends over and smells them, saying, "a . . . a . . . a"
One year, four months, thirteen days:	The child is crawling about the room. His mother says, "Where are the flowers?" He crawls toward the jonquils and holds out his hand toward them.
One year, four months, sixteen days:	In another room, there is a bowl of tulips. His mother says, "Baby, where's the flowers?" He points to the tulips.
One year, six months, fourteen days:	His mother is holding him by a window, through which he can see a bowl of hyacinths in the room. He puts his hand on the window pane and says, "fa fa."

Lewis comments (p. 59) on the evolution of the word "fa fa" from "a . . . a . . . a": "It is clear that in replacing his primary expressive 'a . . . a' by 'fa'—his adaptation of the adult word—the child is making a dual advance. He is able to communicate his delight more effectively, to draw his mother's attention to the flowers and not to any other object in the room. At the same time, he is enabling himself to link up his feeling of pleasure with the flowers, to bring this feeling more closely into relation with the flowers." Lewis' child is attaching the meaning of a sound to an object, and this is an arduous and negotiated process that involves the sympathetic and systematic attention of the listener if consensus and differentiation is to develop.

Third, the speech utterances of the young child, unlike those of the adult, often cluster into sharp vocalizations that take the perceived shape of the cry, the scream, and the yowl. At a very early age, these sounds constitute the most significant gestures of the child. The caretaker struggles to develop a typology of meanings that he can give to different types of cries, perhaps developing some consensus around cries that designate boredom, fear, pain, discomfort, hunger, and danger. Utterances of this order are expected to drop out of the vocal vocabulary of the socialized adult. If such utterances do appear, they must be linked to some ongoing personal or social experience that justifies an adult crying. No such justifications need be apparent for the crying child.

Fourth, unlike the adult speaker, who is quite experienced in separating words and thoughts from action, the young speaker can often be observed to make no such distinction. The mere utterance of a word produces an action sequence that plays out the interactional implications of the word. The child merges the overt and covert sides of the act, and thus he displays little of what Mead (1934) would have termed "act rehearsal." This feature of the child's speech behavior produces problematic episodes for the adult, who, on making a statement such as "We must leave now," often engages in a long leave-taking ritual. The child, hearing that utterance, takes it seriously and perhaps prematurely brings the adult's ritual activity to a close. Until the speaker has acquired the ability to separate word from deed, he or she will continue to be a problematic actor in the world of the adult caretaker.

Candor, Openness, and Truthfulness

Normalized, everyday interaction rests on the tactful doctrine that individuals do not fully disclose their attitudes or reactions to others. Personal repulsion, aversion, and other negative attitudes toward specific others are expected to be withheld or, if acknowledged, done so in a way that minimizes one's aversive reactions to others (see Davis, 1961). Candor, openness, and truthfulness are problematic elements in any interactional encounter among socialized adults; they are even more problematic in encounters between adults and young children. The young child challenges the finer edges of polite society and can be regarded as an obtrusive intruder into the fictional world of adult equality. Davis (1961, p. 129) makes the following observation on the interactional rule violations frequently experienced at the hands of young children by those who are visibly handicapped: "Many of the informants were quite open in stating that a small child at a social occasion caused them much uneasiness and cramped their style because they were concerned with how, with other adults present, they would handle some barefaced question from the child." The obese individual is exposed to similar experiences. A young child, age three years, is accompanying her mother to a plant nursery. While waiting in line at the cash register, the young female notices a middle-aged woman weighing approximately 300 pounds. The following conversation was recorded:

Child: "Mommy, look at that fat lady. What's wrong with her?"
Mother: "Shush." (Smiles at the lady in question.)
Lady: (Looks away, moves to cash register.)
Child: "Mommy! What's wrong with her?"
Mother: (Moves child out of line and gives lecture on talking so loud in public.)

Children not only show a refusal to be tactful toward adults, but they also reveal a similar tendency toward their own peers. For example, a young child aged five years has fallen on the sidewalk and bruised her lower lip, which swells out of proportion. It turns blue and purple and then slightly yellow. At recess the next day at school, she is confronted with a six-year-old male playmate. The following conversation was reported:

Male: "That is the ugliest lip I have ever seen. You are ugly."
Female: "I hate you!"

This episode suggests an additional factor. The failure to summarily uphold the polite fiction that persons with swollen lips do not look ugly leads to the consequence that cruel and harsh evaluations about others is a potentially underlying variable in any interaction sequence. While adults know this and continue to act "as if" such an interpretation is not a potential, children refuse to sustain the "as if" implication. Consider the following exchange in a park, which also bears on any analysis of friendship in early childhood.

An adult has taken three girls, ages six, three, and two, to a neighborhood park. While there, the six-year-old encounters a classmate from school whom she wishes to ignore. He approaches her, stands in front of her as she swings, repeats her name several times. She refuses to acknowledge his presence. Finally he confronts her directly and attempts to force her into recognizing him.

Boy: "You're stupid. You can't even spell. You don't even know my name."
Girl: (Ignores him.)
Boy: "I bet you don't know my name. It begins with *E* and ends with *K* and has *R* and *I* in between. I bet you don't know what that spells."
Girl: (She has turned her back on him while he spells out his name.) She slowly turns, faces him directly and says: "It spells *France*."
Boy: "I hate you, I want to kill you."

To be socialized is to learn how to be cruel, how not to be cruel, and how to read and manage cruelty. Groups and relationships vary in their respective emphases on these processes, with some stressing relatively open, candid expressions of rejection and emotion and others giving greater attention to masking and politeness. (In general, it appears that adult-monitored encounters between children such as preschoolers give greater emphasis to statements such as "You didn't really mean that, now, did you?" "You apologize to Charles for hitting.") An example can be taken from Murphy (1937, pp. 45–46) on preschool observations: "Julius picked up Gregory, carried him into the bathroom and dropped him on the floor, said 'Oops!', picked him up again, then let him walk, went off, returned, picked Gregory up, and said, 'Don't cry,' when Gregory cried, and patted him. . . . The teacher took [Julius] off and said to him, 'He thinks you are trying to hurt him. You weren't, were you?' Julius said, 'No.' The teacher said, 'Tell him.' Julius said to Gregory, 'I wasn't trying to hurt you,' and patted him and stroked his hair." Lies, willful or accidental, are also a prevalent element in early childhood presentations. We do not know if Julius intended to hurt Gregory when he dropped him to the floor in the bathroom. It is a curious paradox that children are punished for lying, while adults are rewarded for engaging in the same activity, suggesting again that polite adult society rests on a set of serious fictions that are maintained through a systematic structure of lies.

Play, Work, and Situated Activity

Goffman (1961b, pp. 5–6) has made the following observation on the social organization of play, work, and situated activity: "A basic social arrangement in modern society is that the individual tends to sleep, play, and work in different places, with different coparticipants, under different authorities and without an overall rational plan." Young children do not conform with this model, and, like inmates in total institutions, they tend to sleep, play, and work in the same company of others twenty-four hours a day. This presents intrusive problems for the child's caretaker, for what the caretaker takes to be work the

child takes to be play. And what the child works at may be regarded by the adult as "playful nonsense." An uneasy relationship exists between the two parties. A father is preparing a salad
for the evening dinner. His daughter, age three years, five
months, enters the kitchen and pulls a chair over to the counter
top. The following behavior was recorded.

Father:	"Hi, sweety, how are you? Leave Daddy alone; he's working."
Daughter:	"Hi, Daddy. I want to help. What can I do?"
Father:	"Go play, sweetheart."
Daughter:	"No. I want to help." (Child picks up head of lettuce, squeezes it, and drops it in the sink. She attempts to lean over to pick it up, and her chair topples to the floor, leaving her dangling in the sink.)
Father:	(Picks the child up. Modulates his voice, and sends the child off to play.)

Elsewhere it has been suggested that the child's play is
often regarded as an intrusion in the adult's world. Adults take
pleasure in watching children play only as long as the child's play
does not disrupt the adult's work or playful activities. Typically,
the child is told to go and play, but to play in a place that is not
occupied by the adult. (Ariès, 1962, suggests that this distinction between child's play and child's work may be a historical
occurrence specific to Western societies. Those social structures
that minimize the differences between children and adults will be
more likely to incorporate the child's behavior into the adult's
behavioral repertoires.)

The serious activities of the child, which the child approaches with the dedication of an adult at work, are similarly
viewed as intrusive and "nuisancelike" in nature. Two boys, ages
four and five, have located four gallons of green paint in the
garage belonging to the five-year-old's parents. They take the
four gallons of paint over to a goldfish pond and proceed to pour
the paint into the pond. They work at this activity for nearly one
hour until they are discovered by the mother of the five-year-old.
The following conversation was recorded:

Mother:	"What are you doing?"
Five-Year-Old:	"We are painting the fish pond green for Daddy."
Mother:	"Stop immediately."
Boys:	"We were only trying to make it pretty."
Mother:	"Out! Now! You two are going to be spanked, and hard, for this!"

The serious actions of the young child either go unnoticed and are regarded as playful in nature, or they are approached with a vengeance, as was the case with this mother. In some instances, these actions are defined as a willful violation of the adult's moral order, in which case the child's play is regarded as a lapse in moral character. Few techniques of neutralization are brought into play when judgments of this order are made (Sykes and Matza, 1959).

Young children are caught in a dilemma. Oftentimes not taken seriously, they are rewarded only insofar as they retreat into their own worlds of play, fiction, and work. Such retreats make children less problematic for adults, although the consequences may be less than desirable, for it encourages the creation of a privatized world that is neither open nor revealed to the adult. This private world may, however, take on a life of its own such that it transcends its childhood origins. A. A. Milne (1939, pp. 47–48) offers an illustration. He and his brother Ken were four and five at the time and had been toad hunting. They had caught a toad and killed it. They regarded this feat with some significance and responded as follows.

A secret so terrific, a deed so bloody, had to be formulated. The initial formula was Raw Toad (as you would have believed, if you had seen what we saw). Raw Toad was *R.T.*, which was *arte,* and Latin for "by, with, or from art." Artus was a limb (or wasn't it?) and the first and last letters of *limb* were *L.B. Lb.* was *pound;* you talked about a "pig in a pound"; *pig* was *P.G.;* and (Greek, now Ken had just begun Greek) πηγη was *fountain.* So, ranging lightly over several languages, we had reached our mystical formula—"FN." Thumbs on the same hymnbook in

Dr. Gibson's church, we would whisper "FN," to each other and know that life was not all Sunday; side by side in the drawing room, hair newly brushed for visitors and in those damnable starched sailor suits, we would look "FN" at each other and be comforted. And though, within six months sharing some entirely different secret, yet, forty years later, the magic letters had power to raise sudden memories in two middle-aged men, smoking their pipes, and wondering what to do with their sons.

Friendship and Shifting Group Alignments

The structured world of the adult rests on a small circle of stable social relationships and friendships that are given some significance in the adult's everyday round of activity. Whether situational or orientational in influence, those others the adult takes seriously are given some degree of credibility. They are taken to be serious others whose influence is legitimate and whose concerns are ones that must be respected (see Kuhn, 1964). Adults have friends. Children have playmates, little friends, classmates, and persons they have "made friends with." The interactive, peer-group others of the child are not accorded the significance or importance that the adult claims for his significant others. The child's playmates are viewed as others who take the child off the adult's hands, often at the adult's convenience. They are a resource to be employed when the adult wishes to seriously pursue the activities of adult work or leisure. This segregative stance toward the child's world drives a further wedge between his world and that of adults and leads to the construction of secret societies and private social relationships. This world, not so freely entered, is viewed with casual or little respect by the adult and is not taken seriously as long as it does not too apparently corrode the adult's conception of who he wants his child to become. Two girls, ages three and four, move into a neighborhood wherein an established play and friendship pattern has been built up among three girls, ages, three, four, and five. The newcomers enter a backyard, asking if they can play. The following behavior was observed:

Newcomer 1:	"Can we play?"
Newcomer 2:	"We are new here."
Regular 1:	"OK, I guess."
Regulars 2 and 3:	"No, we don't like you."
Newcomers 1 and 2:	(Run up and hit Regular 1.) "Damn you. We want to play."
Regulars:	(in unison) "We don't like you."

The parents, overhearing this conversation, drew the regulars aside and said, "We don't play with people who hit one another and swear."

Two elements are of interest in this episode. First, the parents clearly offered a definition of who a proper friend should be. Second, and of greater interest, is the short-lived nature of this attempt to form a friendship. Within one minute, the regulars had decided that they would not play with the newcomers. This rapid conclusion to the transaction supports the adult's conception that perhaps the child's world of interactive others is one that is based on conditions that are not well thought out (although in this instance the adults' grounds for a friendship also seem somewhat arbitrary). The adult is regarded as a competent selector of interactive others; the child is not. On occasion children support this conclusion and on others do not. The following account (reported more fully in Chapter Eight) was given to me by a four-year-old boy to explain his friendship with another child. It both confirms and refutes the typical adult conception of childhood friendships: "He wants to be a friend real bad. But you see it's in his head why he wants to be my best friend, and it's in my head, and I can't know what he feels and thinks. I don't know. He wants to be a friend real bad. It's in my head. We just play together."

The child's free entry to the world of fantasy permits the arbitrary construction of territorial boundaries and gives his sense of group alignment a shifting and "constructed" element. This shifting nature of group boundaries further contributes to the adult's irreverent view of the child's world of interactive others. Five girls, Linda (age thirteen), Nancy (age nine), Rhonda (age six), Janna (age seven), and Theresa (age eight), are swimming in a backyard swimming pool. Theresa is confined to the shallow end. Linda has organized a group of mermaids in the southeast end of the pool. To be a mermaid, you have to swim to the end of the pool. To be included in the mermaid group, you have to kill a shark that lives along the edge of the shallow end. Theresa is the guard of the shark. Janna is the shark, and the shark cannot go beyond the middle of the pool. Mermaids Linda, Nancy, and Rhonda take turns attacking the shark. Whoever kills the shark first is Linda's best friend. Three adults observe the game. In unison, they respond: "Silly kids, they're just playing."

Deference, Demeanor, Tact, Taste, and Young Children

Goffman (1956, 1967) defines deference as a form of activity that symbolically functions to show one's appreciation of the actions, goods, or services another actor has directed toward that individual. Acts of deference may or may not be obligatory. The rules underlying their expression may be symmetrical or asymmetrical. They may be of a presentational nature and be displayed in salutations, invitations, compliments, or minor services. Avoidance rituals, in contrast to presentation rituals, serve to keep persons apart and may signal status hierarchies wherein one class of actors can profane, embarrass, or disturb the self-presentational acts of another class of actors. On avoidance rituals, Goffman (1967, p. 73) comments, "avoidance rituals . . . imply the acts the actor must refrain from doing lest he violate the right of the recipient to keep him at a distance. . . . As Durkheim suggested, 'The human personality is a sacred thing; one dare not violate it nor infringe its bounds.' " Goffman further suggests (1967, p. 87) that in our society some playful profanation is "directed by adults to those of lesser ceremonial breed—to children, old people, servants, and so forth." The implications of this statement for the study of children will be indicated later.

Goffman (1967, p. 77) defines demeanor as "that element of the individual's ceremonial behavior typically conveyed through deportment, dress, and bearing, which serves to express to those in his immediate presence that he is a person of certain desirable or undesirable qualities." The well-demeaned individual "possesses the attributes popularly associated with character training or socialization, these being implanted when a neophyte of any kind is housebroken." Persons who show proper deference behavior and who are properly demeaned can be counted on to sustain other individuals' definitions of themselves. Persons who refuse to show proper deference and demeanor challenge the ritual nature of the social order and may, if they persist in their untoward actions, destroy the very order they are a part of. Goffman (1967, pp. 94–95) suggests another alternative: "Modern society brings transgressors of the ceremonial order to a single place, along with some ordinary members of society who make a living there. These dwell in a place of unholy acts and unholy understandings, yet some of them must retain allegiance to the ceremonial order outside the hospital setting. Somehow ceremonial people must work out mechanisms and techniques for living without certain kinds of ceremony."

These single places, of course, are total institutions. I wish in this section to consider Goffman's combination of children, mental patients, and the elderly into one category. While children certainly act in nondeferential and in nonrespecting ways toward others, they are seldom brought to a single place for ceremonial care or remedial work. Children, unlike mental patients and certain of the elderly, are sprinkled throughout society and are confronted on a regular basis by persons committed to sustaining some version of a social order. That order may be displayed in the enduring relationships central to the primary group or in focused, and perhaps fleeting, encounters produced around dinner tables, in bathtubs, in living rooms, in department stores, and on sidewalks.

The Negotiated Order: An Aside on Deference, Demeanor, and Children

The young child violates nearly all rules of deference and demeanor. They make claims for self-respect in statements like "Mommy, look at me, aren't I pretty?" Proper interactants, Goffman claims, must not make claims for self-respect. They must wait for others to confer (voluntarily) such judgments on them. Young children invade the personal, sacred sphere of the caretaker's body when they climb on a father's knee and play see-saw. Similarly, they find their own personal body territories invaded when they are bathed, changed, spanked, and kissed by a caretaker. Young children "make issues" of themselves when they whine for a third cup of juice, and then cry and hold their head under a blanket when parents are entertaining guests. In making issues of themselves, children are calling attention to themselves, hoping (perhaps in a negotiated fashion) to secure something more from the caretaker, even if it is only a small amount of personal attention. Young children demand small services and refuse to give thanks or compliments. Their parents intervene in such instances, as the following excerpt reveals. A seven-year-old boy arrives with his father at a friend's house to play with the host's four boys. Immediately on entering the house, Len (the seven-year-old boy) asks:

Len: "Can I have juice and cookies?"
Father: "Len, you don't just ask for juice and cookies! What do you say?"
Len: "Please, can I have juice and cookies?"
Host: "Sure, Len, you can have juice and cookies. What kind would you like?"

Four elements are salient in this specimen. First, Len violated the usual rule by requesting a small service. Second, his father acted on the transgression and gave Len the proper clue for making the request. Third, the host willingly offered the service. Fourth, no disruptive action occurred. That is, the encounter did not dissolve, and apparently no party felt offended. The transgression was absorbed into an ongoing line of activity. Goffman's model would have predicted that embarrassment, perhaps of only a mild order, would have been produced.

Two views of socialization and the social order can now be set forth. On the one hand, Goffman offers a view of a relatively fragile order, of a social order made up of individuals involved in mutual facework or supporting social interaction, engaged in jointly sustained efforts to keep focused interaction going on. The slightest error in etiquette, a show of bad face, a failure to control emotions, the invasion of another's personal space, a display of lack of attention, and a host of other variables produce distortions and perhaps eventual collapses in the focused gathering. Well-mannered, properly housetrained individuals do not distort focused interaction. Now children, as Goffman notes, are not well housetrained. Yet children are involved in endless focused interactions with their caretakers, and these interactions do not necessarily collapse.

A second view is suggested, and this one rests on the assumption not only that society may be viewed as symbolic interaction (Blumer, 1962) but also that it is best viewed as a negotiated order as well (Lindesmith, Strauss, and Denzin, 1978). If negotiation is given central consideration in the study of early childhood and the focused gatherings that caretakers have with children, then it can be seen that any disruptive behavior on the part of the child will be differentially defined and responded to. As the child becomes a regular actor in the routine situations of their caretakers and as the child's peculiarities and special attributes become better known, their disruptive effects are routinely processed, and routinized encounters go on. Negotiated responses to the child's failure to show proper deference and demeanor can range from disavowal or overlooking it to an occasional punishment or a temper tantrum on the part of the parent. The refusal to show proper deference can also become an occasion for instilling humiliation and embarrassment in the child's behavior repertoire, as the following episode reveals. Four adults are seated around a dining room table, having drinks after dinner. Ken, the five-year-old son of Mark, comes into the room and says, "Daddy, can we go home now? I'm tired, and I don't want to play with Randy anymore." His father responds, "Ken, what have I told you about asking to go home! Now you go back outside and play and apologize to Chuck (the host) for having said that! And right now!!" Ken says, "I'm sorry, Chuck, I didn't mean it." He drops his head, begins to cry, and goes outside.

In the negotiated order of the family group, wherein actors are committed to one another on emotional, psychological, intimate, and kinship grounds (which does not appear to be the case for Goffman's actors), there will be continual attempts to respond in a deferential fashion to the improper behaviors of others. When selves are not properly acknowledged, claims for acknowledgment will be made. If boundaries are overstepped, such transgressions will not be ignored but will be acted on and absorbed into the *socializing encounter*. The proper encounter between equally housetrained interactants occurs with low frequency in the caretaker-child relationship. That relationship, then, absorbs its own deviance, acts on that deviance so as to reduce its occurrence in the future, and makes that deviance a proper concern in its own right. Clearly, what is needed is another view of deference and demeanor as these concepts fit the special worlds of children and their caretakers.

Conclusions

Childhood is a world that is unique to children and their caretakers, and it is a world that does not readily admit of close-up naturalistic investigation. This factor, in conjunction with the child's special language, with his special view of tact and candor, deference and demeanor, of friendship, play and work, contribute to a view of the child's world as immature and "child-ish." This view has perhaps led sociologists and psychologists to adopt a rather arrogant and irreverent image of children, conceptualizing them less as active organisms and more as vessels into which the values and norms of outside society are poured. There is nothing inherent in childhood or in children that would make them more or less childlike, or more or less adultlike. Rather, as Ariès (1962) has shown with sixteenth- and seventeenth-century France, a child's "childishness" is a consequence of the structure of the situations he or she confronts. These situations are in a large sense structured by adults, and the images adults have of children seem, at least on the surface, reinforced by the very behaviors children engage in. The student of society and symbolic interaction could profit from a systematic study of the unique worlds of childhood, for these worlds make problematic what the adult chooses to ignore on a daily basis.

Chapter Five

Interaction and Language Acquisition in Early Childhood

*M*ounting evidence suggests that the young infant, under the age of one year, acts in a social and socializing fashion toward its caretakers. As Rheingold (1969) observes, the infant begins life as a potentially social organism; he can see, hear, smell, feel heat, cold, and pain (see also Stone, Smith, and Murphy, 1973). Equipped with these abilities, the infant behaves in a social fashion toward others. These behaviors, in turn, evoke socializing behaviors from the caretaker. The infant acts in ways that produce social responses from others. By the age of two months, he can follow others with his eyes. His smiles and cries are rewarded and bring attention from caretakers. The socializing behaviors of the infant produce profound economic, political, and social-psychological alterations in the

76

world of the caretaker. The infant alters the identities of the parents, leading them to view themselves as "caretakers." In Rheingold's words (1969, p. 783), "he teaches them what he needs to have them do for him. He makes them behave in a nurturing fashion." Put another way, the infant acts in ways that teach the caretakers how to teach themselves to do for him what they think he needs to have them do for him. His actions are socially interpreted by the caretakers as indicative of social needs and desires. His actions, as Markey (1928) observed, evoke social and socializing responses and attitudes from the caretakers. In a similar sense, the caretakers socialize the infant. They provide him with a universe of discourse that expands, modulates, and builds his social and socializing skills. As his physical skills are elaborated and as he becomes more physically mobile, the child becomes less and less dependent on his caretakers. At this point, his acquisition and use of language become critical as he becomes physically independent of the caretakers and more dependent on social and linguistic guidance and experience.

Language and its acquisition is central to the socializing process. All available evidence suggests that the average American child who is not visually, auditorily, or vocally impaired has by the age of four mastered the rudimentary elements of the English language (Lewis, 1963; McNeill, 1966a; Slobin, 1971). The processes that move the socializing, yet minimally linguistically responsive, infant from the status of an ill-understood member of his language community into the position of a "relatively" competent speaker and interactant have been debated. Most prominent in this argument has been the position of the transformational grammarians—or psycholinguists. Chomsky (1959) in particular has hypothesized that perhaps deep and innately biological and cognitive processes shape this process of language acquisition (see also Chomsky, 1959, 1964, 1965, 1968). These structures *do not* give the child a grammatical system. They are seen as providing an innate means for processing information and for forming internal cognitive and linguistic systems. When applied to the speech that the child hears, they permit him to construct a grammar of his native language (see Slobin, 1971).

In this chapter, I shall review the issues that surround the language acquisition process. In line with recent research in comparative anthropology, historical linguistics, and child development, I shall propose a model of language acquisition and early childhood socialization that rests neither on biological determinism, nor on a deep structural position, nor on a strict developmental-chronological age phase model. Rather, the model will be consistent with a social linguistic position that extends back to Boas, Sapir, the pragmatic social psychologist George Herbert Mead, and the school of sociological thought known as *symbolic interactionism* (see Markey, 1928; Mead, 1934; Lindesmith, Strauss, and Denzin, 1978).

Three major issues will be discussed. First, a brief critique of the transformational grammar position will be offered; second, a view of the social and socializing relationship between the child and the caretaker will be given. A model of the social act—embedded in a universe of linguistic discourse—will be presented. Third, a view of language acquisition that rests on historical and comparative data drawn from preliterate societies and cultures will be discussed. It will be suggested that the interactive exchanges that make up the child's early world of language acquisition are much like the linguistic interactions that underlie the process by which a member of a preliterate society would acquire his or her language. I believe that many current theories of language acquisition rest on a written-literate conception of language. A more rounded view would consider how a child learns a verbal, as well as a written, language. The place of paralinguistic languages in this process must also be considered.

The Transformational Model of Language Acquisition

In Chomsky's (1959) review of Skinner's *Verbal Behavior* (1957), he forcefully argued that a traditional and strict stimulus-response model of language acquisition could not account for how a child arrives at an understanding of the notions of grammar that make perfect linguistic utterances possible. A probabilistic, left-right model of linguistic reinforcement cannot account for the emergence of new utterances, nor does it explain the fact that many chains of words have no intrinsic left-right order. As Lashley (1961, p. 113) notes, "Depending on what is said, a given word can be followed by a variety of other words." Lashley, anticipating Chomsky, suggested that perhaps there is an underlying schema of order that is responsible for the serial ordering of words. Thus Lashley, Chomsky, and others came to reject a probabilistic, stimulus-response model of language acquisition and competence.

In its place emerged what is now termed "transformational" grammar, which is an attempt to explain how speakers of a language are able to rearrange elements in their native language. Transformational grammar identifies such operations as substitution ("what" for "the ball"), displacement (preposing of "what"), and permutation. It is assumed that these operations are linguistic universals, found in all known languages (see Slobin, 1971). The goal of this syntactic theory is to account for all linguistic behaviors as if these behaviors always involve the transformation of language elements. Slobin (1971, p. 5) comments: "The transformationalists assert that a grammar is a theory of a language. It is a theory which should be able to discriminate sentences from nonsentences, assign degrees of deviance to nonsentences, relate sentence structures to both meanings and sounds, and it is a theory which should be able to account for, or 'generate,' all possible sentences of the language."

Grammar, as a theory of language, must be able to generate all the grammatical sentences of a language. Yet this is not a theory of language in usage. It is an attempt to explain how it is possible for people "(generally linguists) in ideal situations to make judgments of grammaticality, identify grammatical relations, and so on" (Slobin, 1971, p. 7).

Beginning with one set of problems inherent in a stimulus-response, probabilistic model of language usage, Chomsky and the transformationalists have moved to a position that may carry more problems than the perspective they rejected. If a child does not learn how to make proper utterances based on the usual variables of reinforcement, imitation, and indifference, then how does he learn the rules necessary to make such utterances? The transformationalists have removed the problem from direct empirical testing by asserting that an underlying cognitive structure in the human brain determines such acquisitions. Von

Raffler-Engel (1970, p. 16) has suggested that recent work by the transformationalists involves a debate over "whether or not there is a separate Language Acquisition Device (LAD) distinct from all other learning strategies of the child." She proceeds to argue that language is just another of many social activities the child learns to master: "It does not appear to necessitate an autonomous mechanism" (p. 16).

It can be asserted that the position of Chomsky and others has underestimated the capacities of the human organism to learn. It is evident that children do learn beyond mere stimulus-response exercises. Yet one need not resort to innate cognitive structures to explain how that process occurs.

Following Mead (1934), we must assume that the child possesses the physiological and neurological abilities to engage in minded, self-reflexive behavior; that is, the child has the ability to stimulate and respond to his own behavior. He is able to mediate the external environment and his own internal environment through the manipulation and organization of symbols. The child enters an ongoing universe of symbolic discourse, and the progressive acquisition of that universe of meanings leads the child to engage in increasingly complex forms of self-stimulation and self-other interaction. As language and speech abilities are acquired, the child, as Vygotsky noted (1962), is able to produce silent, self-spoken utterances and directions. Language becomes the main mediator between the child and the external world. Through the use of language, the child is able to formulate plans of action and mold lines of activity. In this way, the child becomes an active constructor of his own social reality.

Such a view of the human organism is not present in the transformationalists' view of learning and language acquisition. Indeed, their conception of language in large part impedes their understanding of the learning process. It is this topic to which I turn next.

A Definition of Language

A theory of language and of language acquisition must be more than a theory of the grammar of a given language; it must be a theory of language in use. It must be able to account for how the infant acquires, improvises on, and utilizes the linguistic symbols, meanings, and utterances it receives. It must be a formulation that takes into account nonverbal gestures as well as verbal utterances. Language consists of more than rules of syntax, semantics, and morphology.

Language must be viewed on at least two levels: the verbal and the nonverbal. It is necessary to view language as a set of more or less significant gestures, the meanings of which arise out of specific interactive situations. These gestures are both verbal and nonverbal, and they can be silent or vocalized. They are significant gestures, in the sense that they signify, for the gesturer and the receiver, lines of action that should be taken when they are made and received. The response may or may not be consensual; all the significant gesture need do is call out in the recipient a response or body of alternative responses that will or can be made on reception. This definition of language does not assume that speakers possess a consensual understanding of the utterances and gestures that they produce and receive. Rules of syntax and semantics may be incompletely understood for any group of speakers. Their ability to engage in minded reflexive behavior permits them to interpret and give meaning to the utterances and gestures they receive. This fact is critical, because the neonate's early sounds possess no intrinsic meaning for the caretaker. They are given an understandable meaning as the reactions to them produce "satisfactory" results for the caretaker.

Three forms of linguistic behavior can now be discussed: silent, vocal speech defined as thought; public, verbal utterances that are defined as speech; and paralinguistic gestures, including facial movements, smiles, nods, frowns, as well as movements of the body. The child is thus socialized into a speech community that consists of these three forms of linguistic behavior. Following Lewis (1963), it is assumed that the child is born a speaker in a symbolic universe of speakers. The child vocalizes, hears vocal utterances, gestures, and sees nonverbal gestures. The universe of discourse that it enters consists of speakers who hear these utterances and view these gestures, and by responding to them, thereby give them meaning. However, initially these utterances and gestures carry no intrinsic meaning for either the infant or the adult. The child's acquisition of language must be traced to this universe of discourse and action, for it is here that meaning is learned.

Consider the following example offered by Lewis (1963, p. 43) on how his son learned the meaning of the word *no*. Nine and a half months: "He has seized a piece of newspaper which he is about to put into his mouth. I say 'NO!' in a loud voice. Immediately he stops the movement of his hand and looks toward me. He keeps his eyes steadily on me for a minute or so, then turns back to continue the movement of the paper toward the mouth. I say 'NO!' again. Again he turns toward me and stops the movement of his hand. This time he looks at me for quite two minutes. I look steadily back at him. He begins to cry and continues for some minutes." At the age of one year, eight months, Lewis's son was observed as follows: "He reaches out for a medicine bottle. His mother says 'No bottle, baby.' . . . He replies 'No!' and desists from trying to touch the bottle. Later in the day this happens again" (1963, p. 45). A week later, the same child engaged in the following behavior: "He is offered, for the first time, some clotted cream in a spoon and takes it. His mother offers him more but he turns away his head and says 'NO!' " (Lewis, 1963, p. 45).

We see, in these language specimens, the emergence of two meanings of the word *no*. In the first, the child learns that the word *no* means to desist, or to stop a line of action. In the third, he learns that the word can be used to express refusal; it is used as a statement of intent.

Two other factors are operative in these examples. First, it must be noted that Lewis engaged his child in visual interaction as he uttered the word *no*. Second, in the third example the child states the word *no* when it was not spoken to him by his mother. We can assume that the child called out in his own mind the word *no* and then verbally uttered it. The three forms of linguistic behavior noted earlier are illustrated in these examples. Lewis' son can be seen acquiring a linguistic repertoire that rests on nonverbal gestures, spoken utterances, and silently vocalized thoughts. Furthermore, he is learning the meaning of words, and his learning process occurs within a matrix of interpersonal interaction, which is the next topic to be considered.

Interpersonal Interaction in Childhood

Given the foregoing assumptions and definitions, the following model of interaction can be proposed. The social order as it is known, sensed, and experienced by the caretaker is symbolically presented to the young infant through linguistic and paralinguistic acts. In the first three months after birth, the child hears and makes sounds that are symbolically responded to by the caretaker. The sounds that the child makes and hears carry no meaning, however, and inner thought, as it will later be experienced, is not sensed. Sounds are not yet attached to objects, settings, activities, or other individuals. A relatively simplistic stimulus-response model of learning operates at this level of cognitive development. Yet critical to these early interactions is the fact that the caretaker, as a significant other, provides the verbal and visual stimuli to the infant that provoke the child's verbal and visual response and stimulus patterns of activity. In this first phase of linguistic development, the child hears sound but does not hear words. It will take at least three more months before repeated stimulus-response reinforcement sessions will produce the utterance of sounds that bear some resemblance to words (as they are known and sensed by the caretaker and by any other native speaker of the infant's natural language). Yet the sounds and utterances of the young infant are likely to form a pattern of rhythm, cadence, and intonation that closely resembles the normal pattern of talk and speech in the adult world. On this point, Sullivan writes (1953, p. 180): "Quite early, I suppose by the eighth or ninth month, the infant is spacing things like 'da' so that it comes out 'da-da-da' and presently 'da-*da*-da.' This means that the element of melodic repetition, the rhythmic tonal business, is already being caught on by the infant. In this process, some things like 'dada' happen to be said at an appropriate time, so that an enthusiastic parent is apt to wonder if it isn't an attempt to say 'mama' or 'papa' or something else, and there is a certain amount of response. If by any chance 'mama' is said, that is considered proof that the child has learned to call mother something (which I think is almost infinitely improbable), and there is a strong tender response. I think this is about all there is to it." Those early utterances that are defined as coming close to words are rewarded by the significant other and are often repeated after the infant utters them. They may even be imitated by the adult (see Brown, 1970).

On the other hand, those sounds made by the infant that are not perceived as having the shape or semblance of words are responded to by indifference or are ignored. They get, as Sullivan (1953, p. 181) notes, "no special returns." Thus a large proportion of the early sounds produced by the infant are simply not responded to either because no one hears them or because they do not strike a responsive cord in the listener's ear.

The child's significant others thus become critical variables in the language acquisition process. Their responses of a rewarding, negative, or indifferent nature to the child's sounds and utterances provide the stimulus feedback that leads to a convergence in sound patterning on the part of the child. Such convergences in response, in turn, lead the child to relate specific sounds to words, objects, situations, activities, and so on.

The influence of the significant other on the child's language skills can be posited as follows. The significant other provides visual and verbal stimuli to which the child responds. The critical variable is the child's ability to make a symbolic connection between a verbal or visual stimulus and the response made to the stimulus. As noted earlier, the child's first behaviors are of a relatively simplistic stimulus-response nature. In the *first phase* of language acquisition, stimulus reinforcement principles operate. In the *second phase* of development, which will be termed *imitation,* the child makes crude subjective links between the stimuli of others and his responses to them. Inner thought of a relatively undifferentiated nature is present in Phase 2.

The imitation of the behavior of others is critical, since in Phase 1, the caretaker imitates the child, but the child does not imitate the caretaker. When the child's visual stimuli and verbal responses substitute for or are exchanged with the significant other, then symbolic behavior has occurred (see Markey, 1928). This appears in Phase 2. At this stage, the child is still unable fully or with any regularity to evoke in himself the responses to the stimuli of an absent other. When the child is able to say no to himself as he approaches a plant or ashtray and then pulls back his hand from that object, then he has progressed to the *third level* of linguistic development. In Phase 3, the basis for concerted face-to-face interaction is present. At this stage, the child produces verbal and visual stimuli that are understood and responded to by the significant other. They are conjointly exchanging understandable utterances and gestures.

It must be noted that the child's utterances will be of a shorthand, holophrastic, and telegraphic nature until about the age of two. Short one-, two-, and three-word sentences will predominate. Their utterances in Phase 3, as Markey substantiates, tend to be action oriented, and the symbolic contents of these early utterances tend to reflect the self and immediate surroundings of the young speaker (Markey, 1928). Pronouns are prominent. In Phase 3, the beginnings of a self-conception are emerging. The child begins to express personal ownership of prized objects. He begins to talk out loud to himself. Inner thought flows together with speech, and the child will be observed to literally think out loud. This does not support Piaget's (1962) suggestion that early speech is monologuelike and egocentric in nature. It simply indicates that until the child has fully acquired an elaborated self-conception his thoughts will flow together with his actions and vocal utterances. Furthermore, he will be the center of that universe, because he is the person who has the most constant and direct access to it. It can be argued, following Lewis (1963), that the child likes to hear the sound of his own voice. Vocal utterances are their own reinforcers. Speech and thought become autotelic, self-reinforcing activities that produce more speech, talk, and thought. By engaging in such behavior, the child proves, establishes, and reestablishes his growing symbolic mastery of the world around him. These speech acts also gain the attention of the caretaker, whose response to them can be seen as rewarding; that is, they bring the caretaker directly into the child's visual and auditory field of perception.

Passing on Language

A three-phase model of language acquisition and interaction has been proposed. Thus far the model has only considered the role of one significant other, typically the mother.
The role of the absent other has not been elaborated, nor have
multiple others been considered. Before these two topics can be
treated, it is necessary to consider exactly how it is that significant others pass language along to their children.

Goody and Watt (1962–1963) have proposed a rather
complex model that accounts for the emergence of written language in human history. It is from this model that I draw in the
following section.

It can be assumed that an American or western European child is born into a company of speakers who not only can
speak their native language but can also read and write it. The
young child cannot perform any of these activities. The child's
significant others pass on their conception of their native language to the child both orally and nonverbally. In passing a
language on to the child, they are attempting to transform a nonliterate human being into one who is literate in each sense indicated earlier. Transmitting the verbal elements of their language
to the child involves oral activity, requiring that the child be
exposed to long chains of interconnecting conversations. Children must encounter face-to-face interaction.

Goody and Watt make this observation concerning members of preliterate societies (1962–1963, p. 313): "The transmission of the verbal elements of culture by oral means can be
visualized as a long chain of interlocking conversations between
members of the group. Thus all beliefs and values, all forms of
knowledge, are communicated between individuals in face-to-
face contact; and, as distinct from the material content of the
cultural tradition, whether it be cave paintings, or hand axes,
they are stored only in human memory." A similar process must
operate for young infants. They learn a language through repeated exposures to conversations. These conversations constitute the substance of the linguistic socialization process. Children must learn the etiquette of conversations. They must learn

how to listen, when to speak, and when to be silent. They must learn how to recognize age, sex, and social status differences between speakers; they will also quickly acquire a kinship terminology that permits them to distinguish immediate kin from absent and nonkin persons. As with members of a nonliterate culture, they store what they learn in their memory.

Oral communication has a variety of distinct features, noted by Goody and Watt, that are relevant to the language acquisition process in childhood. It has a directness of relationship between symbols and referents. A child must learn that the word *milk* refers to a white, liquid substance. In the early stages of language development, the child and the significant other have no recourse to the dictionary. They must produce their own interpretations of sounds and, in this sense, the caretaker has to learn an unwritten language: the language of the child. The early utterances of the child do not acquire successive layers of meaning, as they do in a literate culture. Their meanings must be ratified in successive concrete situations and exchanges. Such ratification is typically accompanied by verbal inflections and nonverbal gestures. Goody and Watt remark (1962–1963, p. 313): "This process of direct semantic ratification, of course, operates cumulatively; and as a result the totality of symbol-referent relationships is more immediately experienced by the individual in an exclusively oral culture and is thus more deeply socialized."

The child is a member of an oral culture, and, as in all oral cultures, the elaborateness of his vocabulary will reflect the particular interests and problems he and his caretakers confront and process. To the extent that baby-talk works and functions for the child, he or she will talk within a constricted vocabulary.

Like members of a preliterate culture, the child speaker and his caretakers keep their language alive through memory and through continual use. What is remembered and kept alive will reflect what is important to them, but it is likely the child's early baby-talk language will be short-lived in the collective memory of the family members. My eldest daughter, now nine years old, was recorded at the age of three years, eleven months, using the word *Nanny* to refer to herself. The word was an ap-

proximate attempt to speak the last syllables of her own name.
The word is no longer used. Similarly, the same child used the
familiar "bow-wow" to refer to *the barking of dogs* until the age
of four years, one month. "Cra-cow" referred to *crawl* and
crayon, "wo-wo" to *water*, "pa-pa" to *paper*, "ea-ea" to *eat*.
Other neologisms were prominent in her speech. None of them
exist at this date. They have ceased to play any role whatsoever
in the collective actions of the family. They died as they were
replaced by conventionally spoken words that had their proper
referents.

The social functions of memory and forgetting in the
language acquisition process can now be seen, since that which
is remembered can be stored and reused in the future. That
which is forgotten cannot be retrieved, because it failed to be
recorded in print or memory. Language, in the form of a written
vocabulary, is acquired by the age of six or seven, depending
on a child's educational experiences. Consequently, the young
child has neither access to, nor a great perception of, the past unless his unwritten language was learned and written down, or
firmly embedded in his memory. Otherwise the child's past cannot be reconstructed.

The pastness of the past, then, can only operate, as
Goody and Watt state, when there are historical records of it—
when there is a recorded and recordable language and when
there is someone present who will make such recordings. The
child's efforts at speech are seldom recorded; instead, the significant other's activities are pragmatically directed to resolving
the source of the sound or to fulfilling the vaguely stated request
of the child. The repeated conversational exchanges between the
child and the caretaker thus can be seen as attempts on the part
of two parties to learn two totally different (for them) unwritten languages.

Reflexivity and the "Other"

Given this conceptualization of the child's early speech
patterns, it is now possible to discuss how the child learns to take
the role of and respond to absent and multiple others. The first

three phrases of self-other development outlined earlier assume the presence of one significant other. Clearly, though, the child's world is populated with multiple significant others. He progressively acquires the skill and ability to distinguish, separate, and mold into single and cohesive units the points of view of multiple others. He is able to do this first on a singular, one-to-one basis, shifting from one viewpoint to another, but seldom combining the viewpoints of his entire family unit into a generalized common perspective. Thus the child's coupling of language in use with face-to-face interaction experience moves from what Mead (1934) termed the "play stage" of development, through the "game" to the "generalized other" stage (also see Stone, 1962). The movement from one stage to another is contingent on the development of sufficient language skills and on the presence of interactive experiences with those others. Furthermore, it assumes a working knowledge of the languages that make up his social world.

A child, then, can respond to (1) a single other who is present, (2) multiple others who are present, (3) a single other who is absent, and (4) multiple others who are absent. When multiple others are considered, one may respond to them serially or as a collectivity, jointly combining all of their responses and utterances into a single viewpoint. Responding to the absent other requires more language skills than does responding to the present other, since the child has no verbal or visual cues to utilize when calling forth the viewpoint of the former.

When another perspective is taken into account, the following conditions can occur. First, there may be no response by one of the individuals in the situation: The other responds to the child, but the child does not respond to him. Second, both respond to one another, but not on comparable symbolic grounds: The child cries; the mother picks him up, feeds him, changes him, rocks him, places him back in the bed; and then the child coos. Third, both respond to one another on similar symbolic grounds: The mother talks to the child in a form of preliterate language; she is talking to the child in terms of the child's language, not in terms of her own literate language. Fourth, both individuals talk to one another in a commonly understood verbal and visual language that any speaker of the language could understand and talk in terms of. When the perspective of another is acted on, the person in question may note the perspective, yet not adopt it. The perspective is only dimly grasped; it is not made an explicit object of attention. On the other hand, the perspective may be taken and adopted, as when Lewis' son learned the meanings of the word *no*. Finally, the child may take the perspective of multiple others but be unable to separate those lines of action.

When the child takes the viewpoint of a significant other, he may take the perspective in a passive, nonreflexive fashion, as when an infant permits a mother to slip a bottle into his mouth. At the other extreme, the child may take the perspective of the other and actively define it, identify with it, and use it in novel, or reflexive ways (Turner, 1956).

The acquisition and use of language involves the interconnection of a set of processes that progressively become more and more complex. These processes can now be summarized in terms of three factors, or stages, that are functionally interdependent. Originally developed by Markey (1928), who was building on the early writings of Mead (1922, 1924–1925), they are presented here. The child must have learned through association and conditioning the ability (1) to substitute the visual stimuli and behaviors of the significant other for his own; that is, the child connects his own behavior with the behavior of another. He is able to do this so well that (2) he can now arouse in himself the same behaviors that would be aroused were the other present. He can act "as if" the other were present. He connects visual and verbal stimuli with internal thought processes, which in turn mobilize physical, gestural, and verbal responses and behaviors. Most critically, he is doing this in the absence of the other. At the same time, (3) the child is able to arouse "similar and conditioned responses" to his own visual and verbal responses and utterances (Markey, 1928, p. 35). These responses, in turn, arouse other stimuli and other responses. Thus the child has learned to stimulate his own behavior, and in so doing he enters into the organization of that behavior. He is now able to differentiate his own verbal stimuli and responses from the stimuli and responses of the caretaker. As Markey observes, this differentiation gives some validity to the very utterances the child is able to produce. A crude sense of self-awareness begins to emerge, and the child is now able to recognize the sound of his own voice and to respond accordingly. These utterances, as noted earlier, take on the autotelic, self-rewarding character, so that the infant or young child can be observed talking to himself. He carries on his own monologue and dialoguelike conversations with himself as he makes sounds, forms words, and utters the phrases of absent others. The child has entered the world of symbolic behavior and is well on the way to becoming a literate member of his respective language community and family culture.

No mysterious underlying cognitive structures or "language acquisition devices" need be called on to explain this process. The child as an organism is capable of responding to and manipulating symbols and its body. The child becomes an organism that engages not only in minded behavior but also in self-reflexive behavior. The origins of this process are lodged in the social order that he is born into and not in physiological structures, innate needs and drives, or in age-specific developmental phases. Most importantly, that social order is presented and "represented" to him through the symbolic gestures and utterances of the significant other. It is this interpersonal relationship and the specific symbolic transactions and conversations that it produces that account for the origin and use of language by the average four-year-old American child. The child is, as Lewis argues, truly a speaker born into a universe of fellow speakers. That these speakers at first do not understand one another, yet somehow manage to stage and produce social transactions, simply attests to the strength of the interpersonal relationship, which must be regarded as the nexus of linguistic socialization. That relationship—formed and grounded, as it is, in endlessly repetitive face-to-face interactive episodes—presents the infant or the young child with all he needs to become a competent speaker of his native language, namely, interactional experiences.

Chapter Six

Childhood as a
Conversation of Gestures

Young children, it is conventionally assumed, remain incompetent participants in social interaction until they have mastered the intricacies of adult speech. This conception of the child is embedded in the works of Piaget (1968), who has asserted that until approximately the age of seven children engage in open monologues with one another—they are incapable of aligning their actions with others. Cooley (1908) set the emergence of social, self-directed behavior at the point of correct pronoun usage. Allport (1961) argued that social behavior coincides with an understanding of the personal name.

These and other theorists have assumed a rather special view of language, seeing it as a set of more or less significant gestures, the use of which calls forth in both speaker and listener approximately the same response. In addition, judgments about the "social qualities" of any behavior sequence have been assessed from the perspective of the adult. This dual focus on adult conceptions of language and social behavior has created a rather narrow view of childhood in general and of language and social behavior in particular.

In this chapter, I shall propose that it is possible to view early childhood (from approximately eight to twenty-four months) as a complex social order—a social order that demands for its maintenance a set of coherent symbols, gestures, and languages. These languages are developed through interaction between child and parent. I know of no unit of early childhood conduct that cannot be easily matched with taken-for-granted, adultlike behavior. Although resting on different motivational, meaning, and interactional structures, children engage in behavior that is every bit as humanly social as the sequences of actions routinely undertaken by "normal" functioning adults. (I borrow this assuption in part from Goffman, 1967, p. 147, who asserts in his analysis of mental illness that "I know of no psychotic misconduct that cannot be matched precisely in everyday life by the conduct of persons who are not psychologically ill nor considered to be so.")

Language as a Set of Indicative Gestures

As noted, students of early childhood have traditionally employed an adult conception of language. By stressing the function and importance of personal pronouns, the sequencing of vocal utterances into subject-object patterns, the rate of verb acquisition, and the sheer quantity of understood or vocalized words, investigators have overlooked a number of nuances of early child speech. (For reviews, see Gumperz, 1967; Grimshaw, 1969b.) On the basis of these formal attributes of speech, investigators have concluded that young children are egocentric in their thought patterns.

By examining only spoken and verbalized speech, investigators have tended to give scant attention to the silent, gestural components of language. It is a central thesis of this discussion that early childhood speech—indeed, speech at any age level—cannot be understood without first taking serious account of these silent gestural aspects of language.

Another important bias has shaped the study of language. This has been the tendency to view language as either *caused* by attributes of social structure or to view it as an *independent variable* that shapes variations in social structures (see Grimshaw, 1969b). Although evidence can be gathered to support both views, neither does justice to the interactional qualities of language. It is appropriate to view language as a situated production that varies by the definitions given objects, selves, others, time and place, and the social relationship between speakers. Seen in this light, language becomes a complex gestural system that is created and maintained through symbolic interaction. Its sheer existence serves to give social groups means by which insiders and outsiders can be identified, labeled, and acted toward. Its organization into what may be termed "language communities" gives all members of that community routine and consensual grounds for ongoing interaction.

Embedded within any language structure are a set of rules concerning how words and thoughts are put together. Additionally, all language structures mirror, if not create, interactional rules of conduct. Thus, honorific systems of exchange both inform and dictate to their users how persons in varying statuses (rich-poor, educated-uneducated, clerk-customer, child-adult) are to be spoken to and hence are to be treated. Language brings persons together and at the same time separates them from one another. In this way, a civil, interactional order is maintained. Entry into any language system demands that one play by these rules. For instance, a language system may demand that one speak when spoken to and that one reply "on topic." In short, any language system demands that the speaker make himself available for interaction in ways prescribed by his society's, group's, or relationship's etiquette as well as language rules. I shall show shortly how aspects of adult society are peculiarly present in the world of young children. Failing to enter the adults' language community, the young child creates his own world of symbols and meanings. This world is created *in concert* with adults, namely parents, and also with peers and siblings, if present. This language system leads to recurrent violations of adult etiquette and consequently has misled previous investigators into assuming that young children are "asocial" interactants.

Before returning to alternative conceptions of social behavior, it is necessary to offer an expanded conception of language. Mead's (1934) terms, "significant gesture" and "conversation of gestures," provide this conception. Rather than focusing on the sequence of vocal utterances within interactive episodes, Mead's model calls for a consideration of all the movements, gestures, and vocalizations given and given off by any interactant. His view demands a treatment of the silent, as well as the vocal, aspects of language. It is appropriate then, to view any language, as Herbert Blumer (1969) has suggested, as a set of more or less "significant indicative gestures," the meanings of which arise out of specific interactive situations. Language becomes a situated production. It cannot be understood "out of context." This assertion, commonplace among students of deviance, social relationships, and organizational life, has led to the study of "argot" and special coded speech systems. Unfortunately, this strategy has not been applied to the study of early childhood.

Conceptions of Normal Social Conduct

Students of everyday interaction, especially Goffman (1963) and Garfinkel (1967), have deduced a number of taken-for-granted features of routine adult conduct. Interaction is temporally sequenced and spatially bound. It involves negotiations between interacting selves. Talk is its central feature and talk (or conversation) often ignores actions and objects that are only tacitly recognized. Objects are assigned meanings that hold for the occasion of interaction. When in one another's presence, interactants are expected to maintain a mutual openness of speech, body alignment, and eye contact. They are expected to orient themselves to the utterances and actions of their fellow participants. Consensually defined roles will be worked out by each partner along mutually accommodative lines. Embarrassing attributes of speech, action, or dress are expected to be ignored or suspended from consideration. Mood, affect, and involvement must also be controlled. Emotions must not get out of hand. Their presence is expected to lie inside the private dialogue each person has within himself. Emotions are not to be acted out, except those defined as appropriate to the encounter. This appropriateness will be loosely decreed by taken-for-granted rules of discourse and differentially negotiated by the interactants themselves.

If there is a single theme uniting these conceptions of social behavior, it is that social conduct involves interacting selves capable of conversing within consensually defined language systems. This cannot be disputed. The error is to assume that adult conceptions of language and social behavior provide the grounds for evaluating what is or is not language and social behavior. My thesis thus appears. Children are social interactants far before the appearance of systematic pronoun usage, even before names are fully understood. They are social interactants initially because they are treated as valued social objects by their socializing agents (parents, siblings, peers). Suited out with the barest of neurological equipment, infants are immediately transformed from the status of "thing" to the role of self—of social being. This fact can only be grasped by following the unfolding trajectory of experiences and actions of the very young child. The clue to the emergence of social, self-directed behavior in young children comes from their evolving gestural systems.

Language as a set of indicative gestures becomes the medium through which normal, everyday social conduct appears. Modifications of taken-for-granted language structures signal the appearance of unique social worlds where new and different forms of thought, action, and conduct are sanctioned. Childhood becomes a negotiated world of thought and action that rests on a special system of indicative gestures. It is a conversation of gestures. This language is alien to all persons who have not aided in its production.

I turn now to the distinguishing features of early childhood speech and language. I shall indicate how routine aspects of adult speech and social conduct become problematic features of the child's world. In this analysis, the perspective of the child and of the adult will be alternatively stressed. If I have erred, it is because I have attempted to enter the child's world and view adults from his point of view. Taken on their own grounds, children are engaged in serious action—not play, asocial, nonperson, or unserious conduct, as so many have stressed.

The Language and Conduct of Young Children

The following features are crucial for an understanding of early childhood speech. It is important to underscore the fact that these features have meaning only within the expanded conception of language offered earlier—that is, as a set of *indicative gestures*.

First, it will be found that the same word (*baby, Mommy, bow-wow*) can cover and, to the outsider, can blur the meaning given several distinct objects, moods, and relationships. But while the same word appears to be incorrectly employed, its in-context meaning appears when it is used concurrently with or is followed by a set of body gestures. My oldest daughter (age twenty-five months) employs the word *baby* as a designation of her younger sister (age twelve months). The word *baby*, however, refers to other objects and actions. It can mean a doll or any small child seen on the street, or it can refer to her actions when she sees herself acting as a baby. Of most importance are those utterances of *baby* when her sister is not present. To an outsider, such statements lack meaning. However, the actions her sister (baby) would take toward a problematic object can be best indicated by employing the word *baby*. This utterance thus designates the actions the speaker *would not take* toward the object (a drink, an ashtray, and so on). When accompanied by a shake of the head, hands, or arms, this interpretation is easily grasped by her sister and parents. This interpretation is situated and has reference only within the biographical history of the speaker and listener. It is a consensual gesture for the family, which represents a distinct language community.

This example highlights the historical and biographical components of early childhood speech. I wish to stress another aspect of this first feature, namely the apparent indiscriminate use of words. The meaning of any utterance can only be understood by grasping the character of the actions taken toward the designated object. That is, speech is embedded in action. The following episode illustrates this concept. Two boys (ages three and two and one half years) were talking and looking at a pair of caged rabbits at their preschool. The following conversation and sequence of actions was recorded.

> The two boys, Tommy and Jack, go over to the rabbit cage and begin pointing at the rabbits, saying "Mommy, Mommy, Daddy, Daddy." Tommy points to the water bottle several times and says, "Mommy, Mommy." The instructor, Cathy, comes up and says, "Oh, it's empty; let's go fill it. Would you like to go get some water for it?" (never designating a boy by name or gesture). Tommy leaves and returns with a filled bottle. Cathy places the water bottle in the cage and says to Tommy, "How would you like to put this away" (never referring to 'it' by name, only by pointing), "and then we'll go to get some lettuce?" Tommy removes his jacket ('it') and puts it in his locker. Tommy and Jack cross the room, get the lettuce, and on the way back Tommy says, "habbit, habbit," (for rabbit). They return to the cage and begin stuffing lettuce in the rabbits' cage. A fight ensues (with no spoken words) over who is going to close the door to the cage. Finally Cathy tells them how it is done, and she closes the door.

The episode ended at this point, as Cathy left the room and Tommy and Jack went off to play records. There are several features in this example that defy understanding until the actions and utterances of Tommy, Jack, and Cathy are seen within their relational and interactional context. The initial utterances of "Mommy" and "Daddy" display an early grasp of sex differences in animals. It is clear the reference was made to the rabbits; however, on first hearing this speech sequence I was at a loss, for I knew the children's parents were not at the preschool that morning. I attempted to locate a mother and father near the rabbit cage. There were none. The utterances only had meaning with respect to the rabbits.

A second important feature of this episode is the pointing of Tommy to the water bottle in the cage and his repeated use of the word "Mommy." He felt the mother rabbit needed water, and the water bottle was empty. An observer further than five feet from the rabbit cage would have seen no sense in this statement. The word "Mommy," when accompanied by a gesture designating the water bottle, filled out a proposed action sequence. It is important to note that this entire conversation of gestures was immediately understandable to the instructor. She was a part of the interaction. When Cathy suggested that the water bottle needed to be filled, she made no reference to either boy, yet Tommy left with the bottle. To understand this action, the relationship between the boys had to be known. In their friendship, Tommy was the leader, Jack the follower. It was obvious to both boys that if the bottle was to be filled Tommy would do it.

When Tommy removed his jacket at Cathy's suggestion, the word *jacket* was not mentioned. The jacket was pointed to. This was another instance of a word given meaning by an accompanying gesture.

The word "habbit," at this point in the episode (which lasted two minutes), was, of course, clear. Just as "Mommy" and "Daddy" can now be given correct meaning, there are two kinds of "habbits." The rabbit episode was consensually ended on the closing of the cage door. At this point, Jack attempted to assert himself and close the cage door. After all, Tommy had gone for water. Cathy entered the episode once again and successfully brought it to a negotiated conclusion. She closed the door.

I offer this extended discussion of the "rabbit" episode to point out the significance of silent gestures, special words, social relationships, and ongoing action for the young child's speech. I am convinced that these features are not unique to early language usage.

This first feature of the young child's speech—the use of

gestures to precisely designate a particular object within a broad class of objects—is to be distinguished, if only slightly, from the second characteristic: the use of gestures to give an unclearly enunciated word precise meaning. The vocal utterances of young children are often slurred. For the adult accustomed to clearly enunciated words with proper emphasis on syllables, vowels, and consonants, this early speech is often uninterpretable. Once again, the young child struggles to communicate his thoughts through silent gestures. The sound "jewoush" may designate "juice." It is given additional and clarified meaning by bringing saliva to the lips. Saliva designates the middle phase of the social act the child wishes to carry out toward the object juice; that is, to procure and drink it. Similar gestural differentiations are produced for discriminations between other liquids (milk, Coca Cola, water). In each case, saliva will be brought to the lips but then accompanied by pointing gestures to the location of the desired liquid: milk by pointing to the refrigerator, Coca Cola by pointing to the upper shelf of the cupboard, and so on. This clarifying function of the gesture refers to the child's relational network, wherein a negotiated meaning for juice or other liquids has been settled on. For the gesture to have meaning, it must be acted on by the parent in a way that complements the child's intentions. If it is not, the act is blocked. Frustrated, the child searches for another gesture or utterance. In the last resort, the most significant gesture of all—the cry—will be called forth.

Third, words and gestures are employed by the young child to designate *situational ownership* of some object or set of objects crucial to an ongoing line of action. This feature of early childhood speech is centrally important, because self-declarations (the objectification of self) are made, even though personal pronouns and names are not present in the child's vocabulary. Mead, although never setting precise ages, asserted that for the child to be social and hence to have a self, he or she had to grasp the ongoing character of another's actions. Of crucial importance, the child had to be able to view his actions from the stance of another person or object. This perception leads to the "objectification" of self and others—a necessary condition for all human, self-directed social behavior. It is my thesis that young children objectify the self through nonverbal actions taken toward their valued social objects. These objects can range from dolls, blankets, special pieces of clothing or dress, to themselves, their siblings, and their parents. The *eyes* and *hands* are especially crucial in this early phase of self-objectification. The child communicates who he or she is toward a valued object by fixing the eyes and hands firmly on that object and then by raising the eyes to the level of the adult. *This repeated movement of the eyes from the object to the adult shows that for the moment this is the child's object.* It is the child's distinct object, because the child is a distinct object in his or her own eyes. Visual communication reinforces this definition of the situation.

A peculiar mixture of *repressive* and *restitutive* justice underlies the young child's attempts at self-objectification. When a valued object has been stolen or taken away by a sib or peer, an immediate response is demanded. If the valued object is not returned or substituted by one equally valued, the thief (villain) must be punished and the victim rewarded, if only in the name of justice. This is most evident in the actions of one- and two-year-olds. A young child, perhaps playing with a favored blanket, has it stolen by a sibling. If the blanket cannot be returned by the child's own efforts, what began as a simple game (the tease) becomes transformed into the "moral" arena of sacred selves. The baby's self has been challenged. A petition to higher authority is immediately called for. A deviant act has occurred. A cry, simultaneously joined by flailing arms and legs, announces the offense to the broader interactional community. The villain cannot escape. He has been publicly labeled by the offended. The system of justice now swings into force. Put on the spot, the parent or preschool instructor has little alternative but to intervene. Several options are available. Repressive justice in the form of a spanking or verbal chastizement can be employed. Restitutive justice can be attempted. The victim can perhaps be assuaged by the proffering of an equally valued object. The villain can be persuaded to give up the object—without force. Depending on the severity of the offense, a negotiated settlement is most likely. The offender will be reprimanded; the offended will be soothed.

However, the possibility always remains that a "scene" will be created. Scenes can be created by one or both parties. In such instances, all sense of justice collapses. The selves of all persons (offender, offended, instructor, parent, the watching audience) are collectively challenged. Children are adept at producing scenes. The following two episodes show how the offender (villain) can turn events around to make himself the victim, in this case the victim of the "insensitive" instructor. The scene is the preschool; the participants a four-year-old male, a three-year-old male playmate, and the instructor of the school. Kevin is the offender; Andy, the offended; Mindy, the instructor.*

> Kevin and Andy are playing together in the corner by the stack toys. Kevin tries to take the banana from Andy, and in so doing he knocks Andy down. Andy immediately starts to cry. Mindy appears and attempts to mediate and smooth things over, but as she approaches Kevin backs off. She attempts to assure him that she regarded the "incident" as an "accident" and that she wasn't going to "hit him." He continued to avoid her and backed away. Mindy made a last attempt to approach Kevin, and he ran upstairs to the upper level of the dollhouse and sat on the corner of the bed. He sat with arms folded for one or two minutes. Then he began to amuse himself by making faces in the mirror. Two minutes elapsed during which Andy went off to play, banana in hand, placated and soothed by the teacher's attention. Kevin then ventured down the stairs, interested in the activities of two girls playing at the foot of the dollhouse. Mindy was standing in the middle of the room with her back to Kevin. As Kevin reached the foot of the stairs, Mindy turned around quite suddenly. Kevin's reactions were swift. He ran up the ladder again with the teacher calling after him.

Second scene:

> Some fifteen minutes later, Kevin became involved in another scene. He approached the large

* I am indebted to John Skelton for the following episode.

"rocker toy" in the outer play area and jumped on the middle section as two girls were quietly rocking. The girls immediately jumped off and ran inside. Kevin ran after them and yelled, with a noticeable lack of anger, "I'll get you guys." He chased them inside and then out into the playground again. Giving up the chase, Kevin entered the woodshop, but as soon as the two girls returned to the rocking toy he once again jumped on the middle section and proceeded to violently pitch the rocker back and forth. Mindy, coming outside, walked over to Kevin and said, "I'm sorry Kevin, that's too dangerous." "No!" shouts Kevin, who once again runs away from Mindy.

Kevin's actions were quite deliberate. In both scenes, he refused to take the blame. He would not accept the instructor's definition of the situation. It was not an accident. He would not assume the villain role. Through his actions, he refused the scheme of restitutive justice. The judge (Mindy) and the victims (Andy and the two girls) became the offenders. Kevin emerged from both episodes (at least in his own mind) as the offended party. In both instances, his attempts at self-objectification had been challenged. Through a silent dialogue, punctuated by a few short phrases, his definition of self and situation came forth.

Self-Objectification, Normal Trouble, and Total Institutions

It is necessary to digress and note how the recurrent efforts of the child to objectify self and others lead to what parents call *normal problems* or *normal trouble* (see Sudnow, 1965; Cavan, 1966). Produced in scenes, normal trouble represents any situation where the child calls attention to himself and by direct implication involves the parent in that action. Embarrassment is the outcome (see Gross and Stone, 1963). These actions are problematic only when parent and child (1) find themselves in public settings (stores, sidewalks, restaurants, hotels, and so on); (2) or encounter a private behavior setting (the home) that is transformed, because of the appearance of guests or outsiders, into a public setting. In both situations, the parent is held accountable for the child's "sociable" conduct—the child is expected to complement the parents' line of action by acting properly. When he or she fails to do so, the self of the parent is challenged—the parent has failed to produce a child who will not create scenes. Scenes range from outright screaming tantrums to refusals to walk or sit in a stroller; from getting into display items to demanding food when in a grocery store; from wetting or messing diapers to asking to go to the bathroom when none is available; from talking or jabbering in a loud voice to all who pass to throwing items on the floor or sidewalk. The list of possible causes of a scene is endless. Children are skilled at producing novel variations on normal problems. A parent may feel that a child is toilet trained and then find that every time a grocery store is entered the child demands to go to the bathroom. Food may be purchased immediately on entry into a store and then refused. Distracting items may be brought by the parent and these too rejected.

A constant accommodative tension underlies the parent's attempts to soothe the child's efforts at self-objectification. Tension appears simply because the child is constantly changing, testing out, and trying on new self-conceptions. Each of these conceptions has the potential of creating scenes in public places.

Paradoxically, the persons who staff and enter public establishments develop a remarkably tolerant attitude toward the normal troubles of parents and children (except in those establishments such as bars and theaters where children are explicitly excluded by law or convention). As long as valued items are not destroyed or if parents can demonstrate their ability to pay for such destruction, these scenes are smiled on and accepted.

These scenes appear to be accepted for two reasons. First, all persons who have had or who look favorably on children can locate in their own biographies situations where a child embarrassed them. It is part of the problem of being a parent. Second, children tend to be viewed as "nonaccountable" social interactants (Goffman, 1963, pp. 125–126). Since they lack language ability ("real" selves) and an understanding of right and proper interaction rules, children can be (1) approached by anyone at any time, (2) spoken in front of as if they were not present, and (3) used as "bridges" to their masters (parents) much like dogs and other domesticated animals (Goffman, 1963, p. 126).

Placed in a "profaned" or "nonperson" category, little children are viewed as "unaccountable" objects. But if children are not held accountable for their actions, parents certainly are. And here lies a curious interactional paradox—sacred persons (adults who are parents) produce profane objects (children). This view of children is embedded in socialization theories of childhood and operationalized in preschool and elementary school settings. It leads to the existence of *total institutions* that control the child's every movement from the moment of waking to sleep at night. His food, entertainment items, dress, speech, toilet patterns, and sexual life are under constant surveillance. Although in sheer numbers children cannot be regarded as a minority group, in all other respects and notwithstanding the remarkable folklore defining childhood as blissful and happy, children are treated as members of a biologically inferior class.

The foregoing remarks were meant to suggest that young children actively reject this status. Their efforts at self-objectification represent continual demands for "accountability" and acceptance as full-fledged persons. Their languages offer the most strategic means for obtaining this status. I turn to the fourth distinguishing feature of this language.

The cry, yowl, and scream probably represent the most significant gesture of young children and their caretakers. Yet these utterances are given diverse interpretations, just as the smile, giggle, coo, and laugh are differently defined. There is an important difference between these two utterances. The cry is likely to provoke immediate action, the laugh is not. The cry, however, is a complex sound that is clustered into several categories: expressions of pain, anger, hunger, discomfort, or danger. Each of these categories have subdivisions. Pain can mean wet diapers, stuck with a pin, teething, a fall, or confrontations with a dangerous object (a light plug, a hot stove). Hunger can represent boredom or habit (feeding at a set time). The definition of danger is most likely to arise when the child is out of the adult's

field of vision. In this case, immediate physical action is called
for. This is seldom the case with the other meanings given the
cry. The meaning of the cry, however, arises out of the parents'
and child's ongoing sequence of actions. Its meaning is also
couched in the definitions parents tend to attribute to their children (troublemakers, teases, crybabies). Of interest is the fact
that the cry represents the one utterance of the child that is likely
to produce adult attention. As such, it becomes a central component of the child's speech, and it is continually employed in
those situations where the self is threatened or where demands
are not met.

In the preschool, the cry becomes an effective means of
calling attention to claims that are not met by other children. It
is also utilized to bring the instructor running when the child
perceives that he or she has been improperly treated by another.
The following example illustrates how the cry acts as a petition to
higher authority when a deviant or hostile act has occurred.
Once again, the relational context of the interaction must be
understood. In the following sequence, two girls, Emmy and Rita
(both age two years, eight months), have been playing together
all morning, alternating between the roles of mother and baby.
They have excluded Bobby from their activity. The scene opens
with Emmy and Rita playing the roles of mother and baby in
the lower level of the dollhouse.

> Emmy gets the stroller, and Rita climbs in it
> for a ride. Emmy (mother) gets a blanket for baby
> Rita and pushes the stroller in front of the mirror.
> She gives Rita a kiss on the cheek, and Bobby comes
> running up holding a ribbon in his hand. He makes a
> "mock" hitting action with his ribbon at Emmy
> (mother). Emmy says, "Leave us alone." Bobby per-
> sists in waving his ribbon at her. Emmy looks around
> for the instructor, and, locating her, she begins to cry.
> The instructor comes up, and Bobby runs upstairs
> away from her. The instructor asks of Bobby, "Was
> it an accident, Bobby?" Bobby says, "No!" The in-
> structor replies, "No!! Don't you love me anymore,
> Bobby?"

The episode ends here. Emmy and Rita go on playing in the stroller, satisfied that Bobby has been reprimanded by the instructor. Of greatest interest in this context is the instructor's questions, "Don't you love me anymore?" and "Was it an accident?" If the incident was an accident, it could be easily explained away. Anybody can wave a ribbon at someone else and have that action interpreted as a threat, even if in fact no threat was intended. Bobby denied this definition. Disturbed because he had been excluded from the mother-baby interactions, he fully intended the mock hitting episode to be interpreted as a threat—as an expression of dissatisfaction. Not accepting this definition, the instructor relied on the dictum that "If you love me, you wouldn't do something like this." It can be seen that the cry transformed a normal interactive sequence into a problematic episode involving love and the moral character of the defendant.

Fifth, gestures and words take on special meaning for children as they create personal relationships. There is often an attempt to produce special words that outsiders cannot understand. This word or phrase, when followed by a special set of actions, sets the new relational partners off from all others. Elsewhere in this book, the example is used of two young girls who had just become playmates in the preschool. Within an hour, the two girls had developed the word "Buckmanu" which they chanted in rhythm while swinging their arms in unison. "Buckmanu," as was clear when the girls enunciated "Manuel bucked us off," referred to one of their instructors (Manuel) who played horseback with the children. This word has become "their" word, and cements the unit of the two (they). Words such as "Buckmanu" are common and are not unlike the following: "off you," "ludes," "spaced," and "fox," which are common among various adolescent and adult minority subcultures. These words are neologisms. They lack consensual meaning within adult or outsider speech communities. Indeed, they resist outsider interpretations; this is an explicit function. (Another function is to describe an experience, act, object, and so on to which adults or outsiders have no reference.) In many respects, the language of early childhood can only be understood as a complex set of ever-changing and evolving neologisms. As the child progressively moves into the adult's world of speech, these phrases are dropped and replaced by even more subtle indicators of groups and relational membership. These neologisms are more than spoken words; they are nests of tightly woven verbal and nonverbal gestures.

Sixth, in the early stages of word acquisition, there is little differentiation between the utterance of a word and the actions designated by the word.* In short, the covert and overt act are merged and collectively made public—a feature of speech that is differentially displayed in adulthood. Symbols, as Mead (1934) remarked, are universals. Their use telescopes the emergence of a proposed act. By combining the languages of verbal speech and the language of the hands, young children attempt to ensure that their listeners (and viewers) will understand the proposed act. This merging of the covert and overt act frequently leads children to rehearse and take to completion the proposed act. Children, then, are continually producing *solo acts*. Words such as "bye-bye" are often accompanied by a waving of the arms and on occasion the preparation for actual leave-taking.

This attribute of early word usage vividly highlights the function of words and gestures for adults. While adults seldom speak without gesturing, their use of words merely signals a proposed act. Conversation, not immediate overt physical movement, is the usual outcome. As noted elsewhere in this volume, the phrase "Shall we leave?" may be followed by ten minutes of conversation during which elaborate leave-taking rituals are employed to release interactants from one another's presence. The child is much more likely to follow his utterance with immediate action; the leave-taking ritual is not employed. It remains for future research to identify the points in the life cycle where gestures funnel into spoken words and conversation. In this instance, I am proposing research on the problem of how the covert act remains covert.

The child's use of gestures to fill out and complement his interpretations of a word, object, or proposed action ensures for

* I am indebted to Evelyn Denzin for bringing this point to my attention.

him that his listeners understand what is vocalized. This line of action serves another function. If carried far enough, it provokes adults into acting on the child's declaration of intent. Until the adult or listener is brought into the proposed action sequence, a one-sided social act is produced. For a joint action to emerge, the adult must act on the child's proposals. If a child says good-bye, waves goodbye, secures a coat, and then moves to the front door, the adult is forced into action. Several possibilities appear. The adult can be gently coerced into going bye-bye. This action reinforces the child's gestural system and sense of autonomy. On the other hand, the gesture can be exposed as a fiction by ex-plaining that it is impossible to go bye-bye at the present time. In this case, the child's, not the adult's line of action (as in the former case), is diverted.

A large proportion of early child-parent interactions fall into this coercive-diversionary category. Indeed, one of the prob-lematic features of child production (for parents) is the creation of an interactive relationship with the child wherein the parent does not have to give in more than he or she wants to. Two broad categories of children are then produced: spoiled brats (those who always get their own way) and docile, shy weaklings. The normative structure of American middle-class family life calls for a child somewhere in the middle. Socialization strategies in the family and school are, in part, aimed at such productions.

There is another problem with this tendency for children to act out their proposed actions. This is the separation of fact from fantasy. The reinforcement of a child's gestural system can lead to a language that (for a parent or instructor) bears no relationship to reality. Since the reality of parent-child interac-tions tends toward continual renegotiations, this is often no problem. But on occasion it can become a problem. Children who move completely into their own gestural systems may be labeled autistic or retarded, thus necessitating the creation of special actions and institutions for their care and treatment.

On other occasions, the problem is less severe; it is simply troublesome for the parent to have to act on the child's symbol system. This is most evident in the world of dolls—those objects contributed by adults for child's play. It is one thing to call a doll a baby. But it is another to demand that the doll be changed, given a special bed, fed special foods, and rocked to sleep.

Paradoxically, adults contribute to childhood fantasy. This appears to be related to the conception of children noted earlier; that is, their similarity with other domesticated animals. An examination of the literature afforded children between the ages of two and four reveals one noticeable feature. The most frequently discussed object is either the animal or the doll. Since both objects are nonhuman in nature, the meanings given them by adults and children tend to reinforce the nonreal and fantasy features of childhood. The following interaction between three two-year-old children and a mother at a preschool illustrates how adults participate in the creation of childhood fantasy.

> Larry, a small boy, attempts to climb into a highchair in the play area of the preschool. A mother (Miriam) comes up and says, "No, Larry; that's for little babies and dolls, not for big boys like you, not big boys." Larry makes three attempts to climb into the highchair, and each time the mother repeats her previous statement. Finally she places a doll in the chair, and Larry begins playing around the highchair. Two girls come up and begin fixing breakfast for themselves and the doll. The mother cautions them that the baby must wear a bib if it is going to have breakfast. The mother then puts a bib on the doll and sets a bowl of oatmeal on the doll's plate. The two girls begin feeding the doll oatmeal. In the meantime, Sam (a boy) comes over with a pair of high-heeled shoes on. They keep falling off, and the mother leaves the doll (for a moment) and helps Sam with his high heels. The girls decide that the baby is full, and the mother assists them in taking off the bib, changing the baby's diapers and preparing it for a nap.

We have in this episode the social construction of "irreality." Dolls cannot eat oatmeal, and children know it. Yet the mother persisted in acting on the doll as a human object. There is an additional motive underlying these adult constructions of childhood fantasy. Childhood is seen as a period of bliss, happiness, and laughter. Children are not to be troubled with the problems of everyday adult life. It is not surprising, therefore, that children have been regarded by some (Ariès, 1962, p. 68; Stone, 1965, p. 28) as forming "the most conservative of societies." My observations lead to the opposite conclusion. Although the myths, stories, tales, and toys of childhood remain remarkably stable across generations (see I. Opie and P. Opie, 1959), this stability is contributed by adults, who pass on the myths, stories, and tales from their childhood to their own children. Stability is also produced in the marketplace. The toy market is based on what sells, and there is little feedback from children and their parents to the manufacturers of toys and books (see Ball, 1967). It is adults, then, who are fanciful and conservative in their actions toward children.

Making Society Real

Childhood socialization has received little sociological attention. It is conventionally assumed that children, once grasping adult language, move rather systematically into the roles, values, and perspectives of adulthood. Socialization thus becomes the inculcation of adult values into the child's personality.

I should like to propose another conception of socialization. Many have remarked that socialization is never ending—it proceeds throughout the life cycle. Yet this assumption has seldom been taken seriously. My research suggests that socialization is but one aspect of the process by which interactants (of any age) attempt to make society real through the process of self-objectification. At the heart of socialization and the role-taking process lies a bundle of special symbols, gestures, and nested languages. These languages are lodged in social selves and become the medium for interaction. Socialization research must be directed to the many language and gestural communities that make up any society. It is here that selves, personalities, roles, and perspectives are created. From this stance, society emerges as a negotiated social order. It is an ongoing network of lodged selves, symbols, and objects. No object carries intrinsic meaning. Interactants must settle for themselves what languages and meanings they are going to employ as they go about their daily routines.

Early childhood represents one of the most problematic periods of socialization—for both the parent and the child. Society, as it is known and experienced by the parent and child, is under constant revision. This suggests that the child's control over the parent becomes a direct function of the *complexity* of his indicative gestural system and the degree of consensuality assigned that system by adults. The child's contributions to the social world of family and school life is similarly a direct function of these two processes. It is here, in the interactions between children and parents, that society appears. Each family, as a distinct community, creates its version of right, of proper conduct—its version of what society is and ought to be.

The study of how children are treated by parents, peers, siblings, and instructors reveals what is problematic for adults. Thus, prior research on young children, which has stressed the acquisition of language and the rate of learning, simply suggests that for those investigators the most problematic features of adulthood are language and knowledge.

My evidence suggests that a completely different set of problems confront parents as they produce children. These problems involve the control of normal trouble and the legislation of a system of justice, sanctions, and rewards.

Problems not treated in this essay include invasions of privacy in childhood and the play of young children. Nor have I offered evidence from other cultures and groups where children are seen as different kinds of objects (see Mead and Wolfenstein, 1955). If childhood is seen as a complex status passage, comparative research into other cultures, groups, and societies must be examined (see Glaser and Strauss, 1970). This suggests comparative research into situations where children are produced in solitary nuclear families, in groups of siblings, or in the absence of parents. Those cultures where children are seen as "young adults," not as unaccountable objects, should also be studied. It would be expected that the languages, symbols, gestures, and selves of children would vary by the situation of production. That is, the meaning of an object resides, in large part, in the interactions brought to it. A child, then, is a complex social object. The meanings brought to the child will be reflected in his actions. I have attempted to show that American middle-class children resist the definitions brought to them by parents, instructors, and social scientists.

Chapter Seven

Genesis of Self
in Early Childhood

My intentions in this chapter
are to examine the Mead-Cooley-Piaget theory of self-development.* Consistent with a symbolic interactionist position, I hold
that any theory of society must ultimately answer the question,
"How do selves develop out of the interaction process?" (See
Strauss, 1969; Lindesmith, Strauss, and Denzin, 1978; Blumer,
1969.) Aside from the early observations of Baldwin (1897),
Mead (1934, 1938), and Cooley (1922), few sociologists have
directly addressed themselves to the subject of the genesis of self

---

* Doby (1970) provides a very useful review of Mead's and
Piaget's theories of self and cognitive development. Strictly speaking,
Piaget's formulations are not directed to self-development, but Kohlberg's
1969 revisions of Piaget make the self of central concern. Piaget's work,
more properly, refers to language development and to the refinement of
cognitive skills in early childhood.

114

in early childhood. (For important exceptions, see Bain, 1936; Kuhn, 1954; Allport, 1961; Shibutani, 1961; Blumer, 1969; Parsons and Bales, 1955; Parsons, 1968; Stone and Farberman, 1970). These exceptions, however, have seldom been grounded in empirical observations; they represent conceptual additions or revisions of the Mead-Cooley perspective or, as in the case of Parsons, Freud. (See Swanson's 1961 attempt to wed Mead and Freud. Doby's 1970 discussion extends Lindesmith and Strauss's synthesis of Piaget, Vygotsky, Flavell, and Mead, and it is also a point of departure for the present analysis.)

The works of Piaget or of his revisionists (see Kohlberg, 1969; Flavell, 1963; Flavell and others, 1968; Miller, Kessel, and Flavell, 1970; Devries, 1970) are often incorporated into the symbolic interactionist view of selfhood. This research however, seldom touches on the growing literature in developmental linguistics that is central to Mead's position on the importance of language acquisition in early selfhood (see Doby, 1970; Brown, 1958, 1964, 1965, 1970, 1971; Brown and Bellugi, 1964; Brown and Ford, 1961; Brown and Fraser, 1963; Brown, Fraser, and Bellugi, 1964; Ervin-Tripp, 1964, 1969a, 1969b; Bernstein, 1964; Luria, 1966; Fishman, 1960; Vygotsky, 1962; Piaget, 1970; Hymes, 1964; Miller, Shelton, and Flavell, 1970). Even though this literature is central to the interactionist position, it is seldom cognizant of the role of the self in social interaction. Except for Brown, Gumperz, Piaget, and Ervin-Tripp, most researchers in linguistics view learning from a maturational approach, from a stimulus-response perspective, or from an innate ability position (see Chomsky, 1966; Piaget's review of structuralism, 1970; Kohlberg, 1969; Zigler and Child, 1969; Miller and McNeill, 1969).

There is an additional difficulty with this literature. As Deutscher (1969–1970, p. 6) observes: "We are not linguists; we are sociologists, and it is a sociological concept of language to which our attention is directed. Under some conditions, it could of course be disastrous for the sociologist to ignore the concepts employed by linguists; the categories employed by natives are an important part of the object of our study. As in all fields of sociological endeavor, it is the perspective of sociologists as outsiders reflecting upon the categories of insiders, which provides our unique contribution. . . . The categories employed by the native are important, but as data, not as theoretical or analytical tools. I suspect that the sociologist who assumes the linguists' perspective is as likely to achieve success in understanding language as is the sociologist who assumes the legal perspective in understanding crime."

Last, this literature fails to conceptualize language either sociologically or as symbolic interaction. It views language (see Grimshaw, 1969a, 1969b) either (1) as a social institution independent of the people who use it (Piaget, 1970), (2) as a product of innate genetic abilities (Chomsky, 1968), (3) as a product caused by attributes of social structure, or (4) as a product independent of culture and structure. (See also Hymes, 1964; Hertzler, 1965; Brown, 1958; Lieberson, 1966; Gumperz, 1967.) Consistent with the symbolic interactionist tradition, I view language as a situated production that varies according to the definitions that people give objects, selves, others, time, place, and the social relationships between speakers. I will treat language as a complex gestural system (both spoken and silent) that is created through symbolic interaction. Language is best seen as a set of indicative gestures that have differential universal relevance both for speaker and listener and for linguist, sociologist, and psychologist. (Herbert Blumer, in conversation, suggested this view of language. Elaborations of this position can be found in Cicourel, 1970; Cicourel and Boese, 1975; R. Turner, 1970; Speier, 1970; Zimmerman, 1970; and Manning, 1970. Also see Birdwhistell, 1970.)

Briefly then, I shall review the Mead-Cooley-Piaget-revisionist perspective on the genesis of self, summarize the literature on developmental linguistics, and present field data from my own observations on young children between the ages of one and three. My aim is to bring current sociological thinking on self-development more into line with recent research than it has been. My strategy will be to subject the most salient hypotheses from the Mead-Cooley tradition to the empirical observation that such researchers as Glaser and Strauss (1967) and Denzin (1970a) have proposed. I hope to present a more grounded image of self in early childhood. My last goal is to provoke more interest in studies of children in their natural habitats: in pre-schools, schools, and nurseries, in streets, yards, and on side-walks, and in parks, stores, and homes. (See the work of I. Opie and P. Opie, 1959, 1969, for work in this tradition; the papers collected by Mead and Wolfenstein, 1955; and the argument of Goodman, 1970.)

The Mead-Cooley-Piaget Perspective

Mead, Cooley, and Piaget present views of early self-hood that may be termed *interactional, cognitive,* and *developmental.* (See Kohlberg, 1969, for this view of Piaget; also Flavell, 1963. The views of Piaget, however, are more biologi-cally and socially oriented than those of Mead and Cooley.) In a sequential fashion, the self develops out of the universes of dis-course and experience that are routinely confronted by the infant and young child (primary groups). Mead stressed three phases of selfhood: the anticipatory or play stage, the game stage, and the generalized other phase. (See Stone, 1962 for an elaboration and critique of these stages.) In each phase, the child is pro-gressively able to differentiate self from other, to view the rules of the game as constructed rather than as invariant, and to con-ceptualize the attitudes of fellow selves into an organized whole (that is, to show the ability to take the perspective of the gen-eralized group). Holding a similar view, Piaget (1968; Piaget and Inhelder, 1969) presents several phases or stages of develop-ment; his basically threefold scheme distinguishes interactions that are imitative, absolutistic, and reciprocal; or autistic, ego-centric, and logical. (In this sense, Piaget's scheme parallels H. S. Sullivan's, which also stressed three developmental stages: prototaxic, parataxic, and syntaxic.) Reciprocal interactions represent the appearance of intuitive thought and the culmina-tion of abilities for abstract reasoning. As the child moves through the advanced developmental stages, his accommodative and imitative actions give way to reflexive and assimilative con-duct. He relinquishes his egocentric view of self, rules, and the world around him. He ceases to think in animistic, artificial, finalistic, and narrow moral terms. In essence, he becomes a reflexive self.

These three theorists agree with each other on five major points. First, they emphasize the importance of affective and cognitive processes in self-development. (Cooley, more than Mead, stressed affective features of the self as central to self-awareness. In his observations of early childhood, he employed the strategy of recording fights, scenes, and temper tantrums as a means of revealing the child's definition of the situation.) Second, they view each stage of development as qualitatively different from the previous stage. Third, they emphasize the role of interactional processes in cognitive development and in early selfhood. Fourth, they reject associationist and stimulus-response theories of learning. To them, the organism progressively acquires the ability to stimulate its own conduct and to formulate its own plans of action: Objects and stimuli carry no intrinsic meaning. (According to Kohlberg, 1969, Piaget treats learning as a complex process of differentiation and assimilation, which is in itself contingent on the development of language acquisition.) Fifth, they emphasize comparable empirical methods for the study of self. Each used a variation on the ethnographic, case study method (Piaget and Cooley both studied their own children). Each emphasized the importance of linguistic utterances as central indicators of selfhood. (Cooley observed pronoun utterances, and Piaget recorded conversations.) Each attended to gestures, to performances, and to nonverbal actions as indicators of self.

Piaget, however, differs from Mead and Cooley on two major points. First, he emphasizes that cognitive processes are continually striving for reciprocity between the demands of self and other and for equilibrium between assimilative and accommodative modes of conceptualization. Second, he emphasizes that each developmental stage can be fixed at a specific age; he asserts, for example, that children until the age of seven engage in egocentric thought and conversation (1968, pp. 20–21). Apparently in response to recent criticisms concerning these age levels (for example, Vygotsky, 1962), Piaget and Inhelder (1969, p. 3) state, "Ages indicated in this book are always average and approximate." Notwithstanding this disclaimer, the book is filled with specific age predictions concerning cognitive development and so on.

In my judgment, the basic difference among these three theorists rests on the invariant character of their development stages. Some have severely criticized Piaget for setting specific ages for cognitive development. (See Flavell, 1963; Kohlberg, 1969; Zigler and Child, 1969. Kohlberg presents the best version of Piaget's theory. Although Piaget treats age levels as fixed entities, Kohlberg treats them as variables influenced by social processes.) Some observers have criticized Piaget's works on four accounts: He underemphasizes situational factors in selfhood; his age levels are not cross-culturally universal; his age levels are products not of age per se but of psychological and interactional processes; and learning is basically the same at all levels of development. (For a review of these criticisms, see Zigler and Child, 1969.) In his own defense, Piaget contends that he has little interest in variations among children and that he is not a student of children but a student of thought.

The present chapter also challenges Piaget's concept of age levels at which certain actions will either appear or not appear. If one adopts an interactional view of self and of the social process, then one does not believe that age in itself elicits reflexive abilities. Rates of self-development are indeed contingent on the character of the symbolic world of the child and of his significant others. This view is consistent with Mead's formulations (1938), which suggest that a child's reflexive ability varies according to the play situation (for example, consecutive versus singular) and to symbolic abilities. In fact, Mead (1938) noted that children of the same age engage in qualitatively different reflexive acts. His generalized actor-manager, the child who directs, applauds, and criticizes his own roles and those of others is acting quite differently from the child who docilely takes directions. This same point is reflected in Cooley's (1922, p. 198) description of M. at fifteen months: "She had become a 'perfect little actress,' seeming to live largely in imaginations of her effect upon other people. She constantly and obviously laid traps for attention and looked abashed or wept at any signs of disapproval or indifference. At times it would seem as if she could not get over these repulses, but would cry long in a grieved way, refusing to be comforted. If she hit upon any little trick that made people laugh she would be sure to repeat it, laughing loudly and affectedly in imitation. She had quite a repertory of these small performances, which she would display to a sympathetic audience, or even try upon strangers."

On the basis of these perspectives, one would then expect that observations of young children (ages two to four years) in a common setting (such as homes or preschool) would reveal variation in such skill dimensions as systematic language usage, role-taking ability, conversational reciprocity, seriousness of play involvement, and an understanding of the rules of the game. Although Piaget's work suggests that in children between the ages of two and four few complex and reflexive acts may be observed, Mead and Cooley have left this question open. For them, the self develops as the child acquires abilities to call out in himself the attitudes of others; the child must separate self from other and take the attitude of the other. The self is a social process, a product of symbolic interaction that is observable in the interaction process. It also represents not a cognitive process alone but all the activities of the individual that call out responses in him that are similar to those being called out in another individual.* According to Cooley's formulations, the self involves affective, cognitive, and interactional activities. It is not a fixed entity, a rigid structure of attitudes, nor a strict reflection of the attitudes of others. It reflects its own private conceptions and its consensually public designations. Covertly, the self arises in the individual's conversations or dialogues with himself, and in his symbolic encounters and retrospective acts (see Saltiel, 1969; Kuhn, 1962; Faris, 1940). On the other hand, the self is overtly or behavioristically observed through a person's announcements, proposals, declarations of intent; through his gestures, his special languages, his manner of dress; and through his movement, his special styles of performing, and his public and private names

---

* This view of Mead's position was suggested to me by Robert L. Stewart.

(see Stone, 1962). The self, then, is "created, established, and presented in the communication process" (Stone, 1962, p. 394). It represents all the indications of self and reflections that a person makes to himself as a distinct object (see Blumer, 1969).

The Literature on Developmental Linguistics

It is impossible to give a complete review of the research in developmental linguistics. My emphasis will, therefore, be on the most salient work pertinent to language development and to the genesis of self. (For reviews, see Brown, 1958, 1970, 1971; Lindesmith, Strauss, and Denzin, 1978; Hymes, 1964; Miller and McNeill, 1969; Cottrell, 1969; Greenfield and Bruner, 1969; Blumenthal, 1970; Kohlberg, 1969; Bandura, 1969; Jenkins, 1969; Gumperz, 1967.) As I have indicated, this literature has as its major problems a limited conception of self, language, and social interaction. (See also the essays on linguistics by Cicourel, Wieder, Turner, Speier, and Manning in Douglas, 1970.)

A desired goal of the linguist who studies early childhood speech is the construction of a word dictionary (Miller and McNeill, 1969). Here the observer begins by charting the speech sounds of the young child (phonemes). He then moves to the morphemic analysis of semantic units by breaking these units into the functional units of speech (noun, verb, adverb, adjective). He next describes the child's syntactical system (for example, rules of construction) and finally examines the semantical or meaning system employed by the subject. Descriptive linguists focus on inventorying the elementary sounds of the child. Developmental linguists, however, give attention to such matters as linguistic performance and linguistic competence, perhaps using Brown's (1958) original word game acts as their paradigm of analysis (see Miller and McNeill, 1969).

Studies of early childhood speech (Miller and McNeill, 1969; Brown, 1971) reveal its telegraphic character; that is, the child uses one sound to characterize an entire act. Utterances, until at least the age of three, tend to be holophrastic or in the form of one-, two-, and three-word sentences. Neologisms are continually constructed, but there is disagreement on this point. Some observers assert that onomatopeic words are not inventions, but crude imitations of adult sounds (see Nice, 1925). At least initially, children learn language through imitations of adult utterances. Much research indicates that three-year-olds know many more words than they routinely speak and that their ability to imitate sounds is more advanced than is their ability to understand (see Fraser, Bellugi, and Brown, 1963).

A child's linguistic skills are contingent on the actions taken by his parents. As Miller and McNeill (1969) and also Brown (1964) and Ervin-Tripp (1964) noted, the adult may expand, reformulate, or even ask for repetition of the child's utterances. The adult may also ignore or challenge the utterance. Preliminary research by Brown (1964) indicated that adults may repeat a child's utterances no more than 30 percent of the time. (Unfortunately, his records come from academic parents in Cambridge, Massachusetts.) This finding alone, however, gives significant support to an interactional view of language development and selfhood.

McNeill's (1966a, pp. 34–38) analysis of early childhood speech is informative and opens the way for a sociologically informed view of language development. He stated: "At about the age of one, a normal child, not impaired by hearing loss or speech impediment, will begin to say words. By one-and-a-half or two years, he will begin to form simple two- and three-word sentences. By four years, he will have mastered very nearly the entire complex and abstract structure of the English language. In slightly more than two years, therefore, children acquire full knowledge of the grammatical system of their native tongue. This stunning intellectual achievement is routinely performed by every preschool child, but what is known about the process underlying it?"

If the preschool child displays in his speech, even if only crudely, a knowledge of the grammatical system of his speech community, then one can analyze such talk in ways that reveal the child's ability to take account of others. One would expect that the young speaker, like more skilled adults, would make grammatical errors, construct new words, mispronounce, repeat, and stutter. One would also expect that an interactional account of the preschooler's speech would reveal the salient objects in the interactional process (that is, repetitions of key words would reveal problematic objects or proposed acts, and so on). One may well use Ervin-Tripp's (1964, 1969a) suggestions for distinguishing setting, act, and episode or Firth's (1964) suggestion for studying types of language and speech situations (for example, honorific and interrogative greetings, greetings governed by custom or etiquette, or greetings expressing flattery, lovemaking, praise, blame, and persuasion).

In summary, students who study the genesis of self in early childhood would examine syntax and semantics only as indicators of the peculiar features of the child's speech community. Here the analyst would attempt to learn a new language and not attempt to force that language into his own grammatical and semantical system. (See Gudschinsky, 1967, for suggestions in learning an unwritten language.) They would isolate certain linguistic categories (for example, nouns and pronouns) if they were studying expressions of selfhood. They would examine emotional phrases to highlight the affective tone of the interaction sequence (see Cooley, 1922). They could catalogue variations in speech abilities (and perhaps role-taking skill) by recording sentence length (one, two, or three words). They could study expressive skill by recording the frequency of nonverbal utterances and by relating these gestures to spoken words. They could study the nonconsensual character of the child's speech by recording the ratio of consensual utterances in single or multiple speech acts. (Consensuality would be judged here (1) by the observer's ability to comprehend the utterance and (2) by the actions taken toward the utterance by the other speech partners in the setting, such as parents, sibs, or peers.) They could study the salient interactional objects in the speech episodes under analysis by recording the repeatability ratio of all words in the episode. They would consider those words with the highest repeatability ratio as indicators of the salient or problematic objects. Such a mode of analysis permits the observer to focus centrally on the

question, "How do children take account of one another?" I
will now present the data obtained from my ongoing study of
preschool children.

The Research Setting

The data were primarily obtained from direct personal
observations of children who attended a racially mixed, uni-
versity-related, and parent-cooperative preschool center that was
located in a large metropolitan city on the West Coast of the
United States. This center was one of the eleven outstanding preschool centers in the United States, according to the report by
Abramson (1970). Owned by the local university, the center has
one wing that is operated by the university and another wing that
is operated by the city's public schools. Morning and afternoon
sessions are offered for three- and four-year-olds, and each session has approximately twenty children. The university wing is
staffed by professional child care workers, and the city wing is
staffed by parents who work on a cooperative basis. At the time
of my observations, ages of the children ranged from two years,
eleven months, to three years, ten months, for those in the three-
year-old sessions, and from three years, eleven months, to four
years, ten months, for those in the four-year-old sessions. The
children in the three-year-old sessions had an average of 1.63
siblings at home, whose ages ranged from one to seventeen years.
The children in the four-year-old sessions had an average of 1.36
siblings at home, whose ages ranged from one to sixteen years.
The occupational and educational backgrounds of the parents of
the children in both sessions ranged from parents with university
appointments to blue-collar workers and college students. Mexi-
can-Americans, blacks, and Asians, although strictly in the
minority, were represented.

The staff in each wing routinely structured the activities
of the children into the following time periods: for the morning
groups, children's arrival at 9:00; self-selected activities from
9:00 to 10:00; serving of juice from 10:00 to 10:30; indoor
group play from 10:30 to 11:00; story time or small-group ac-

tivity from 11:00 to 11:20; final putting-away time at 11:20; children's departure at 11:30. I have discussed the functions of these timetables elsewhere in this book.

This setting is not unlike those of other preschools, but the parental backgrounds of the children and the special features of the city may introduce factors that restrict the external validity of my observations. In substance, this setting is similar to those reported by Brown (1970) and his colleagues. Although the university attempts to recruit, for purposes of doing research, preschoolers with widely varying backgrounds, one can hardly view the study group as representative of preschool children in the United States today. My findings, which were based on participant observation and informal interview, may be specific only to this situation and thus may be historically specific. (Such appears to be the case with most, if not all, research on preschool children. Piaget's observation often came from his own family or from Montessori schools; Brown's came from a university preschool; Ervin-Tripp's from those children whose parents permitted them to be studied.) The usual criteria of willingness, geographical nearness, and convenience appear to prevail in studies of this age group. I defend this approach because important contributions to existing linguistic theory have come from these case history and ethnographic approaches. This suggests that the researcher must alter the usual canons of scientific conduct to fit the character of the empirical world. Blumer (1969), Becker (1970b), and Glaser and Strauss (1967) stress this naturalistic approach to theory construction and the research act. (See Kohlberg, 1969, for a criticism of this position.)

The Strategy of Analysis and Presentation

My strategy, as an observer, was to sit, play, eat, and drink juice with the children. I often took notes on the spot. To assess my reactive effect in the situation, I also gathered observations from behind a one-way screen that ran the length of the center. As I developed hypotheses and hunches about the children's conduct, I employed teachers as resources so that I might check my account of a child's behavior against their interpretation. In the early phases of my observations, I was guided by Piaget's age level formulations; but I subsequently dropped that perspective because it became apparent that this prediction failed to hold true for my study group. In forming and testing hypotheses, I employed a rough approximation of analytic induction (Denzin, 1970a; Becker, 1970b) and the constant comparative method (Glaser and Strauss, 1967). My strategy was to form a hypothesis while I was in the field and then to check that hunch against the next series of observations. In this way, I attempted to refine progressively my perspective and to ground it in the data.

The evidence that I present reflects what I regard (from my field notes) as *representative* cases, types, or examples of the behavior that I describe. I distinguish representative cases from *anecdotal* cases by their frequency of appearance in the field experience. An anecdotal case may appear only once or, at best, infrequently. It may provoke negative case analysis, but it should not be taken as firm foundation for an emergent hypothesis. Examples of anecdotal cases were each of the five children who failed to become members of the play group: One was under drug sedation, another was autistic, another was a latecomer to the group, another was periodically ill, and a last was suffering from problems stemming from separation between parents. Each of these cases, hardly representative, sharpened my conception of what it means to be a member of a preschool. Representative cases, then, should appear at a frequency that is sufficient to cover accurately the range of behaviors explained or described by that case. (See Becker and others, 1961, for a more elaborate treatment and presentation of this strategy; see also Chapter Three.)

My strategy will be to present evidence on the ways in which young children in this preschool "take account of one another." My basic hypothesis is quite simple and follows from Mead's discussion. Wide variation in role-taking ability will be present in children of this age, and these variations will reveal differential levels of self-awareness. I, however, assume that, to the degree to which these children have grasped the rudiments of the English language, their behavior will reveal differential levels of reflexivity.

Language Usage Patterns

The Use of Personal Pronouns. Cooley (1922), employing a variety of empirical indicators of self-development, stressed the importance of the personal pronouns in the young child's vocabulary. (He noted its appearance with his daughter M. when she was only sixteen months old, and Bain, 1936, observed a similar occurrence in his daughter Sheila shortly after she was two years old.)

My observations, which were consistent with McNeill's (1966b) reanalysis of Brown and Fraser's (1963) study of Adam (a two-year-old), revealed that pronouns occupy an important and central role in the three-year-old's speech. The following three examples are representative.

Two girls are standing below the large dollhouse inside the preschool.

First girl: "They're people up there." (Points to three girls playing upstairs.)

Second girl: "Shall we go up there?"

First girl: "No, they'll say 'You can't come up here.' "

A three-year-old girl has just finished working at the painting table. She gets up and goes across the room to get a book. An instructor confronts her:

Instructor: "Are you through painting? Don't you want to hang up your painting?"

Girl: "No, I don't want to!"

Instructor: "Don't you really?"

Girl: "No." (Shakes her head and walks off.)

Instructor: "I'll do it for you." (Grimaces.)

Three girls are standing in a semicircle admiring one another's clothing.

First girl: "Mary, can you help me get the pink dress down?"
Second girl: "Yes, I'll help you."
Third girl: "I'm three and a half years old."

Each example showed that the children use both personal and impersonal pronouns with no difficulty and in direct reference to some ongoing activity system where selves are involved. In the first example, a decision not to go upstairs into the dollhouse was made because there were people who would not want them to come up. The use of the term *people* represented an attempt to take the collective perspective of several individuals and to assess a line of action against that imputed perspective. The two girls had moved outside their own behavior and had formed a line of action on the basis of which they thought others regarded them. Similar conclusions can be drawn from the other excerpts. In the second example, the pronoun *I* clearly represented a self-conscious decision not to do what the instructor wanted. In the third instance, the response, "I'll help you," represented an "interiorization" of the other's perspective and the organizing of a line of action on the basis of that interpretation.

The pronoun is only one indicator of selfhood. Its presence in the child's vocabulary can be taken as evidence that self-consciously organized lines of action are forthcoming. Its absence, however, must not be taken as evidence that such conduct will not appear. Cooley (1922), for example, noted that although his oldest son was slow in using the pronoun, he engaged in acts that displayed a differentiation of self from other. Similarly, he also observed confusion in the use of the first-person *I* in which self represents the social object or the material self (the child's body). (See also Bain, 1936; Baldwin, 1897; James, 1910; R. H. Turner, 1968, 1970.) Conversation samples of my own daughter, who was between the ages of two and three at the time of observations, had yet to reveal the use of a personal pronoun in her vocabulary. Yet she engaged in the kinds of stage-managing performances noted by Mead and used, in the place of the personal pronoun, her own name. Her younger sister followed the same pattern. This suggests that a child's speech repertoire reflects the character of her larger speech community.

If the family uses few pronouns, so too will the child. Because preschools represent the intersection of several distinct speech communities in which each, in differential fashion, emphasizes names, pronouns, and possessives, one would then predict that the child would (1) speak differently at school than at home, (2) develop some version of the dominant preschool rhetoric and vocabulary, and (3) fit that version into his repertoire of verbal utterances. This suggests that observers may find more expressions of personal pronouns in preschools than they would find in their "home ethnographies."

Taking Others into Account

Most researchers who have been influenced by Piaget's distinction between accommodative and assimilative thought have proceeded in their research to dichotomize the young child's behavior into one or the other of these categories. (The same can be said for students of Mead who distinguish reflexive and nonreflexive action.) Thus, either the child is autistic, egocentric, and imitative, or he is sociocentric and intuitive. Such a distinction does injustice to the complex character of human social interaction, whether the interaction be among children, infants, or adults. A preferred line of analysis would ask, "How do interactants take account of one another?" Casting the question in this fashion permits a flexible examination of human interaction and does not prejudge the cognitive, affective, or interactional skills of the people in question. It suggests that as soon as the basic organic equipment is operative and as soon as elementary cognitive and linguistic skills are acquired, humans, wherever they gather, will take account of one another (see McNeill, 1966a).

So that interaction sequences may occur, persons as social selves must identify and make claims on one another and must acquire information about the scene, the upcoming interaction sequence, and the intentions of the other. They must negotiate sequence movements (for example, act as equals, as superior or subordinate). They will evaluate and monitor, either visually or physically, one another's acts. They will differentially acknowledge the intentions of the other, form exchanges, and attempt to establish a central focus for their joint action. They will act in terms of some shifting set of standards, which are probably based on etiquette or on legal or relational criteria. They will locate themselves in a common time-place frame and act in ways to protect that territorial spot. Their actions will carry differential biographical consequences that depend on the focus of the interaction and on the sequence and relational rules brought into operation. (This is a highly condensed summary of Strauss, 1969; Couch, 1970; Goffman, 1963; and Garfinkel, 1967.)

Self-Taking and Behavioral Repertoires

In taking account of one another, interactants may engage in qualitatively different modes of role or self taking. (See Couch, 1970; Turner, 1956; Coutu, 1951; Cottrell and Dymond, 1949.) In most, if not all, interactional sequences, persons orient action toward the standpoint or the line of action of those whom they confront. These standpoints represent unique configurations of meaning and interpretation, and I term them *behavioral repertoires*. Such repertoires are characteristic lines of action associated with a particular self or person. When a class of actors across situations share the same or similar repertoires, it is appropriate to speak of a "common interactional role." All interactants are obliged to assess the special line of action taken by any person whom they confront, and in such assessments they must turn some amount of attention to the special features of alter's definition of the situation. Accordingly, all interactants will display some mix of self and role taking. (As an empirical directive, I suggest that students initially give attention to the special features of an actor's behavioral repertoire, because these very features establish the boundaries for his proposed action.)

To study how persons take account of one another means to distinguish what Ralph Turner (1956, pp. 316–328) calls *role taking, role playing,* and *playing at a role*. Role taking, in my terminology, becomes self taking and represents the person's imagined construction of another's line of action. Self playing represents the person's imagined construction of another's line of action. Self playing represents a person overtly acting on the imagined perspective of the other. Playing at a self describes dramatic encounters with self that reside within the covert features of the act. Here the person converses with alter while he is casting him in a variety of different stances and is assessing each stance against past, present, or future action.

Self-taking ability can be studied in empathic dimensions as Cottrell (1969) and his students have done. Here an actor's ability to take accurately another point of view would be judged. In studying self-taking ability in early childhood, one could use R. H. Turner's (1956) criteria for inferring a role. Children may observe another person's behavior and act on that observation. They may imagine that behavior, they may project themselves into the other's position, or they may act on the basis of past experience. In assuming another's standpoint, the child may take the other as an object to act on, but he must separate himself from the other person. On the one hand, he may adopt the other's perspective entirely and act in an imitative or parallel fashion. He may also assume the perspective of an absent third party or play to a surrounding audience; in this case, he finds himself obliged to separate his own line of action from the multiple other. In making these separations, the child may anticipate the effect of another's perspective on future interactions, and in this case, reflexive conduct is observed.

Turner identified six types of role taking. Each represents a form of reflexive or nonreflexive thought and is distinguished by the actor's taking into account of a single or multiple other and by his anticipation of future interactional efforts. Turner's formulations are amplified by Miller, Kessel, and Flavell's (1970) study of children thinking about people thinking about other people. Although they gave no recognition to Turner's work, their study noted four distinct levels of role taking or reflexive thought. The first represents a child thinking about contiguous objects or people; the second, thinking about action (talking); the third, thinking about thinking; and the fourth, thinking about thinking about thinking. At the most com-complex level (Type 4), a two-loop recursive sequence is implied. An actor must put himself in the position of three people (for example, a boy thinking that a girl is thinking of a father thinking of a mother). Flavell and others (1968) found that an understanding of recursive thought is not complete by the sixth grade and that it may not appear until adolescence. This finding is consistent with a finding from an earlier work by Flavell (1963) and by Devries (1970) that revealed a stagelike developmental sequence for role-taking ability. For present purposes, I suggest that any interactional sequence involves multiple levels of reflexivity that range from imitative recognition of the role of the other to refusals of taking the other's role or to highly imaginative variations on the other's behavioral repertoire. Further, it must be recognized, as Turner noted, that any action sequence will itself display shifting levels and degrees of reflexivity. In the early stages of an encounter, reflexivity may be high, and then it may move to an imitative or repetitive level that is governed by custom or habit. Shifting degrees of awareness (Glaser and Strauss, 1964) thus characterize all interactional sequences. Actors of all ages will vary in their reflexive ability, and these variations will be shaped by the dimensions noted earlier (sequence and conduct rules, intents and purposes, and so on). Custom, tradition, habit, ritual, and force will also influence the degree of reflexivity present in any interactional episode. Imitating another's actions, that is, perfectly replicating another's gestures, can itself be a reflexively conscious act. When ego extends a hand to meet alter's, the position of alter has been assumed, acknowledged, and accepted. Ego has separated self from alter yet has engaged in a parallel act. This suggests that prior conceptualizations of imitation and reflexivity have oversimplified the cognitive and interactional dimensions of self taking.

Self-Conduct and Self-Other Interactions in the Preschool

The preceding discussion suggests that young children in the preschool will orient themselves to one another in several different ways; that is, different levels of reflexivity will be observed. While early observers of young children suggested that parallel play (not reciprocal play) was most characteristic of preschool conduct, my observations are more in line with those of Miller,

Kessel, and Flavell (1970), Devries (1970), and Elkind (1962). That is, I observed extremely elaborate forms of cooperative and reciprocal play, and I observed children engaging in rather complicated forms of role and self assignment. The following episodes describe instances of joint action and self role taking among three-year-olds. Joint action: Three children are seated around a table and are having juice and crackers.

Mary:	"Pam, here's your juice. Why don't you sit down here?" (Pam takes juice and sits down beside Mary.)
Jan:	"Norma, here's a chair for you." (Norma sits down beside Jan who has pulled the chair out.)

Three girls come over to the big dollhouse.

Amy:	"Come on; let's get into the dollhouse."
Mary:	"I forgot my shoes; let's see if they're in my locker." (They leave for a moment to go to look for the shoes, and then they return to the dollhouse.)
Amy:	"Come on, Mary and Jan. 'Here baby,' someone's been in our house."
In unison:	"Oh, oh, someone's been in our dollhouse."
Mary:	"I know who it was. I know it was Tina, and that's a bad thing."

(They then go upstairs into the dollhouse, and the following observations were noted.)

Penny:	"I want to be the baby."
Mary:	"I'm going to be the mother."
Tina:	"I want to be the baby, too."
Mary:	"You be the big baby."
Penny:	"I have to be the little baby because I have the highchair."

(Another girl comes up.)

Mary:	"She has to be the daddy. Little girl, you have to put your shoes on in the morning."

(A boy, Wendall, comes up.)

Mary:	"Wendall, what do you want to be?"
Wendall:	"I'll be the daddy."
Mary:	"We'll have two daddys, then. Where do you sit?"

The last episode is more complex than the first. Each child who arrived at the dollhouse was assigned a behavioral repertoire to play (big baby, second mother, and so on). This assignment was guided by Mary, who was the stage director. She based her assignments on situational contingencies (the number of mothers already present) and on the line of action characteristic of the child in question (for example, smaller children or those who assumed docile stances were assigned the position of baby). Of equal importance in this sequence was the expression by each child of a preferred role to play. Here Mary was forced to work between a child's requests and behavioral assignments that she had previously made; the past was influencing the present and the future. Behavioral assignments were made finally according to a child's location in the dollhouse (highchair). This episode continued uninterruptedly for forty-five minutes. The assignments, once made, lasted for the duration of the activity. Once a repertoire was assumed, special lines of action were adopted (a baby putting on shoes and a mother helping). Here is an instance of cooperative, joint action where roles and selves are forged into a meaningful activity sequence.

This episode reveals several different levels of reflexive conduct. Mary displayed the most reflexivity and acted on a third-party perspective (mother at home). Mary fitted that perspective to the concrete situation, made it an object to act on, and used it as her guiding rhetoric for assigning the other children their places in the dollhouse. Penny made a differentiation between big and little babies and shored up a behavioral claim by sitting in the highchair. After an opening sequence of "position negotiations," the children settled into rather routine conduct in which they revealed their interpretations of mother, father, and baby sitting around a dinner table. This episode revealed shifts in reflexivity. At one point, Mary engaged in what approaches Flavell's notion of two-loop recursive thought. She stated that Tina was in the dollhouse (absent third party), indicated where Tina was (dollhouse), and make an announcement to the surrounding children. Thus, she reflexively differentiates first parties, third parties, and setting (territorial invasion) and even invokes a rule that was violated (entry into their dollhouse).

It is likely that role- and self-taking ability varies by the situation and by the audience to whom the child plays. More reflexive conduct is probably present in a world of children, where distinct structures for authority, dominance, and dignity are created, than it is in the home, where the child is often forced to submit to the stance of the parent or of an older sibling. Situational variations produce variations in self-conduct.

If these examples reveal rather sophisticated skills in reflexivity of children at the age of three, then the following excerpt from field notes on my two daughters (whose ages were two years, ten months, and one year, nine months, at the time of observation) suggest that reflexivity is differentially present even with children at these ages. Jody (older) and Ramona had been taken to the doctor earlier in the day. The time was early evening; the setting, the family living room. Jody enters the room with a set of nose plugs around her neck. She picks up her red bear and places the nose plugs on the bear's back, ears, and stomach just as a physician would use the stethoscope. Emily (mother) asks Jody what she did at the doctor that day. (This utterance by Emily not only clarifies Jody's act but also justifies its occurrence and makes it public.) Jody points to her "stethoscope" and says, "doctor." Ramona moves to the sofa, lays her head down; Jody examines her with the nose plugs. Jody climbs on Nick's lap (the father), examines him and, again, says "doctor." She then points to the various parts of Nick's body (back, knee, ear) and names and examines them with the nose plugs.

There was little verbalization in this episode, yet the focus of the act was clearly established (nose plugs). The point of the act was the examination; monitoring was nonverbal; and the audience was the general family. Knowledge of a social role was displayed, and the behavioral repertoire associated with that role was acted on (doctor and examination). A set of "object transference" rules was called forth. For example, the everyday nose plug became a piece of medical equipment, and the bear (via animism) became a patient (Goffman, 1961a). Ramona played the role of patient and thus made the doctor performance a joint action. An absent third party was invoked (doctor); an absent setting (office) was reproduced; and the doctor's perspective was redefined to fit the available objects in the setting (nose plugs, and so on).

A second episode, which involved a television show, also indicated third-party invocation. Nick is on the sofa, and, sitting next to Nick, Jody is watching television. Ramona is riding her plastic horse. The character on television (a children's program) is showing how rockets go up in the air. Jody calls him Bob. As Bob moves a rocket, Jody says to Ramona and Nick: "Daddy, Roma, Roma, air, air, up, up, Bobby." She then points up in the air. Translated, her utterance said: "Daddy, Ramona, look, Mr. Bob is showing how something goes up in the air." This is a rather complicated linguistic utterance, which is similar to those reported by Brown (1964). The points, however, are that the perspectives of three people and an inanimate object were called forth and that joint action involving three people was proposed. It can be argued that as Jody separated her line of conduct from Ramona and Nick, she put herself in their perspectives. (Even if such were not the case, the outcome was as if this were so; that is, Nick and Ramona complied with Jody's directive.)

Selves

Piaget, Cooley, and Mead propose a progressive, developmental model of selfhood. Although elementary forms of self-directed conduct appear in the anticipatory and play stages, the child still lacks a clear conception of self and other. This is so because he has not yet acquired the necessary linguistic skills. To have a self, the child (1) must view himself as a distinct object and realize that his self is not the same as the material-body self and (2) he must be able to see himself as both subject and object. That is, he must be able to distinguish himself from other objects. He must, then, be aware of other perspectives. Only then can he become an object of his own actions. In the early phases of self-development, as Piaget, Mead, and Cooley note, the child will not only make a distinction between self and other objects but he will also impute to those objects an invariance that reveals an inability to grasp the socially constructed features of reality. That is, he will think that rules are finalistic, that objects are imbued with animistic qualities, and that reality can be bent to his fancy.

The genesis of the self involves a simultaneous awareness of self and of other. While Cooley, Mead, and Bain stressed the point that the child must come to know other perspectives before he can know his own, my observations suggest that the temporal order of events is less than clear-cut and certainly quite variable. Depending on the symbolic and interactional features of his world, the child may come, as did Bain's daughter, to know others before self; but this is influenced by birth order and alternative self-child models. (On birth order, see McCandless, 1969.) The genesis of self in my older daughter Jody appeared at the point when she grasped the fact that she had a name. By the age of fifteen months, she could identify objects that were hers and those which were her mother's. An awareness of self as a distinct object merged quickly into an awareness that certain objects in her environment did not belong to her. Calling herself by Jody's name until the age of one year, ten months, Ramona (my second daughter) had not fully grasped the meaning of her own name. Her development of self followed an awareness of Jody as a distinctly named object. Thus, Cooley's hypothesis is supported, not by Jody's development of self, but by Ramona's development of self. Self-development is contingent on reciprocal knowledge of self and other. So that developed and reflexive thought may appear in the child's repertoire, self must be conceptualized as a distinct object.

This suggests a naming or labeling hypothesis for self-development. The child's knowledge of self is contingent on a separation of self from others. Central to the creation of self as social object is an identification of that object that will be called *self*. Identification involves naming (Stone, 1962; Strauss, 1969; Allport, 1961). Once an object is named and identified, a line of action can be taken toward it. For a child to act toward self, he must be able to identify himself in opposition to other selves. The most important linguistic aid becomes the name (Allport, 1961). While the appearance of pronouns in the child's vocabulary indicates that a sense of self is developing, the prior use of personal names (or other familial referents—for example,

Mommy, Daddy) suggest a growing awareness of self as a distinct object. Thus, the child *may* differentiate self first and others second. As I indicated earlier, this sequence is contingent on the character of the child's symbolic and interactional world. It would be predicted that the more complex the interactional world of the child is, the more rapid would be the genesis of self and the closer in time would be the self-other differentiation. (This hypothesis offers a more social psychological explanation of Bowlby's 1953 analysis of maternal deprivation and development in infancy.)

This model more accurately fits the data reported by Bain (1936, pp. 767–775) on his daughter Sheila. By the age of ten months, twenty days, she was answering the question, "Where's Sheila?" with the response, "She-e! She-e!" Although she also had a sense of mother and father, she did not make these designations until the age of one year. The first-person singular pronoun appeared at the age of fifteen months, but she did not systematically use it until five months later. By the age of two years, nine months, according to Bain's vocabulary count of his daughter's speech, she was using seventy-one proper nouns (persons) and fourteen pronouns (I, me, my, mine, myself, we, us, you, your, something, it, both, any, none).

Bain concluded that these data confirm Cooley's hypothesis that the child knows other selves before he knows his own. The evidence, however, leads to the opposite conclusion. His daughter's first attempts at personal names and personal pronouns were in reference to herself, not to other persons.

Allport supports this conclusion. Although he presented no data, he suggested (1961, p. 115), "By hearing his name repeatedly, the child gradually sees himself as a distinct and recurrent point of reference. The name acquires significance for him in the second year of life. With it comes awareness of independent status in the social group." This hypothesis is supported by my observations. In the first two weeks of the preschool year, all children are given name tags, and every morning (or afternoon), introductions are made as each child arrives. In addition, instructors make it a point continually to introduce children to one another as they are playing. Names are also heavily stressed in the songs that are sung near the end of every play period.

These songs, which have simple melodies, locate each child by name and identify the child by describing one activity in which they engaged that day. The following excerpts from my notes describe these two features of the daily routine of the school.

A three-year-old girl enters the preschool at 9:03 with her mother. The mother helps her take off her coat. Her daughter gets out a crumpled name tag with her name on it and attempts to put it on.

Mother: "Don't you think they know your name by now?"

Daughter: (Shakes head and puts on the name tag.)

Six children are seated in the corner of the large play-room. The instructor begins a song that goes as follows.

Instructor: "What did Teddy do today? What did Teddy do today? Teddy jumped off the tree house, Teddy jumped off the tree house."

Group: (Repeats song in unison. Then instructor identifies another child by name, and the song is repeated, only now with a different child and with his activity of the day. All members of the group are included in the song.)

I am suggesting that the ritual order of the preschool teaches identity.* It is clear that children vary in their awareness of names and things. The child must, as Lindesmith, Strauss, and Denzin (1978, p. 340) noted, "learn that things have names and that names have things." He must grasp the link between conceptualization and appearance, between object and subject. Until he learns that his name refers to him and that other people's names refer to them, he cannot separate self from other. The child must relate conceptualization to objectification. For some three-year-olds, names must be printed and "tagged on" before they (name and self) exist. This appears to be the case for the girl who insisted on wearing her name tag.

* A reviewer suggested this interpretation and proposed that, from the child's view, things have names only when a lettered label can be perceived. Thus, any abstract conceptualization of the name may follow after the "situated" view of the self is grasped.

On the other hand, uncertainty over one's personal name is also revealed in a desire to have the name publicly announced. Such announcements ensure that the child will be acted on in at least one consistent fashion across encounters (that is, by the name). Wolfenstein's (1968) discussions of name games in early childhood amplify this conclusion over identity uncertainty for three-year-olds. Wolfenstein treats such games as name switching, name reversals, name calling, and name loss. She notes that frequently a child who has a name taken away or who is called by a different name becomes uneasy. As mentioned in an earlier chapter such children, it would be predicted, have yet to be committed fully to their own personal identity. Loss of name makes the child a nonperson; his essential self as a distinct person has been denied.

Strictly speaking, these observations cannot be taken as acceptable tests of the naming and self-identity hypothesis. If my perspective is correct, then names will have appeared in the child's repertoire prior to preschool. Thus, observations of self-hood must be pushed further back in the child's biography. (This, of course, was Cooley's strategy.)

The Genesis of Self in Early Childhood: A Proposed Sequence

I have suggested that selves in early childhood emerge in a sequence something like the following. The object called *child* is given a name, which is distinct to his family's collective identity (see Rossi, 1965). Bombarded with this name from the moment of birth, the infant comes to associate the material-body self with that name. As the child acquires linguistic skills and begins to explore its physical and social environment, a crude differentiation of material and social self appears (see Rheingold, 1969). Seen initially as an awareness that special objects belong to self, the child begins to respond to its own actions in ways that parallel and imitate parental actions. The child imitates parental demands, and, as he moves into the ritual order of the family, a sense of self-identity solidifies. This identification of the self as a distinct object is nearly simultaneous with awareness of other—with the knowledge that there are perspectives other than those of the child that must be taken account of.

Parental selves and behavioral repertoires become incorporated in the child's identity or self-system at this point. Progressively, the self becomes more differentiated than it was at a previous stage; assimilative modes of thought alternate with accommodative and imitative stances. As the child moves from setting to setting and begins to encounter "outside others," regressions to earlier modes of self-taking will occur. (That is, the child falls back on past behavioral repertoires in problematic or strange settings. A process of "setting generalization" occurs. To say that he regresses is to say that he employs what worked in the past.) Thus, names that are taken for granted in the home become problematic in the preschool. Increased situational awareness and an expanding breadth or range of interactional others further develop the child's ability to take the role of different others in different settings.

This sequence represents an attempt to treat the self as a social process and to account for differential levels of reflexivity on the part of the child by looking into the social setting where the self arises.

Studying the Genesis of Self in Early Childhood

The foregoing suggests that previous students of early childhood have erred, at least in part, in their search for indicators of self. By focusing only on verbal utterances (especially pronouns), they have overlooked the fact that the self is a social process. As a process production, the self can be observed behavioristically; but behaviors go beyond verbal declarations. Nonverbal actions, dress preferences, protections of territories, fights and battles, tantrums and scenes, pats and touches, stumbles and falls, all reveal attempts by the child to act on his environment, to make that environment sensible and orderly.

Thus, while verbal interrogations, responses on tests, and adult recollections can be employed as one class of indicators of early self-hood, investigators must be alert to the range of actions just noted (see Birdwhistell, 1970). Selves must be studied naturalistically. The ploys and devices used by persons to communicate self (Goffman's work represents developed examples) must become the sociologist's indicators of self as a process.

Chapter Eight

Play, Games, and Interaction

*I*n this chapter, I will briefly review and critique existing theories and definitions of play, games, and socialization. A view of interaction and socialization consistent with the formulations of G. H. Mead and the symbolic interactionist perspective will be offered.

Play, Games, and Childhood Socialization

The import of play and games for early childhood socialization experiences has long occupied the interests of sociologists, social psychologists, psychologists, and students of child development, among them, Mead, Cooley, Groos, Hall, Huizinga, Caillois, Piaget, Freud, Herron, Sutton-Smith, Lueschen, Ellis, I. and P. Opie, Ariès, Singer, Stone, Goffman, Waller, Berlyne, and Merton. Research and theory has typically been concerned with one or more of the following questions: How can play be defined and what is unique to childhood play? (Huizinga, 1939; Piaget, 1962; Mead, 1934). Are there different forms of play? (Caillois, 1961; Groos, 1901; Piaget, 1962). Why do people, and children in particular, play? (Huizinga, 1939; Freud, [1922] 1959). What are the consequences of play and games for the socialization process? (Stone, 1965; Merton, 1957).

In general, play is seen as serving anticipatory socialization purposes for the young child. It is conceptualized as a form of social behavior that results in children learning to cooperate and interact with others. It is variously seen as infantile or sophisticated in nature. Play and games are seen as establishing the vehicles for teaching the child how to take the perspective of others (Mead, 1934). Play is seen as displaying shifting degrees of the fantastic and the real. Piaget (1962), for example, views the play of young children as lacking in accommodative abilities and in this sense as revealing the limited cognitive abilities of the child player.

Classical, contemporary, and recent theories compete for attention, yet by and large no consistent theory or definition of play and games relevant to the socialization process currently exists in the literature (Berlyne, 1969). Central to current misunderstanding in this area is the failure of all theorists to distinguish systematically play from games. Furthermore, existing formulations typically attempt to bracket or separate play from work. It will be necessary to make a distinction between these interactional forms in the discussion that follows. Playing a game of marbles, for example, is clearly different from playing dolls or pretending that a blanket is a baby that will not go to sleep. Yet current formulations confuse these two processes: The first is rule governed and gamelike; the second is not. A set of distinctions separating play, games, work, playing at play, and playing at games, will therefore be made, and the impact of play on early childhood socialization will be discussed. Finally, data drawn from naturalistic studies of young children will be offered in support of the perspective presented.

Existing Theories of Play and Games. In an excellent review of play and games, Ellis (1973; also see Gilmore, 1971) lists some thirteen different definitions and theories of play and games. These include the surplus energy theory of Groos (1901), the play-as-relaxation theory of Sapora and Mitchell (1961), the instinct theory of McDougall (1923), the recapitulation theory of Gulick (1902), the psychoanalytic theory of Freud ([1922] 1959) and Erikson (1950), and, more recently, the cognitive-developmental theories of Piaget (1962). Underlying each of these separate formulations are such arguments as that people play because they have too much or too little energy to expend; that they play because they have inherited instincts that make them play; that in play the player recapitulates the history of his species; that in play people play out crises or reverse social roles, so as to resolve unpleasant experiences. In play, people thus confront or avoid problems, produce or lose energy. Ellis summarizes his review by arguing that no existing definition of play or games is workable. He proposes to define play as arousal-seeking activity, yet admits that his definition is too broad. He concludes by suggesting that it is perhaps impossible to separate play from games and work. His review provides a convenient point of departure, for it points to the current state of conceptual confusion in this area. I turn next to perhaps the two most influential theorists on play and games: Caillois and Piaget. (I have cited these several definitions of play so as to establish this state of conceptual confusion. I have not analyzed or discussed these formulations in detail, for my main concern is to establish an interactionist framework for the study of play and games in early childhood. My remarks are also intended to point in the direction of a more general theory of games and sports. The interested reader should consult Ellis, 1973, for his systematic critique and review of these other perspectives.)

In all of the existing formulations of play, the following attributes are commonly ascribed to this interactional form: It is seen as an end in itself, it is spontaneous, it is an activity pursued for pleasure, it has a relative lack of organization, it is characterized by an absence of conflict, and it produces no economic gain or loss for its players (see Berlyne, 1969; Piaget, 1962; Caillois, 1961; Huizinga, 1939). So play is an autotelic or pleasurable and self-contained form of activity. Yet exceptions to each of these criteria can be found. Some play is not spontaneous, some play is pursued so as to achieve an end beyond the playing episode, and some forms of play are highly organized. Also, many playing episodes display high degrees of conflict, emotion, and tension, and some players (for example, gamblers) do lose commodities of some form or another during their playing activities.

It is problems of this order that led Caillois (1961, pp. 9–10) to define play as an activity that incorporates the following essential elements. First, it is *free*—playing is not obligatory; if it were, it would at once lose its attractive and joyous quality as diversion. Second, play is *separate;* that is, it is circumscribed within limits of time and space and is fixed in advance. Third, play is *uncertain*. Its course cannot be predetermined nor its result attained beforehand, and some latitude for innovations is left to the player's initiative. Fourth, it is *unproductive,* in that it creates neither goods, nor wealth, nor new elements of any kind. Except for the exchange of property among the players, play ends in a situation identical to that prevailing at the beginning of the game. Fifth, play is *governed by rules.* These rules operate under conditions that suspend ordinary laws and for the moment make new legislation, which alone counts. Sixth, play incorporates an element of *make-believe,* accompanied by a special awareness of a second reality or of a free unreality, as against real life. Caillois remarks (1961, p. 10) that "These diverse qualities are purely formal. They do not prejudge the content of games."

Herein lies the problem, for Caillois has confused play with games. He begins by listing the attributes of play and concludes by offering a now-familiar typology of games: games of competition, change, simulation, and vertigo. These four game forms are analyzed along a continuum of "structuredness": from *paidia* (unstructured) to *ludus* (highly regulated). It is not clear, then, whether Caillois offers a theory of play, or a theory of games, or a typology of neither one.

Caillois' failure to separate play from games is also evident in Piaget's highly original formulations, which postulate a stagelike, cognitive-developmental model of childhood play. He begins by assuming that the thought processes of the young child move between the polar extremes of assimilation and accommodation. He also establishes four major phases in the development of the child: sensorimotor (birth to two years), preoperational (two to seven years), concrete operational (seven to eleven years), and formal operational. With increasing age, the child's cognitive abilities increase, and the preceding schemata of the stages is reordered. The processes of assimilation and accommodation underlie the child's intellectual development. In assimilative thought, children impose their own reality on the physical world. They do not adapt to it but force reality to fit their limited cognitive conceptualizations of it. In the process of accommodation, children alter their cognitive structures to meet the obdurateness of reality. Piaget defines intelligence as the primacy of accommodation over assimilation. He defines play as assimilative behavior, and he distinguishes three forms of play: sensorimotor practice games, symbolic games, and games with rules. Games with rules, Piaget argues (1962), rarely appear before the ages of four to seven, and they belong mainly in the third period of development (see Flavell, 1963; Ellis, 1973). Like Caillois, Piaget fails to separate play from games. Thus he confuses what occurs in a game, which is properly termed *playing at a game,* with what occurs when a child "pretends to eat a green leaf and calls it spinach" (1962), which should be termed *playing at play.*

Piaget's model has been criticized on several scores. His data are primarily drawn from the behaviors of western European children playing during their free time at school. His model gives no room for games of chance (Caillois, 1961). He treats play as an aberration on the thought processes and sees in it none of the elaborate pretense elements Stone (1965) and others have observed in the play of little children (Sutton-Smith, 1966). His model of cognitive development assumes that intelligence and thought are relatively unresponsive to the influences of social context and social interaction. He postulates that social behavior originates in the organism (thus he can speak of a movement from autism to egocentricism to sociocentricism). He views the child under the age of seven as an egocentric interactant who is unable to fully take the views and attitudes of others (Piaget, 1926). It is not until after the child reaches the age of seven that Piaget views socialized thought and action as appearing. His choice of the term *socialized* is unfortunate, and, as Markey (1928) observes, it implies that social behavior does not appear prior to the age of seven. This clearly prejudges the cognitive and interactive skills of the young child and overlooks the fact that the young child is, in a fundamental sense, the center of his own universe of discourse. That he occupies such a position in no way implies that he is unable to take the positions and attitudes of others. The observations that are reported hereafter reveal young children to be differentially skilled interactants. By neglecting these qualities, Piaget denies the symbolic interactionist view of mind and self, for it is the social context of socialization experiences that shapes the thought processes of the young child (see Vygotsky, 1962; Mead, 1934).

This brief sketch of existing theories of play and games serves to support the following conclusions: With the exceptions of Huizinga, Caillois, Mead, and recent symbolic interactionists, students of play and games have tended to divorce these interactional forms from the interpersonal contexts that produce them. Thus the majority of existing formulations are context-free typologies, divorcing play and games from social setting. Furthermore, they seldom take account of the player's perspective in the playing or gaming episode, young child or otherwise. We have typologies of games, but few theorists make a distinction between play, work, and games. (The major exception is Huizinga, 1939.) Too often games are confused with play, and play is confused with games. There exists in these current theories no firm discussion of the uses to which persons put play and games. There is little treatment of the implications that play and games carry for their players. The data base of existing studies tends toward the study of formally structured games observed in laboratories or child development settings. With the exception of the Opies' (1969) large catalogue of games in Great Britain, few students have recorded and analyzed the spontaneous play and games of young children. The language or medium through which the gaming encounter is produced and presented seldom receives empirical attention. The verbal and nonverbal gestures that go into the focused action of play and games have seldom been studied. In summary, existing theory gives no firm inter-actional basis for a comparative study of these social forms.

Elements of a Theory of Play, Games, and Interaction

In their decontextualization of games and play, contem-porary theorists have failed to grasp the fundamental fact that all instances of play and games involve the interactions (which may not be face to face) of one or more persons who are orienting their cognitive, physical, and symbolic behaviors toward them-selves, one another, or animate and inanimate objects (the case of solitary play with animate and inanimate objects was brought to my attention by two anonymous reviewers). There are forms of play in which the child does not directly and physically inter-act with another person. They may, however, symbolically mock or imitate that individual, perhaps taking on the mannerisms of a mother, father, or hero or idol. Yet the physical absence of the other does not stop the child from bringing elements of that per-son's line of action into play. In play that is not face to face, the child imaginatively acts out the attitude of the other. In face-to-face play, of course, the child reacts directly to the actions and utterances of the other. A definition of play, then, must be capa-ble of handling the solitary player. Similarly, such a definition must include playful and playlike actions with animate and in-animate objects that the child has "personalized"—perhaps given a name to or assigned a role to in a game. The child trans-forms the object into a playmate and may or may not anthropo-morphize that object in the process.

Accordingly, a theory of play and games must rest on a consistent image of the interaction process, and it must address the place of persons and situations in that interaction. Also, as the foregoing suggests, it must treat solitary as well as joint play-ers, and the objects of play (whether animate or inanimate) must be considered.

Interaction (whether playful or worklike) occurs in *place* (Goffman, 1971). Place consists of the following interrelated elements: differentially self-reflexive actors; place or setting itself (that is, the physical territory); social objects that fill the setting and are acted on by the actors in question; a set of rules of a civil-legal, polite-ceremonial, and relationally specific nature that explicitly or tacitly guides and shapes interaction; a set of relationships that binds the interactants to one another; and a shifting set of definitions reflective of each actor's co-ordination to self and other during the interaction sequence. The total amount of time two or more actors spend in place shall be termed the *occasion of interaction*. Every focused exchange between those actors shall be termed an *encounter*. Thus, places furnish the occasions for interaction, which in turn provides the conditions for encounters (see Goffman, 1961a).

Any interactional episode between one or more persons can be studied in terms of the dimensions of place that are acted on and played out. Every instance of focused interaction displays a unique configuration of these six elements of place. Each element can assume different parameters over time, within and across the same encounter. The players can stand in varying degrees of "knowingness" to one another. The relationships that bind them together will be of shifting equality, moving between the extremes of subordinate and superordinate, and they may be of the intimate, stranger, friend, colleague, or enemy variety (see Davis, 1973). The setting may be rigid or flexible, known or foreign, public or private, rented or owned. The objects may or may not be taken as concrete extensions of the actors' selves. The objects may be owned, rented, borrowed, sacred, or irrelevant to the action at hand. The rules that shape interaction will be differentially flexible, and they will vary in their bindingness on the actors. They will be differentially reciprocal. The degree to which rule violation influences the interaction process will be specific to each place, occasion, and encounter.

The action that occurs within place will be of shifting temporal length, differentially reciprocal. The degree to which rule violation influences the interaction process will be specific to each place, occasion, and encounter.

The interaction that occurs within place will be differentially focused or unfocused. Its biographical implications for the players will also vary. Some episodes carry no implications, while others (turning point encounters) are heavily consequential (Strauss, 1969). The degree of seriousness or "pretense" that hovers over place, occasion, and encounter will be variable (Glaser and Strauss, 1964; Stone, 1965). The players may be seriously embedded in the action or take it lightheartedly. They may pretend to be serious or seriously pretend not to be serious.

Play and Games Defined. Play, work, and games are interactional forms: They are situated productions that differentially mold the elements of acts, interaction, and place that have been outlined. Definitions are in order.

Play and games, as Caillois noted, exist along a continuum of interactional structuredness. A *game* shall be defined as an interactional activity of a competitive or cooperative nature involving one or more players who play by a set of rules that define the content of the game. Skill and chance are the essential elements that are played over. Played for the amusement of the players and perhaps also for a set of spectators, games are focused around rules that determine the role that skill and chance will have. The objects of action are predetermined (checkers, kites, chess players, dice). Furthermore, the elements of pretense are known beforehand and are specified by the rules of conduct deemed appropriate to the game at hand. These rules specify the number of players, tell the players how to play, and determine how they will relate to one another as game players. Typically these rules hold constant outside game relationships and make each player a co-equal (subject to the variations of skill and chance) during the game itself. (However, some games deliberately build on inequality; they assign in sequence, or by chance, undesirable roles to their players—for example, "wolf-wolf," "hide-and-seek.") And of course, many games have winners and losers.

Yet location in those roles is determined by the game, not by relationships that exist between the players when they are not gaming (see I. Opie and P. Opie, 1969). While the factor of pretense is known before the game is entered, the players may exaggerate pretense during the game—for example, players of monopoly, poker, or "button-button." In this sense, emotion is central to the game, and players may enter the game precisely because its outcome is problematic and emotional, if not pre-tenselike in nature.

The temporal duration of the game is typically not known; only its outcome is known—it will produce a winner and a loser. Thus the length of a game will be determined solely by how long the players take to play it and by how long they are willing to play. Some games are suspended, broken productions that never reach a rule-determined conclusion. Rule violation is crucial to the game, and all games have players who cheat, or break, or distort the rules. (Highly structured games—for example, professional football—have their own judges or referees who determine when a rule has been broken. Less structured games rely on their players to be one another's judge—and jury.) On rule violation, Caillois (1961, p. 7) has observed: "The confused and intricate laws of ordinary life are replaced in this fixed space and for this given time by precise, arbitrary, unexceptionable rules that must be accepted as such and that govern the correct playing of the game. If the cheat violates the rules, he at least pretends to respect them. . . . one must agree with the writers who have stressed the fact that the cheat's dishonesty does not destroy the game. The game is ruined by the nihilist who denounces the rules as absurd and conventional, who refuses to play because the game is meaningless. His arguments are irrefutable. The game has no other but an intrinsic meaning. That is why its rules are imperative and absolute, beyond discussion."

The biographical consequences of any given game, for any player, will vary by the nature of the game and by the player's attitude toward what the game furnishes him or her. The seemingly inconsequential nature of games can establish for the player a sense of self not otherwise attainable in daily life. Goffman (1967, pp. 269–270) observes: "When persons go to where the action is, they often go to a place where there is an increase, not in the chances taken, but in the chances that they will be obliged to take chances. . . . On the arcade strips of urban settlements and summer resorts, scenes are available for hire where the customer can be a star performer in gambles enlivened by being slightly consequential. Here a person concurrently without social connections can insert coins in skill machines to demonstrate to the other machines that he has socially approved qualities of character. These naked little spasms of the self occur at the end of the world, but there at the end is action and character."

The place or places of the games are differentially fixed. Some games can be moved from place to place, as in checkers or chess or hide-and-seek. However, once the place of the game has been set, it is typically seen as "playable" only in that place, at least for its current duration. It may be played elsewhere on another occasion. Other games require a fixed place for play that is borrowed or loaned, rented, or owned. Such places require that players come to them. The more formalized the game, the more likely it will be fixed by place or by classes of place. And the more fixed the place, the more likely that the game is played for the amusement of an audience as well as for the players themselves. In either case (movable-negotiated place or fixed place), games can be seen as relatively intransient productions. (This point will be elaborated later, when it is shown that play—as an interactional form—is relatively impervious to the needs of a fixed place.) During the production of the game, players are granted a "place legitimacy" that is often not granted the player of play.

In the present context, play shall be given two meanings. On the one hand, it will describe the activities that occur during the gaming encounter. Persons as players play games; they are playing at a game. *However, some persons play at games, but are not playing a game.* Witness the following episode: Three daughters—ages six years, four months (Sara), six years, one month (Jody), five years, one month (Ramona)—are seated in the center of a family living room.

Jody says to Sara and Ramona:	"Sara and Ramona, let's play cards. I'll deal."
Sara:	"Okay, but do I have to sit next to the fireplace?"
Ramona:	"I don't want the joker."

(Jody sorts the cards into three equal stacks, and play begins. Each player has to get an ace to win a hand.)

Jody:	"I've just changed the rules; if you get a pair, you win."
Sara and Ramona:	"No, no [in unison]. That's not fair."
Jody:	"Okay, Sara, want to have an ace?"
Sara:	"No. Let's play by your rules."

(The game goes to conclusion. Each player wins one hand. The cards are stacked up, and the girls leave to watch television in another room of the house.)

In other instances, these three players have played bridge and poker, slightly altering the rules on each playing occasion. Here the players have a sense of a game, have a knowledge of playing in turn, can understand the concept of the deal and the shuffle, but are not playing a specific game of cards. They are "playing at playing at a game of cards," playing within a constructed pretense context that permits them to be something other than what they ordinarily are. (Further exceptions to our formulations can be noted. A player can play with himself and focus the effects of play solely on himself. And many players play with no sense of a game in mind.)

When persons engage in the production of a pretense awareness context that is not framed by the specific rules of a game, they shall be said to be "playing at play." Playing at play, unlike playing at a game, involves the use of flexible rules, and it is much less tied to any specific place. Playing at playing involves players engaged in a "free-floating" set of interactions that takes them from place to place as the focus, needs, and demands of whatever is being played shift and take on new forms.

Consider the following interaction, based on thirty minutes of observation. Jody and Ramona and Sara enter the kitchen. To Jody and Ramona's mother (Emily), they ask:

Jody, Ramona, Sara:	"May we have juice and crackers?"
Emily:	"Yes, wash your hands first." (The three comply and then go to the kitchen table.)
Sara:	"Let's play we're princesses. Jody, you be the king. Ramona, you be the queen."

Ramona and Jody:	"Alright."
Ramona:	"Let's play the king died last night. Oh dear, your husband is dead."
Jody:	"What shall we do? Let's go on a walk through the forest and look for another king."

(The three leave the kitchen, enter the dining room, and crawl under the dining room table.)

Sara:	"King, king, where are you?" (She moves a chair and places a stuffed dog in front of her.) "Bow-wow, King, King, Bow-wow."
Ramona:	"Oh no! Your doggie has to go to the bathroom." (The three exit and go upstairs to the bathroom. They come back downstairs.) To Emily, they state: "The king is dead, and we found him."
Jody:	"Come, Madame, we will go to the desert island." (They move to a green circular rug near the front door of the living room.)
In unison:	"Oh no, the crocodiles are out again; quick, get on the island."
Sara:	"Bow-wow, my dog will kill them."
Ramona:	"Oh boy! Thank you."

Three different playing at play behaviors are displayed in this specimen, and they move from setting to setting, irrespective of the actual place of play. At the kitchen table, over juice and crackers, they moved into playing princess. The dining room table saw the dog enter the picture. The upstairs bathroom permitted them to elaborate on the playing of princess, and finally the dog saved them from the crocodiles who were attacking them on the desert island. In this sense, players of play can pick up their play and play it anywhere. (Some forms of playing at play do become place specific. In many nursery schools, the play involving mother, daddy, and baby often attaches itself to the school's playhouse. Construction play similarly becomes attached to the block corner or the sand box. This attachment is typically encouraged by the designers, owners, and managers of these establishments. The child players are taught to attach their various forms of play to these settings. This often gives rise to place invasions, and battles over territory ensue. See Joffe, 1973; Suttles, 1968; and Thrasher, [1927] 1963, on play and territorial invasions.)

Play is an expansive and expandable interactional form. It is not tied to the demand of time or place. Unlike games, which have concrete rules specifying who may play and how many players there will be, the number of players who can play is limited by the number of persons present and by the relationships the players have with one another. Often these relationships stand outside the moment of play itself, unlike the game as noted earlier.

The following specimen is drawn from a West Coast university preschool. Female Cindy (three years, two months), male Wally (three years, six months), and John (three years, one month) are making pumpkin muffins the day before Halloween. They are seated around a table mixing their batter and filling their baking cups.

John: "My mommy has a grandma, and she lives in L.A., and her name is Grandma Kaye."

Wally: "I have another grandmother, and she lives in New York."

(Two children pass by the door to the kitchen.)

In unison: "Hi, Mary; hi, Gary, come on in."

Mary: "Hi, John; hi, Wally, hi Cindy." (Each child says hi to every other child.)

Wally: "Hi, John." (He says this to Cindy. He then proceeds to alter the name of each child around the table, calling each one by the name of the child seated next to them.)

John: "Hey, that's a mistake, I'm not Cindy!"

Cindy: "We're just pretending, silly, we don't mean it." (They then go through name alterations for all of the children sitting around the table. The number has now climbed to six.)

Two points are relevant in this specimen. First, making pumpkin muffins, a form of work and play, provides the children with an opportunity for focused interaction. Thus making pumpkin muffins is an ancillary activity, and telling about grandmothers is more important. Notice there is nothing about making pumpkin muffins that would necessarily lead one to talk about grandmothers. (This point will be developed later.) Second, as indicated earlier, play is an "incorporating" activity—it expands to fit the number of possible players who are present. Thus, three persons are added to the gathering, and an emergent form of play is produced—the name alteration game (see Wolfenstein, 1954, on name games). It must be noted, however, that play can be an exclusionary form of activity, as when two seven-year-olds refuse to play with three four-year-olds. This also sets play apart from games, for once a game is started its addition or exclusion (loss) of players is predetermined.

Pretense is central to play, more so than in games. Kendon (1930, pp. 57–58) in his autobiography, comments on pretending: "Pretending is a child's art alone, and grown-ups cannot practice it; they can only act. The pretender has no audience but himself, he is not trying to appear like the character he presents, he is that character and feels like it. If he has put a towel around the muzzle of a rocking horse and is driving through rain and storm to catch a train, his feelings will be very nearly the real feelings which he would enjoy if the horse were a real horse, the towel a real bridle, the rain wet, and the storm loud." Play permits the child to symbolically transform reality into new forms and into new configurations. The pretense nature of play rests on a set of tacitly known rules that permit objects to become anything the player wants them to be. The object is what it is during the moment of play. When play is over, the object may be returned to its rightful place, but during play it is what the player says it is. The young child has yet to assign a fixed character or meaning to these objects of play. A towel can become a bridle, a stuffed dog a real dog, a dining room table a cave, scrawls on a page can depict an elegant castle, a female can become a male or a king, a chair can become a bed. Isaacs (1933, p. 35) reports the following behavior of Frank (age four years, eleven months): "Frank was making a 'bed' with chairs when Harold took one of the chairs. Frank threw a cylinder at Harold, which Harold caught and threw back at Frank. Frank was going to throw it again, when Mrs. I intervened. He protested, saying, 'It didn't hit him!' as if that gave him the right to throw it."

The failure to support and validate another player's definition of an object, especially when the object is a scarce resource, provokes object battles, and these battles are often seen by their players as another form of play. While games have object-transference rules (for example, checkers can be played with bottle caps, Goffman, 1961a), these rules are fixed before entry into the games. In play, the rules are made up as play is produced. They may assume a fixed form over time, especially if the same players play with the same objects again and again.

Rule violation, which focuses on one or more players' refusal to treat an object(s) in a desired way, potentially destroys play. Like the game, play cannot tolerate the nihilist; it is, however, much more tolerant of rule violations.

Because play is not tied to specific places, it is often performed in the unwilling presence of others. And, while the player typically plays only for his and his fellow player's benefit, his play is often seen as an intrusion into the worlds of others. Persons come to see players play games, but seldom do they come to see persons play at play. These actions are regarded as intrusions. The child is told to go play but is admonished to play elsewhere.

Ramona and Jody are playing on the living room cocktail table. Ramona has a Barbie doll, who is talking to her rabbit, who is named Bunny. Jody is counting doubloons and is dropping them on the table. They are watching a television show that the parents Emily (mother) and Nick (father)—Nick in particular—are engrossed in. Ramona complains, "No! Jody, you hit my doll." Jody denies it. "I did not. Get out of my way." Ramona appeals to her mother: "Mommy, Jody hit my doll!" Nick interjects, "Go upstairs and play!"

The biographical consequences of play are more difficult to assess. They are not predetermined, as they are in games, but refusals to play with a particular player can be seen as especially devastating, at least by the denied player. He has not been permitted to enter the pretense world of the other players.

Thus, it is often regarded (by the child player at least) as a
privilege to play, a privilege that carries biographical implications into the future. One knows that if one has played in the
past with a certain player the likelihood of playing together in
the future is increased. In this way, players become friends. The
following excerpt from an interview cited in Chapter Four, with
Fred (age four years, seven months), supports this conclusion.

Interviewer: "Which guys do you know here?"
Fred: "Well, I don't know all the guys, Bob, Chuck, Eddie,
                Andy, Tom, Sam."
Interviewer: "Who are your best friends? Who do you know
                best?"
Fred: "Chuck and Eddie."
Interviewer: "Why Eddie?"
Fred: "He said one day, 'If you let me play with one of
                these puppets, I'll be your best friend.' If he wants to
                play with me, he can."
Interviewer: "What's a best friend?"
Fred: "He wants to be a friend real bad. But you see it's in
                his head why he wants to be my best friend, and it's
                in my head, and I can't know what he feels and
                thinks. I don't know. He wants to be friends real
                badly. It's in my head. We just play together."

    The matters of skill and chance are less relevant in play.
Indeed, unlike games, which are built around the role of skill and
chance, playing at play often reveals the players cooperating with
one another. Willy (four years, three months, male) and Bonnie
(three years, eleven months, female) are working with puzzles.
Willy's mother is observing them helping one another. The
mother says, "Oh, good, Willy, you need only one more piece."
Bonnie repeats, "Willy only needs one more piece." The mother
says to Bonnie, "Yeah, you need a whole bunch more, better get
busy." In this instance, each player has a puzzle. Initially, they
cooperate in this individual activity by helping one another, so
it becomes a joint endeavor, to end when both of them have suc-
ceeded in completing their respective puzzles. But now the

mother has introduced elements of adult "gamelike" competition into their play.

If competition and skill and chance are kept at a minimum in the child's game, boasting about one's abilities is often taken quite seriously. While players of games can boast after a game is over, they are under constraints not to do so during the playing of the game, because one play does not constitute a game and one who boasts too early may later be the loser. Since play seldom establishes winners and losers (childhood play, at least), boasting and bragging about one's abilities take on central import—the player seeks praise for his or her accomplishments, abilities, and pretensions. Three males (Andy, three years, eight months; Bob, three years, ten months; Ken, four years) are sitting in the corner of the playroom in the preschool described earlier. They are assembling small pieces of plastic into ships and airplanes. Andy starts:

Andy: "I'm Superman." (He was wearing a Batman tee-shirt.)
Bob: "I'm strong man, I'm so strong I can blow the whole world into pieces."
Ken: "I'm so strong I can blow the United States into pieces."
Andy: "Oh yeah?"
Bob: "Oh yeah?"
Ken: "Yeah!"

Three forms of play have been distinguished and they range along a continuum of rule-embeddedness, or degree of structure and formality. *Playing at play* describes the free-floating interactions of the young child who moves from place to place, playing at whatever concerns him at the moment. *Playing at a game* describes the young card player who draws and deals and forms pairs, yet has no firm knowledge of how a specific game of cards is played. A good deal of the play of young children from the ages of three to seven falls in this category. *Playing a game* describes the skilled game player who works within the rule-constructed boundaries of a specific game wherein matters of skill and chance are rigidly controlled.

If our earlier statements concerning solitary and joint play are reconsidered, six types of play are actually produced. Thus, the child players can play at play alone, as when they stage a conversation with a stuffed bear, or they can conjointly produce a conversation with another player who has a stuffed animal. Similar considerations hold for playing at a game and playing a game. Prior typologies of games, in particular Piaget's, Huizinga's, Caillois's and Mead's, have confused these play forms, and in so doing they have failed to dissect the unique configurations of place and action that occur within each of them. They also prejudged or underestimated the interactional skills of the young child player of play and games.

Further complications are introduced when the topic of work is considered. It is necessary to introduce a conceptual discussion of work at this point for, as noted earlier, existing theories of play and games typically begin by first defining work (see Caillois, 1961). That is, work is seen as a form of activity that can be neatly separated from play and games. However, such a separation seldom stands the test of critical analysis, as I hope to show in the following discussion. This is especially the case if work is considered in processual, not static terms. Like play and games, work is a situated production, and it may be approached from a playful or gamelike perspective. Indeed, one person's work is another person's play. And it often takes a class of workers to produce for other persons the context of play. Furthermore, the moment of play can be transformed into the actions of work, just as work can be transformed into play (Bernstein, 1973).

Like play and games, work is a situated production that involves the six elements of place. Unlike play, it is situationally fixed (although some workers can do their work wherever they are—for example, painters and novelists). The rules of work, as in games, are known beforehand. Work involves the transformation of objects from one state to another—ideas into printed words, images into pictures, steel into nails. Games and play are different in this respect, for when play or the game is over players typically return to their preplay and pregame conditions. Thus, play and games seldom produce lasting economic effects or rewards. And they are less likely to affect the biographies of their players, while work does. The persons that one works with assume a fixedness that need not be present with the players of games. Players of play tend to establish fixed playmates. Work builds up a set of "working relationships" that are differentially rule grounded—subordinate, superordinate, equals, colleagues, buyers, and sellers. These relationships are assumed to hold during the work transaction. We have shown that this need not be the case with play, and games work on the deliberate suspension of existing relational ties. Work is entered into with a known and often predetermined degree of pretense and illusion. This is not to say that the worker cannot approach work as an autotelic act (as the player does), but he is less likely to sustain the autotelic spirit for the duration of any working occasion. Work is structured so as to attempt to control the play of skill and chance. While workers are ranked by skill, it is assumed that the degree of chance that enters into the ranking is kept to a minimum.

   Play, Work, and Games: Process. So far I have regarded play, games, and work as more or less static interactional forms. In this section, I treat them as processual forms, and use the verb, not the noun form, for each word. There are six interrelationships between play, work, and games. Persons can work at work, work at playing, or work at producing a game. They can play at work—the young child helping a mother fix a salad or the university employee who plays at being a faculty member—or they can work at work. They can play at play—our young children discussed earlier. They can play at games, and they can actually play games (Caillois' and Huizinga's typologies only fit persons who play games). Each of these conditions constitute different variations on place. Each is a situated production that will vary by the attitudes brought to it by the persons or players in question. And each varies by the self-other relationships in question. Furthermore, any occasion of working at work, working at play, working at a game, playing at work, playing at play, and playing a game can be transformed—during its production—into any of the remaining other forms. A game can be approached with enthusiasm, as can play, but during the interaction one or more players can alter their definitions of the situation. The effects of the game, or the play on them, is suddenly (or gradually) defined as undesirable. The consequence is a bad game or a bad instance of play.

Play, work, and games must be approached historically. That is, they must be viewed as temporal productions that have a life within the lifetime of their participants. The temporal dimension of these interactional forms are especially crucial when the topic of interest is the socialization experiences of young children. With increased interactional skills, they become sophisticated players of games and work. Indeed, it is not uncommon to observe the two-, three-, and four-year-old child engaged in the work of the adult (see Kuhn, 1954, on the Iowa Amish; this social collectivity sets its children to work on adult chores at the age of two). The matter of history raises three interrelated questions: What is the actual chronological or biological age of the player? What is the actual age of the interactional form the player works or plays at? and What is the interactional age of the player? Piaget's (1962 and elsewhere) formulations of child's play treat only the biological age of the player. Thus, with conviction he argues that only after the age of seven does the child know how to play rule-bounded games—for example, marbles. In no instance does Piaget consider the interactional age of the play form, nor does he trace out the interactional experiences the player has with that play form. Therefore, his model is irrevocably embedded in a biological image of cognitive development. Interactional age references the actual amount of time the player has spent in the play or work form under consideration.

Interactional age is not an age per se, for it is not grounded in the usual psychological conceptions of physical or mental age (see Markey, 1928). Rather, it is based on the number of interactions the child (or adult) has had with a specific unit of behavior. Thus, it is quite easily measured, although measurement is confounded by the fact that the person can have symbolic interactions with the behavior in question while never displaying physical actions toward it. This, in a qualified sense, would reference what Merton (1957, p. 265) terms "anticipatory socialization." In this sense, it might be more appropriate to label this concept *interactional experience*. It is introduced at this point so as to direct the researcher's attention away from a singular concern with just physical or mental age. Such concerns have led investigators away from the actual study of social interaction in early child development. As a consequence, they have not adopted a historical view of the interactional process. Nor have they considered how that process is built up and incorporated in the behavioral repertoires of the child. A rather blinded view of child development has emerged in the social and psychological literature as a result of this neglect. Mead's (1934) model of the play, game, and generalized other phases of development suggests that interactional age is crucial in the socialization process. Furthermore, nowhere does Mead attach age specifications to these three phases. Implicit in his formulations is the suggestion that some persons may never progress to the generalized other phase of taking the other's attitude. Such a view is accepted in this discussion.

Accordingly, a child's expertise in playing or gaming would be expected to be a direct function of the actual amount of time that child had spent in that play form. Thus, the longer our three card players play at playing at cards, the better skilled they will become. Consequently, if biological age is held constant and if interactional age or experience is allowed to vary, it would be expected that a biologically younger child might show greater play skills than would a biologically older child who had a low interactional age with the play form. Unfortunately, existing data on player age seldom take account of interactional age (see, for example, Herron and Sutton-Smith, 1971). Some studies have considered the interactional age of games (for example, I. Opie and P. Opie, 1969), yet they fail to connect those ages with the interactional ages of the players. As a consequence, there are two bodies of data that exist side by side, but the crucial variable that would bring them together into some meaningful interpretative network is pitifully absent. By way of illustration, consider the following example of playing a game. The players are the three girls (Jody, Ramona, and Sara) discussed earlier and an eight-year-old boy named David. The game that is played at is termed "animals," and it appeared in the behavioral repertoires

of the three girls on March 10, 1972. At that time, the players
were approximately four, four, and three years of age, respec-
tively. David was introduced to the game fourteen months ago.
At that time, the following behavior specimen was recorded.
The game consists of each child taking on an animal identity
(lion, tiger, and bear) and then crawling through the house as
quietly as possible so as to come up behind an adult and then
roar as loudly as possible. If any player is seen by an adult before
the other two players are in a position to roar, she is chastized by
the other playmates. At issue, then, is quietness, and the aim of
the game is to provoke a startled reaction from the adults. This
play form can be repeated over and over again. The act began as
follows:

Jody:	"Come on, Ramona and Sara. Let's play animals. David, do you want to play?"
David:	"Sure, what do I do?"
Sara:	"You can be the big lion. Get down on the floor. You can follow Jody."
Ramona:	"You have to be real quiet. Wait until we growl."

At this point the players began to work their way down the stairs.
They entered the living room. Emily, the mother, was in the kitchen.
They moved across the living room. Jody accidentally coughed.
David roared the sound of a lion. Jody and Ramona and Sara turned
on him.

Jody, Ramona, Sara:	"David, you ruined it. You weren't sup- posed to roar until Jody did. You ruined it!"
David:	"I'm sorry, can we start over again?"

This is not a particularly elaborate example, and unfortunately David's failure to keep quiet was based more on accident, as on a failure to understand fully the rules of the play
form.

The following episode is more to the point. A birthday
party has been given for Ramona on the occasion of her fifth
birthday. Present are Jody, Sara, David, and Linda and Larry
(ages ten and eleven) and Elsa (age six). The game "button-

button, who-has-the-button?" is proposed. Elsa has never played the game. Linda and Larry coach her on the rules. She says she understands. On the first play of the game, when the player (David) in the center yelled "stop!" Elsa, who had the button, stuck her hand out and gave David the button—a clear violation of the rules. Play was started again, and this time Linda was in the center. The button ended up in David's hand, and Jody knew it. As Linda looked around the circle, Jody smiled and giggled, as did Larry. Linda pointed to Jody, who exposed two empty palms. Next Linda pointed to Larry; she was fooled a second time, and as a consequence lost the game. Here the ability of the player to fool another player is seen as a function of past experience with the game and with face-to-face interaction itself. Linda argued that because she had not played the game since the last birthday party she should be permitted another turn.

These two episodes point in the direction of needed research on children's play and games. Until researchers have combined the conceptions of interactional age just outlined, they will be in no position to make arguments connecting biological age to rate of cognitive and moral development (see Kohlberg's 1968 efforts in this direction).

One final issue on age needs to be considered. The longer a play form is played, the more gamelike it becomes. The child player, then, is seen as moving along a continuum of play complexity; yet this continuum must be viewed in multidimensional terms. That is, the child's first form of play will be of the elementary sensorimotor nature observed by Piaget. Here the child manipulates its own body and surrounding objects in its immediate environment. It talks to play dogs, to favorite blankets, yet it displays no complex mix of rules concerning how the dog or the blanket is to behave. Soon thereafter, with the acquisition of more sophisticated linguistic skills—the elaboration of inner speech into longer thought episodes—he or she will be observed playing not only at play but at games as well (see Vygotsky, 1962). The second form of play will be playing at play and playing at games. The final form will be playing games. Yet, at any point after the age of three, if the child has had sufficient interactional experience, he or she can engage in any of these three play forms. Consequently, depending on the child's experience with the form under consideration (that is, the amount of time spent with it) and depending on the age of the form, he or she can display sophisticated or ill worked-out actions toward that form. Thus, the players of any game or play form will display differential role-taking skills that are directly related to their amount of familiarity with that form. The critical variable in this model is interactional experience, not biological age or level of cognitive development. A thirty-year-old male with a Ph.D. in sociology may be a quite inept player of a play form developed and played over and over again by three children ages four, five, and six.

One final topic remains to be treated. This involves the symbolic and interactional effects of play and games on the young child's socialization experiences. In this respect, I wish to discuss the attitudes of the young player toward play and games. Here work is of utmost relevance, for players can approach play and games with a studied seriousness that suggests they are actually working at play. Thus, play as a quasi-autotelic interactional form transcends itself and provides the contexts for working out such important matters as pride, deceit, self-respect, and friendship formation. Paradoxically, then, when players enter the pretense world of play, they enter a world that allows them to become what they will become in everyday, "real" life: differentially skilled participants in the business of face-to-face interaction. By learning to play, young children learn what elements make up place. They learn to attach different meanings and interpretations to self, other, and object; and to take the point of view of civil-legal, polite-ceremonial, and relationally specific rules. They learn how to form, break, and challenge social relationships; how to measure time and its passage; and how to assume (or avoid) the biographical consequences of any set of actions. The player at play is seen as acquiring the skills requisite for future moments of focused interaction. Playing at play, playing at games, and playing games give child players the interactional experience of taking one another's perspective in concrete, focused interpersonal exchanges. In this sense, play as an autotelic interaction form transcends itself, for play becomes life and life becomes play.

What play does for the child player is to give him or her interactional experiences. Socialization quite simply turns on such experiences.

In the present context, *socialization* represents the progressively cultivated ability of the individual to take and act on the attitudes or lines of action of others. In the words of Simmel (1921, p. 349), "Socialization is thus the *form,* actualizing itself in countless various types, in which the individuals—on the basis of those interests, sensous or ideal, momentary or permanent, conscious or unconscious, causally driving or purposefully leading—grow together into a unity and within which these interests come to realization." The present argument suggests that play is but one of many interactional forms crucial to early childhood socialization experiences. While it is clear that Simmel's view of this concept is no longer in prominent use in the social sciences (see Parsons and Shills, 1959; Clausen, 1968), it is also evident that any functional and psychological catalogue of play effects will always be lacking. For play certainly teaches roles, clarifies rules, produces and reduces tension, creates and recreates the problematic. It exhausts energy, and it produces energy. Yet, play only sets the contexts of conjoint interaction, and once that context is entered the focus of the child's actions shifts beyond the initial focus of play to other emergent activities. Play, then, is a socially legitimate activity that is seen as appropriate for its players and, as long as it does not splash over into the worlds of the unappreciative audience, the child will be encouraged to play and play and play. Unwittingly, this carefree activity called *play* constitutes the most important interactional experiences of the young child, for in play he or she becomes a more sophisticated member of the outside social world where work is taken seriously and play is regarded as inconsequential.

Children enter the world with no conception of self, other, object, situation, or place (Lindesmith, Strauss and Denzin, 1978). Out of the symbolic processes of interaction, they soon acquire an ability to take the attitude of the other (Markey,

1928). A matrix of self-other relationships, at first only dimly sensed, make up the child's universe of discourse. Viewed as a semiincompetent actor, the young child is encouraged to play and is typically provided with a stock of objects to play with (Ball, 1967). The adult caretaker teaches the child to play and in doing so produces and provides the contexts for solitary and conjoint play and interaction. In solitary play, the child learns to attach labels and meanings to objects that previously were meaningless. In play, the child brings into his own universe of experience other objects of discourse and in so doing learns to transcend his own immediate physical and symbolic reality. At first the child's ability to take the attitude of the other is limited, and this is at least partially determined by his linguistic skills and by his amount of interactional experience with the object or other in question. The child's early actions thus display what has been termed *playing at play*. The child is learning how to play. As interactional experience increases, the child moves from the playing-at-play stage to a stage termed *playing at games*. Now the child is grasping the various elements of place developed in this chapter. He or she has an understanding of rules, of objects, of others, and of himself or herself. Although an understanding of sequence, propriety, and rule violation has been developed, the child has yet to understand firmly all of the elements that go into proper "gamelike" behavior.

As their interactional experience increases, children become more competent game players, and soon (I have presented evidence from three- and four-year-olds) they actually become players of games. At this point, they have advanced to Mead's (1934) conception of the generalized other, for they are now able to call out the collective attitudes of a group of individuals. The concept of interactional age or experience suggests a "multidimensional" approach to the study of child development since a child may be quite sophisticated in one interactional form and quite ill-equipped to handle another. Thus, single, linear models of socialization, or development, gloss over the variously developed interactional skills of the young child.

Charged by their caretakers to play, children often approach play with the studied seriousness of work. Thus, the work of the young child may, on occasion at least, be termed *play*. It would be erroneous to argue that play is the single necessary condition for the production of self-competent interactants. Other interactional forms of a routine and ritual nature clearly enter into this process. Yet play, in its solitary and conjoint forms, assumes a dominant position in the cycle of activities of the young child.

Chapter Nine

Child's Play
and the Construction
of Social Order

So—here I am in the dark alone,
  There's nobody here to see;
    I think to myself,
    I play to myself,
  And nobody knows what I say
    to myself;
Here I am in the dark alone,
  What is it going to be?
I can think whatever I like to think,
I can play whatever I like to play,
I can laugh whatever I like to laugh,
  There's nobody here but me.

—Christopher Robin, speaking to Winnie-the-Pooh
(A. A. Milne, 1974, pp. 101–102)

The play, games, and leisure time activities of children have been carefully studied by generations of scholars (for reviews, see Ellis, 1973). The functional, interactional, recreational, educational, and socializing effects of such behaviors have been catalogued, recorded, and placed within competing typologies and theories (see Chapter Eight). While no consistent theory or definition of play, games, and leisure behavior has been adopted in the literature, it is generally conceded that such activities do occupy a central place in the development of the child's cognitive, emotional, linguistic, and socializing skills (Menninger, 1960; Avedon and Sutton-Smith, 1971).

Child's Play: Overview and Intentions

The play and games of young children have been viewed not only as social productions but also as social institutions that mirror the outside world of the adult (Ariès, 1962). Within play arise matters of morality, crime, deceit, deception, competition, winners, losers, and bad players. Like the adult's world, child's play has its own rules, judges, moralities, codes of law, jurisprudence, and taken-for-granted understandings. In this chapter, the constructed and negotiated nature of child's play is examined in light of naturalistic observations gathered on children between the ages of seven and eight years.

Specifically, I shall focus on the tightly bounded board games of checkers and dominoes; these games have handed-down, printed rules that must be interpreted and understood before consensual play can begin or end. The negotiations that surround the use of these rules when employed by the young or novice player will be examined. Such an examination should reveal the underlying constructed, as opposed to institutional-structural, nature of play and games. It should highlight the shifting abilities of the young player to bring order to a situation that at the outset has little or no meaning (Goffman, 1961).

In this vein, the analytic model of Durkheim and Piaget is reversed or at best suspended for purposes of discussion. It will be suggested that the constructed social orders observed in child's play reveal the same patterns of interaction that are present in any constructed social order when the participants are obliged to align their actions with one another for any period of time. The study of child's play should apply to the analysis of any social order, whether constructed by children or adults.

Constructing Social Order and Playing Games

A *social order* is here defined as a produced network of identities and social relationships. It consists of the rules, objects, situations, identities, and social relationships a set of individuals has produced through interaction. This social order transcends the specific individuals who have produced it and takes on the semblance of a routinized network of acting, thinking, behaving, and interrelating. A *social world* consists of patterns of communication and interaction that link individuals into ongoing universes of discourse and experience. Their boundaries are set by the limitations of face-to-face and symbolic interaction. Social worlds arise out of social orders and connect social orders to one another. Any player of checkers, chess, or dominoes, accordingly, is involved in the production of a social order that is effectively linked to previous, as well as ongoing, social worlds of experience and discourse.

Games provide the resources and contexts for the construction of specialized social orders. For the duration of play, that order implicates the players in the special realities of the game in question. (Of course, those who become experts in certain board games—chess, for example—can establish a "game world" that may extend several centuries into the past. Here the specialized order of the game transcends any given play of the game, or any given player of the game.) The social order of the game is constructed around the respective definitions, strategies, intentions, self-identities, imputed identities, and social relationships its players bring into and thrash out during the moments of play. This order may resolve into a multiplicity of orders, as when outsiders are brought in as arbitrators or when friends and playmates enter the gaming arena and take sides for or against particular players. In fact, there may be as many social orders to a given game as there are moves, players, viewers, or historians of the game. The more participants, the more complex are the social orders constructed, although this complexity may escape the attention of the player, at least during the moments of play.

Elements of Constraint

The child's world of play, whether solitary or conjoint, involves active participation in an ongoing network of interconnected social worlds that are differentially bounded and framed by what is termed the "rules of the game." The player may have complete freedom to construct the rules as he or she wishes; he can think what he wishes and play whatever he likes. On the other hand, he may be constrained to utilize only boards of fixed size or certain colored and shaped objects. Freedom and constraint are, therefore, representative of a constant dialectic underlying all of child's play. The worlds of play are not just given or handed down; rather, they are constructed worlds that are interpreted, negotiated, argued over, debated about, compromised, and—on occasion—suspended, abandoned, destroyed, or thrown away.

These worlds may be elaborately staged down to the finest dramaturgical detail (international chess championship), casually put together (hop-scotch on the sidewalk), rigidly framed through a nonnegotiable set of rules (chess), open for negotiation as rules are constructed (building a new game—for example, playing baseball with frisbees), highly ritualized (Chinese kite-flying contests), loosely routinized (checkers played with tops from beer bottles), entered with great seriousness (championship play-offs), or played for the sheer fun of playing (touch football between the sexes).

Checkers and Dominoes: Enter Rules and Other Elements

Games, it has been suggested, are complex social and interactional productions. They may take on the attributes of an open-ended negotiated order; they may rest on a set of taken-for-granted meanings; they may be routinized, ritualized, dramatized, or made highly rigid.

All board games, including checkers and dominoes, have the following elements: (1) a set of rules that (2) specifies moves, turns, stopping, and starting; (3) judges or persons who make judgments concerning proper and improper play; (4) a set of players, set by the rules; (5) a class of objects to play with and, on occasion, a board to play on.

Rules, moves, judges, players, and objects constitute the negotiated elements of the game's social order. The *rules* can be modified, suspended, accepted, rejected, ignored, misunderstood, overlooked, deliberately set aside, or forgotten. Moves can be "replayed," necessitating other "replays." Turns can be taken in starting, as in checkers when players agree to shift from black to red after each game. The *moves* can be disallowed, as in dominoes when a player of "sniff" plays a wrong first doublet, or when a player of checkers attempts to jump with a newly crowned king immediately after "crowning." Moves can be compromised or suspended, and this may arise in the more complicated phases of a game of dominoes when a single play may alter a player's school by fifteen or twenty points. Compromise moves produce future compromises and may progressively lead the players away from the formal rules of the game.

The *judges* in checkers and dominoes are the players and the written rules. For young children, outside judges may be brought in, or the eldest, most skilled, or most literate player may be assigned the role of the judge. Ideally, games are self-contained units and need no outside governing agency. The entry of players into the sterile world of the game's rules, however, necessitates some negotiations concerning who will adjudicate moves, turns, and scores.

The number of and the relationships among players is rule related. Checkers can only be played by two persons. Dominoes can be played by up to nine players. The rules of the game make no reference to the relationship the players have with one another outside the boundaries of the game. It is assumed that outside relational affinities, hostilities, alliances, hatreds, and friendships will be held in abeyance during the career of the game. The objects of the game—central to its production—tend not to be problematic, for only certain things can be done with them; there is a fixed number of them; they are typically assigned randomly (in dominoes, by the draw) or are all of the same initial value (checkers).

There are fourteen basic rules in checkers. Only two persons can play on the board, which is a large square of sixty-four smaller squares that are alternately dark and light. The board is placed so that each player has a light square in the corner to his right. Each player has twelve pieces of his own color. Pieces are single men and kings. Black moves first. There are two types of moves: noncapturing and capturing. Play ends when one player cannot make a move or has lost all his pieces. Play can only move forward along the dark diagonal, one square at a time for single men; multiple moves are possible for the king.

There are nine basic rules in dominoes. In "draw domino," the simplest of the domino games, the two-person game has each player draw seven bones. After all the bones are mixed, the highest doublet starts. Play rotates to the left. The layout has two open ends. All doublets are played crosswise. A play is made by adding a bone to an open end of the layout with like numbers touching. A player not having a playable bone must draw from the boneyard until he gets one. The lightest hand, when the play ends in a block, or with a player out, wins the total of points left in all other hands. Games can be fixed at fifty to sixty points. (See Moorehead and Mott-Smith, 1958, pp. 195–197; 207–209, for a statement of these rules as taken from *Hoyle's Rules of Games*.)

Checkers and Dominoes: Enter Players, Relationships, and Careers

Ideally, the rules of checkers and dominoes make irrelevant such topics as who the players are, what their relationships are with one another, or how long they have played the game. Nor do these rules make any specifications concerning negotiations, the length of time a game should last, how intensely one should be involved in the game, one's mood at the time of playing, or whether one can read or not. The rules are assumed to be universal in nature. They are taken as a set of regulations governing conduct, action, and all procedure during the game itself. These rules also refer to customary practices or normal conditions—for example, the game ends when sixty points are reached by one player. The universalism of the rules assumes that they are equally binding to all players, and they are assumed to hold for all past, present, and future moves or plays. When they are questioned, it is assumed that they can be resolved in the immediate present through recourse to the most recent play or through an examination of the rules. Rules are accepted for what they are, and the game rests on the belief that they will not be rejected, negotiated, suspended, altered, forgotten, or thrown aside. (The game, however, ultimately has no say over how it is played.) The rules are subject to varying interpretation when memory lapses, knowledge fails, or a unique situation arises.

Rules, however, are multifaceted in nature. Their sheer existence implies a right to exercise authority, and the player who can invoke a rule can thereby gain authority over the direction the game takes. To rule on a rule, furthermore, implies that one can "rule out" a move or proposed negotiation on the part of another player. Rules specify rights, obligations, duties, and privileges. The "authority" on the rules thus takes control of the game and makes the rules more than a passive set of directions for governing conduct (Goffman, 1971).

This discussion of rules has made the games of checkers and dominoes more complicated, for it suggests the emergence of an authority figure within the social order of the game who gains a set of rights not formally specified by the rules. Once persons as players are brought into the game, their relationships with one another outside the social orders of the game and their interactive careers within the game soon rise to prominence (Glaser and Strauss, 1964). Players, as persons with identities and relationships that transcend gaming encounters, personalize or make particularistic the universalistic specifications of the game in question. Depending on their inclinations, they can rewrite the rules completely—to suit themselves. They may decide to suspend a portion of the rules, or one person may take control and define the rules in his or her best interest.

Playing Checkers and Dominoes: Enter Ramona and Jody

Ramona and Jody are sisters, ages seven and eight at the time they learned to play checkers and dominoes. Ramona learned first, at school. Nick (the father) taught them how to play dominoes, as did Emily (the mother), who played checkers and dominoes with both of them over a consistent two-month period. At the time they were taught the two games, Jody could read the rules for dominoes off the box. There were no printed rules for checkers available for either player. They learned through repetition, error, and correction. Jody first played checkers with Nick and over eight games lost every game. She then played Ramona and won two out of three games. Ramona then proceeded to play twelve games between herself and an imaginary player and in the next set of three beat Jody all three times. Ramona played her mother five times and won two times.

Ramona and Jody both learned dominoes at the same time. Jody's ability to read the rules on the side of the box were of little aid, for they only clarified how to start and stop the game and how to add up points. Nick introduced a modification into the game that held that the double five was the only doublet that could start play.

Developing Strategy and Quasi-Illegalities

Within two weeks, Ramona and Jody, through the assistance of Nick and Emily and the visit of a grandfather, became skilled players of checkers and dominoes. Ramona's practice sessions with herself aided in the development of her own strategies. She also observed her sister when Jody played Nick and Grandfather.

The two sisters' respective strategies soon altered the ideal-typical image of checkers and dominoes. Each developed her

own version of the rules; each developed her own strategies for
faking rules. Each learned how to make illegal moves. Each
learned how to invoke a higher authority in the face of ambi-
guity. Ramona became adept at feigning ignorance of a rule and
utilized the strategey of a bad mood when she was losing. As was
Jody's, Ramona's ultimate weapon was that of the nihilist. She
would destroy the game by shattering the arrangement of all
checker pieces or dominoes. For each player, the game became a
contest between sisters and a contest between themselves and
the game. Hierarchies of losing emerged. A score in dominoes
was better than no score at all. Placing the double five became a
score or coup. Refusing to move players out of king row became
a mark of defense for Jody. Gaining as many kings as possible
became Ramona's strategy.

Jody's added year in age was soon neutralized by
Ramona's strategies, and the probability of winning any given
game was approximately equal, depending on who could maximize illegal or quasi-illegal moves. In checkers, Ramona would
break the diagonal move rule. She would draw Jody's attention
to a television program and move or make a jump or move one
of Jody's pieces out of place. Frustration was a strategy development by Jody. She would maneuver into an untrappable corner,
protect king's row, and not give Ramona a chance to capture
and crown. In dominoes, Jody made it a point to memorize
where the double five was after every shuffle of the bones. When
Jody was exposed to the more complicated form of dominoes
(sniff) wherein the player only scores when the total of all exposed bones is a multiple of five, she refused to play and broke
off a game after feigning ignorance failed.

Careers as Players and the Careers of Games

After three weeks, Ramona and Jody had learned one
another's cheating strategies, and each had carefully memorized
the rules of checkers and dominoes. The rules, earlier fitted to
each player, were now tightened up and began to transcend each
player. Particularism gave way to universalism. Quasi-illegal
strategies gave way to legitimate playing strategies (to planning

moves, watching each other's patterns of movement, scoring, and so on).

Three factors seemed to be operating. First, each player began on an approximate par with the other. The interpersonal relationship of being sisters introduced in the gaming situation an element of competition not contained in the rules. This competition produced the quasi-illegal behaviors noted earlier and gave each a slight edge over the other. Second, as their careers as players expanded, as their skills became better developed, and as they learned one another's strategies, the rules of the game tightened up—it moved from a loose, personal, highly competitive encounter to a gaming encounter guided by very specific known and shared rules. Third, the behaviors of Ramona and Jody suggest that all games, as they are introduced into interpersonal networks of relatively young novice or unskilled players, will move through a series of gaming phases that progress from intense personalism to neutralized affectivity (Parsons and Shills, 1959). It is important to note that this specification may be unique to board games, although casual observations suggest that it is not.

Conclusions

Games have careers through the careers of their players. Games are social productions differentially negotiated, differentially fixed and immutable. The player's attitude, stance, and experimental frame shapes his or her approach to the gaming situation. Games that are introduced into existing interpersonal networks will at first be molded to the relational configurations of that network. If the players sustain a commitment to the game, it will become decreasingly personalized and increasingly impersonalized. It is in these ways that games transcend the lives and games of their respective players. Their abstract, depersonalized rules do, after all, have a place in those social orders wherein they are played. That these rules can somehow surmount the identities and interpersonal relationships of players attests to one feature of the game that no player can alter: If the rules are strictly adhered to, all players are "co-equals" during the moment of play. That is, rules of chance and probability should, over the long run, tend toward equality for each player. (Players, however, can have "hot" or "cold" streaks, believing that chance is either for or against them—see Goffman, 1967.) The co-equality of play and games sustains the illusion that inequalities between persons and players can somehow be controlled, if not neutralized, during those "nonserious" encounters arranged around the objects of checkers, dominoes, chess, and cribbage. (In this respect, solitaire would appear to hold the greatest challenge to the player seeking equity.)

If child players can seriously approach the topic of play and games and render those topics first personal and then impersonal in nature, then perhaps all social orders rest on some complex mix of these two attitudes. Games as prototypes of everyday life suggest that the matters of authority, seriousness, legitimacy, rules, competition, and common understanding are commodities basic to any sustained social endeavor. The persistent effort to segregate work from play and leisure in modern Western societies may rest on the felt conception that moments of play deny the self the seriousness it somehow deserves. Only children appear to think otherwise. That is, play is only rightfully engaged in by children. Adults must legitimate their playful moments, and there may be a penalty for such activity, as A. A. Milne (1939, pp. 13–14) observes: "Life offers quite tolerable diversions apart from games; but for a prolongation of ecstasy one must return to the flying trapeze: the year at the spring, morning at nine, and oneself a few months younger. Childhood is not the happiest time of one's life, but only to a child is pure happiness possible. Afterward it is tainted with the knowledge that it will not last and the fear that one will have to pay for it."

Chapter Ten

The Work of
Little Children

When I was One
I had just begun.
When I was Two,
I was nearly new.
When I was Three,
I was hardly Me.
When I was Four,
I was not much more.
When I was Five,
I was just alive.
But now I am Six,
I'm as clever as clever.
So I think I'll be six
now for ever and ever.

—Christopher Robin, speaking to Winnie-the-Pooh
(A. A. Milne, 1974, p. 104)

Societies and people organize themselves into interacting moral orders: families and schools, rich people and poor people, the educated and the uneducated, the child and the adult. Relationships between them are grounded in assumptions that justify the various social evaluations. Thus, it is taken as right and proper that the rich should have more privileges than the poor and that children cannot engage in adult activities. These assumptions are institutionalized and routinely enforced, so that those people who are judged to be less competent are kept in their place. In this chapter, I shall look at some of the ideologies that surround the adult-child relationship. Data will be presented from an ongoing field study of young children in "preschools," in recreational areas, and in families that challenge the view of children that is taken for granted, at least in America.

Conceptions of Childhood

Childhood is conventionally seen as a time of carefree, disorganized bliss. Children find themselves under constant surveillance. They are rewarded and punished so that proper standards of conduct can be instilled in their emergent selves. The belief goes that they enjoy nonserious, play-directed activities. They avoid work and serious pursuits at all costs. It is the adult's assignment to make these nonserious selves over into serious actors. In America, this belief lasts at least until the child enters the world of marriage and gainful employment.

There is a paradox in these assumptions. Even if a child or adolescent wants to take part in serious concerns, he may find himself excluded. Thus, when the state of California recently passed a law, along the lines already adopted in Britain, giving the vote to eighteen-year-olds, members of the state assembly refused to accord them drinking privileges, and one argument held that eighteen-year-olds were not yet competent enough to incur debts and assume other adult responsibilities (such as signing contracts).

The paradox extends beyond exclusion. Even when children go so far as to act in adultlike ways, these actions are usually defined as unique and as not likely to occur again unless an adult is there to give guidance and direction. This assumption serves to justify the position of the educator. If children could make it on their own, there would be no place for the teacher. This is best seen in American preschools, where instructors assume that little children have short attention or concentration spans. The belief is quite simple. If left to their own ingenuity, little children become bored. Time structures must be developed, so that the child does not become bored. In California, these timetables typically go as follows:

9–9:15—Hang up coats and say "Good morning" to other children.
9:15–10—Play inside on solitary activities (painting, puzzles, toys).
10–10:30—Go outside for group activities on swings, in sandbox, dancing, making things.
10:30–11—Juice and biscuit time in small groups around tables.
11–11:20—Quiet time; small groups around instructors where instructor reads a story.
11:20–11:30—Get coats and jackets and prepare to be picked up by parents.
11:30—Session over; instructors relax and have coffee and cigarettes.

When there are clashes over timetables—if, for example, a child refuses to come in for juice and biscuits—an instructor will be dispatched to inform him that it is time to come in.

These revealing timetables serve several functions. They tell the instructor what he will be doing at any given moment. They state that children, if left on their own, could not organize their own actions for two and a half hours.

Another paradox is evident. Although children are systematically informed of their incompetence and rewarded for the quality of their nonserious conduct, adults appear to assume that something important is happening at these early ages. In fact, it is something so serious that normal, everyday adults cannot assume responsibility for what occurs. As rapidly as possible, the child is taken from the family setting and placed in any number of child care, educational, and babysitting facilities.

The Place of Schools

My interviews with, and observations of, 100 American parents, who delivered their children to a cooperative and experimental preschool, revealed two assumptions. Firstly, the school was a cheap and effective babysitter. The parents had no fears for their child's safety when he was there. Second, if the child was an only child, or if the parents lived in a neighborhood where there were no other playmates, the preschool would expand and cultivate the child's skill at getting on with other children. These parents feared that if their child appeared later in kindergarten he would not know how to interact with other children. Because preschools do not formally assess how a child is doing, the parents felt fairly safe. They transferred the function of looking after their child's sociability from themselves to a neutral party—the preschool instructor.

The school, then, gave the parents a year to get the child ready for his first encounter with formal education. The task of the preschool was to shape up the child's speech and to teach him or her how to be polite and considerate to others. A side function was to give the child different toys and play experiences—finger painting, say, which many parents defined as being too messy for their homes. Economically stable families with several children were less likely to send their child to the preschool. Brothers and sisters performed the sociability function of the preschool.

Let me now note a final paradox. Observers like Iona and Peter Opie—in their *Lore and Language of Schoolchildren* (1959) and their *Children's Games in Street and Playground* (1969)—have found that, when left on their own, children produce complex societies and social orders.

The fact that many children's games are often spontaneously produced, yet are passed on from generation to generation, and that their songs and stories are made to fit special selves must indicate the child's ability to be a serious, accountable actor.

An example from the Opies' study (1969, p. 333) of children's games reveals the serious character of play. Here the game is "playing school": " 'The most favorite game played in school is Schools,' says an Edinburgh nine-year-old. 'Tommy is the headmaster, Robin is the schoolteacher, and I am the naughty boy. Robin asks us what are two and two. We say they are six. He gives us the belt. Sometimes we run away from school and what a commotion! Tommy and Robin run after us. When we are caught, we are taken back and everyone is sorry.' " In their attendant analysis of this game, the Opies observe: "Clearly, playing school is a way to turn the tables on real school: A child can become a teacher, pupils can be naughty, and fun can be made of punishments. It is noticeable, too, that the most demure child in the real classroom is liable to become the most talkative when the canes are make-believe."

Urie Bronfenbrenner's recent study of child-rearing practices in the Soviet Union (1970) shows, too, that Russians take the games of their young children quite seriously. Such games are used to instill self-reliance and collective respect on the part of the child. Here is one instance: "Kolya started to pull at the ball Mitya was holding. The action was spotted by a junior staff member who quickly scanned the room and then called out gaily: 'Children, come look! See how Vasya and Marusya are swinging their teddy bear together. They are good comrades.' The two offenders quickly dropped the ball to join the others in observing the praised couple, who now swung harder than ever." Bronfenbrenner notes that such cooperation is not left to chance. From preschool on, Soviet children are encouraged to play cooperatively. Group games and special toys are designed to heighten this side of self-development.

The point I want to make is that when they are left on their own young children do not play—they work at constructing social orders. "Play" is a fiction from the adult world. Children's work involves such serious matters as developing languages for communication, defining and processing deviance, and constructing rules of entry and exit into emergent social groups. Children see these as serious concerns and often make a clear distinction between their play and their work. This fact is best grasped by entering those situations where children are naturally thrown together and forced to take account of one another.

Many specialists have assumed that young children lack well-developed self-conceptions. My observations show, on the contrary, that as early as age four a child can stand outside his own behavior and see himself from another's perspective. I carried out intensive interviews with fifteen four-year-olds. These revealed support for the general hypothesis that a person's self-concept reflects the number of people he interacts with. The more friends a child had or the larger his network of brothers and sisters, the more elaborate his self-conception.

Keith, who was four years, seven months old at the time of the interview, described himself as follows: (1) "My name is Keith ———"; (2) "I am a boy who plays at a nursery school"; (3) "If I was asked, 'What do you like to play best?' I would say, 'I like to dance to my favorite records' "; ["What are your favorite records?"] " 'Yummy, Yummy'; 'Bonnie and Clyde' "; (4) "If someone asked me, 'Where do you live?' I'd say '[name of street]' "; (5) "If someone said, 'Do you know how to do cartwheels?' I'd say, 'No!' "; (6) If someone said, 'What kind of picture can you draw?' I'd say, 'I can draw my favorite things. I like to draw a man's head.' " ["Why?"] "Because so much can be added to it. I'd put hair, a chin, eyes, a forehead, a nose, a mouth, and a chin on it."

Keith was a leader of the boys' group at the preschool, had nine good friends, and was one of a family that had two other children. Nancy, on the other hand, was an isolate, having only four acquaintances at the school. However, her family also had two other children. Her low integration in the social network of the school is reflected in the fact that she could only give two self-descriptions: (1) "I'm at school"; and (2) "I live in [name of city]."

Small Adults

As extremes, Keith and Nancy point to a basic feature of life at the preschool. Insofar as a child is a member of the social life of the preschool, the more adultlike will be his, or her, behavior. The social life of the school, then, makes the child into a small adult.

Name games—which take many forms—reveal another side of the child's serious self. Children may reverse or switch names. (See the Halloween muffin example in Chapter Eight.) There is a clear separation of play, fantasy, and serious activity in these games. Martha Wolfenstein (1954), in a study of children's humor, has observed that inevitably some child will find these games disturbing, refusing to accept the identity that goes with the new name. Probably such children are not yet firmly committed to the identity designated by their proper name.

Name calling is another game. Here, the child's proper name is dropped and replaced by either a variation on that name, or by an approving/disapproving term. Wolfenstein noted names like "Heinie," "Tits," "Freeshow," "Fuckerfaster," and "None-of-your-business." In name-calling games, the child's real identity is challenged. He or she is singled out of the group and made a special object of abuse or respect. (Parenthetically, it must be noted that adults also engage in such games. Special names for sports and political figures are examples.)

A more severe game is where the child has his name taken away. The other children simply refuse to interact with him. By taking away his name, they effectively make him a non-person, or nonself. In name-loss games, the child may be referred to as a member of a social category ("young child," "honkie," "brat," "dwarf"). In those moments, his essential self, as a distinct person, is denied.

The Opies have described another name game, which is called "Names," "Letters in Your Name," or "Alphabet." Here, a child calls out letters in the alphabet, and contestants come forward every time a letter contained in their name is called.

All of these games reflect the importance children assign to their social lives. A name is a person's most important possession simply because it serves to give a special identity.

In preschools, the children are continually constructing rules to designate group boundaries. In those schools where sexual lines are publicly drawn, boys and girls may go so far as to set off private territories where members of the opposite sex are excluded. One observer working with me noted boys and girls in a four-year-old group carrying posters stating that they were "Boys" or "Girls." On another occasion, I observed the

creation of a "Pirate Club" that denied entry to all females and
to all males who did not have the proper combination of play
money for paying their membership dues. This group lasted for
one hour. At juice and biscuit time, it was disbanded by the instructor, and the boys were made to sweep out their tree house.
Adult entry into the club seemed to reduce its interest for the
boys.

The study of early childhood conversations reveals several similarities to adult speech. Like adults, young children build
up special languages. These languages are silent and gestural.
What a child says with his eyes or hands may reveal more than
his broken speech. As children develop friendships, "private"
terms and meanings will be employed. To grasp the conversations
of young children, it is necessary to enter into their language
communities and learn the network of social relationships that
bind them together. Single words can have multiple meanings.
The word *baby* can cover a younger brother or sister, all small
children, or contemporaries who act inappropriately. To understand what the word *baby* means for the child, it is necessary to
understand (1) his relationship to the person called a *baby,* (2)
the situation where he uses the word, and (3) the activity he is
engaging in at the moment.

Neologisms are especially crucial in the development of
new relationships. The involved children attempt to produce a
word that outsiders cannot understand. Its use sets them off from
the other children; it serves to give a special designation to the
newly formed relationship.

Summary

Preschool children work at the construction of social
structures and social orders, and these constructions are evident
in their playful activities. Indeed, their play becomes work and
in it one can observe serious attempts to be taken seriously by
adults. Yet, adult ideology denies the child any serious inten-
tionality and thus their world is one that often stands outside
everyday adult understanding. The observations reported in this
chapter suggest that preschool children routinely defy the "child-
ish" definitions adults confer upon them.

Chapter Eleven

Children and
Their Caretakers

*S*chools are held together by intersecting moral, political, and social orders. What occurs inside their walls must be viewed as a product of what the participants in this arena bring to it, be they children, parents, instructors, administrators, psychologists, social workers, counselors, or politicians. A tangled web of interactions—based on competing ideologies, rhetorics, intents, and purposes—characterizes everyday life in the school. Cliques, factions, pressure groups, and circles of enemies daily compete for power and fate in these social worlds.

Children and their caretakers are not passive organisms. Their conduct reflects more than responses to the pressures of social systems, roles, value structures, or political ideologies. Nor is their behavior the sole product of internal needs, drives, impulses, or wishes. The human actively constructs lines of conduct in the face of these forces and as such stands over and against the external world. The human is self-conscious. Such variables as role prescription, value configurations, or hierarchies of needs have relevance only when they are acted on by the humans. Observers of human behavior are obliged to enter the subject's world and grasp the shifting definitions that give rise to orderly social behavior. Failing to do so justifies the fallacy of objectivism: the imputing of motive from observer to subject. Too many architects of schools and education programs have stood outside the interactional worlds of children and adults and attempted to legislate their interpretation of right and proper conduct.

Such objectivistic stances have given schools a basic characteristic that constitutes a major theme of this chapter. Schools are presently organized so as to effectively remove fate control from these persons whose fate is at issue—that is, students. This loss of fate control, coupled with a conception of the child that is based on the "underestimation fallacy," gives rise to an ideology that judges the child as incompetent and places in the hands of the adult primary responsibility for taking care of the child.

Schools as Moral Agencies

Schools are best seen not as educational settings, but as places where fate, morality and personal careers are created and shaped. Schools are moral institutions. They have assumed the responsibility of shaping children (of whatever race or income level) into right and proper participants in American society, pursuing with equal vigor the abstract goals of that society.

At one level, schools function, as Willard Waller argued in 1937, to Americanize the young. At the everyday level, however, abstract goals disappear, whether they be beliefs in democracy and equal opportunity or myths concerning the value of education for upward mobility. In their place appears a massive normative order that judges the child's development along such dimensions as poise, character, integrity, politeness, deference, demeanor, emotional control, respect for authority, and serious commitment to classroom protocol. Good students are those who reaffirm through their daily actions the moral order of home, school, and community.

To the extent that schools assume moral responsibility for producing social beings, they can be seen as agencies of fate or career control. In a variety of ways, schools remind students who they are and where they stand in the school's hierarchy. The school institutionalizes ritual turning points to fill this function: graduations, promotions, tests, meetings with parents, open houses, rallies, and sessions with counselors. These significant encounters serve to keep students in place. Schools function to sort and filter social selves and to set these selves on the proper moral track, which may include recycling to a lower grade, bussing to an integrated school, or informing a student that he has no chance to pursue a college preparatory program. In many respects, schools give students their major sense of moral worth—they shape vocabularies, images of self, reward certain actions and not others, set the stage for students to be thrown together as friends or as enemies.

Any institution that assumes control over the fate of others might be expected to be accountable for its actions toward those who are shaped and manipulated. Within the cultures of fate-controlling institutions, however, there appears a vocabulary, a rhetoric, a set of workable excuses, and a division of labor to remove and reassign responsibility. For example, we might expect that the division of labor typically parallels the moral hierarchy of the people within the institution; that is, the people assigned the greatest moral worth are ultimately most blameworthy or most accountable. Usually, however, moral responsibility is reversed. When a teacher in a Head Start program fails to raise the verbal skills of her class to the appropriate level, she and the project director might blame each other. But it is more likely that the children, the families of the children, or the culture from which the children come will be held responsible. Such is the typical rhetorical device employed in compensatory education programs where the low performances of black children on white middle-class tests are explained by assigning blame to black family culture and family arrangements. Research on the alleged genetic deficiencies of black and brown children is another example of this strategy. Here the scientist acts as a moral entrepreneur, presenting his findings under the guise of objectivity.

What Is a Child?

Any analysis of the education and socialization process must begin with the basic question, What is a child? My focus is on the contemporary meanings assigned to children, especially as these meanings are revealed in preschool and compensatory education programs.

In addressing this question, it must be recognized that social objects (such as children) carry no intrinsic meaning. Rather, meaning is conferred by processes of social interaction— by people.

Such is the case with children. Each generation, social group, family, and individual develops different interpretations of what a child is. Children find themselves defined in shifting, often contradictory ways. But, as a sense of self is acquired, the child learns to transport from situation to situation a relatively stable set of definitions concerning his personal and social identity. Indeed, most of the struggles he will encounter in the educational arena fundamentally derive from conflicting definitions of selfhood and childhood.

Child Production as Status Passage

The movement of an infant to the status of child is a socially constructed event that for most middle-class Americans is seen as desirable, inevitable, irreversible, permanent, long term in effect, and accomplished in the presence of "experts" and significant others such as teachers, parents, peers, and siblings.

The child is seen by the white middle-income American as an extension of the adult's self, usually the family's collective self. Parents are continually reminded that the way their child turns out is a direct reflection of their competence as socializing agents. These reminders have been made for some time; consider this exhortation of 1849: "Yes, mothers, in a certain sense,

the destiny of a redeemed world is put into your hands; it is for
you to say whether your children shall be respectable and happy
here and prepared for a glorious immortality, or whether they
shall dishonor you and perhaps bring you grey hairs in sorrow to
the grave and sink down themselves at last to eternal despair!"
(Sunley, 1963, p. 152). If the child's conduct reflects on the
parent's moral worth, new parents are told by Benjamin Spock
that this job of producing a child is hard work, a serious enterprise. He remarks (1970, p. 19) in *Baby and Child Care:*

> There is an enormous amount of hard work in
> child care—preparing the proper diet, washing di-
> apers and clothes, cleaning up messes that an infant
> makes with his food . . . stopping fights and drying
> tears, listening to stories that are hard to understand,
> joining in games and reading stories that aren't very
> exciting to an adult, trudging around zoos and muse-
> ums and carnivals . . . being slowed down in house-
> work. . . . Children keep parents from parties, trips,
> theaters, meetings, games, friends. . . . Of course,
> parents don't have children because they want to be
> martyrs, or at least they shouldn't. They have them
> because they love children and want some of their
> very own. . . . Taking care of their children, seeing
> them grow and develop into fine people, gives most
> parents—despite the hard work—their greatest satis-
> faction in life. This is creation. This is our visible
> immortality. Pride in other wordly accomplishments
> is usually weak in comparison.

Spock's account of the parent-child relationship reveals
several interrelated definitions that together serve to set off the
contemporary view of children. The child is a possession of the
adult, an extension of self, an incompetent object that must be
cared for at great cost, and is a necessary obligation one must
incur if the adult desires "biological immortality."

These several definitions of childhood are obviously at
work in current educational programs. More importantly, they
are grounded in a theory of development and learning that rein-

forces the view that children are incompetent selves. Like Spock's theory of growth, which is not unlike the earlier proposals of Gesell, contemporary psychological theories see the child in organic terms. The child grows like a stalk of corn. The strength of the stalk is a function of its environment. If that environment is healthy, if the plant is properly cared for, a suitable product will be produced. This is a "container" theory of development: "What you put in determines what comes out." At the same time, however, conventional wisdom holds that the child is an unreliable product. It cannot be trusted with its own moral development. Nor can parents. This business of producing a child is serious, and it must be placed in the hands of experts who are skilled in child production. Pressures are quickly set in force to move the child out of the family into a more "professional" setting—the preschool, the Head Start program, and so on.

Caretaking for the Middle Classes

Preschools, whether based on "free school" principles, the Montessori theory, or modern findings in child development, display one basic feature. They are moral caretaking agencies that undertake the fine task of shaping social beings.

Recently, after the enormous publicity attendant to the Head Start program for the poor, middle-income Americans have been aroused to the importance of preschool education for their children. "Discovery Centers" are appearing in various sections of the country, and several competing national franchises have been established. Given names such as We Sit Better, Mary Moppet, Pied Piper Schools, Les Petites Academies, Kinder Care Nursery, and American Child Centers, these schools remind parents that their children have a special genius for learning. The discovery center will help the child develop those skills to an advanced level, thus preparing them for kindergarten. Caretaking for the middle classes is a moral test. The parent's self is judged by the quality of the product. If the product is faulty, the producer is judged inadequate, as also faulty. This feature of the socialization process best explains why middle-class parents are so concerned about the moral, spiritual, psychological, and social development of their children. It also explains (if only partially) why schools have assumed so much fate control over children; educators are the socially defined experts on children.

The children of lower-income families are often assumed to be deprived, depressed, and emotionally handicapped. To offset these effects, current theory holds that the child must be "educated and treated" before entrance into kindergarten. If middle-income groups have the luxury of withholding preschool from their children, low-income, Third World parents are quickly learning they have no such right. Whether they like it on not, their children are going to be educated. When formal education begins, the culturally deprived child must be ready to compete with his white peers.

What Is Cultural Deprivation?

The term *culturally deprived* is still the catchall phrase that at once explains and describes the inability (failure, refusal) of the child in question to display appropriate conduct on IQ tests, street corners, playgrounds, and classrooms. There are a number of problems with this formulation. The first is conceptual and involves the meanings one gives to the terms *culture* and *deprived*. Contemporary politicians and educators have ignored the controversy surrounding what the word *culture* means and have apparently assumed that everyone knows what a culture is. Be that as it may, the critical empirical indicator seems to be contained in the term *deprived*. People who are deprived—that is, people who fail to act like white, middle-class groups—belong to a culture characterized by such features as divorce, deviance, premarital pregnancies, extended families, drug addiction, and alcoholism. Such persons are easily identified: They tend to live in ghettos or public housing units, and they tend to occupy the lower rungs of the occupation ladder. Their culture keeps them deprived. It is difficult to tell whether these theorists feel that deprivation precedes or follows being in a deprived culture. The causal links are neither logically nor empirically analyzed.

The second problem with this formulation is moral and ideological. The children and adults who are labeled *culturally deprived* are those people in American society who embarrass and cause trouble for middle-income moralists, scientists, teachers, politicians, and social workers. They fail to display proper social behavior. The fact that people in low-income groups are under continual surveillance by police and social workers seems to go unnoticed. The result is that members of the middle class keep their indelicacies behind closed doors, inside the private worlds of home, office, club, and neighborhood. Low-income people lack such privileges. Their misconduct is everybody's business.

The notion of cultural deprivation is class based. Its recurrent invocation and its contemporary institutionalization in compensatory education programs reveal an inability or refusal to look seriously at the problems of the middle and upper classes, and it directs attention away from schools, which are at the heart of the problem.

There is another flaw in these programs. This is the failure of social scientists to take seriously the fact that many lower-income people simply do not share the aspirations of the middle class. Despite this fact, antipoverty programs and experiments in compensatory education proceed as if such were the case.

Schools are morally bounded units of social organization. Within and from them, students, parents, teachers, and administrators derive their fundamental sense of self. Any career through a school is necessarily moral; one's self-image is continually being evaluated, shaped, and molded. These careers are interactionally interdependent. What a teacher does affects what a child does, and vice versa. To the extent that schools have become the dominant socializing institution in Western society, it can be argued that experiences in them furnish everyday interactants with their basic vocabularies for evaluating self and others. Persons can mask, hide, or fabricate their educational biography, but at some point they will be obliged to paint a picture of how well educated they are. They will also be obliged to explain why they are not better educated (or why they are too well educated) and why their present circumstances do not better reflect their capabilities (for example, unemployed space engineers). One's educational experiences furnish the rhetorical devices necessary to get off the hook and supply the basic clues that will shore up a sad or happy tale.

The School's Functions

I have already noted two broad functions served by the schools: They Americanize students, and they sort, filter, and accredit social selves. To these basic functions must be added the following. Ostensibly, instruction or teaching should take precedence over political socialization. And, indeed, teaching becomes the dominant activity through which the school is presented to the child. But if schools function to instruct, they also function to entertain and divert students into "worthwhile" ends. Trips to zoos, beaches, operas, neighboring towns, ice cream parlors, and athletic fields reveal an attempt on the part of the school to teach the child what range of entertaining activities he or she can engage in. Moreover, these trips place the school directly in the public's eye, and at least on these excursions teachers are truly held accountable for their class's conduct.

Caretaking and babysitting constitute another basic function of schools. Their babysitting function is quite evident in church-oriented summer programs where preschools and daycare centers are explicitly oriented so as to sell themselves as competent babysitters. Such schools compete for scarce resources (parents who can afford their services), and the federal government has elaborated this service through grants in aid to low-income children.

Formal instruction in the classroom is filtered through a series of interconnected acts that involve teacher and student presenting different social selves to one another. Instruction cannot be separated from social interaction, and teachers spend a large amount of time teaching students how to be proper social participants. Coaching in the rules and rituals of polite etiquette thus constitutes another basic function of the school. Students must be taught how to take turns; how to drink out of cups and clean up messes; how to say please and thank you; how to take leave of a teacher's presence; how to handle mood; how to dress

for appropriate occasions; how to be rude, polite, attentive, eva-
sive, docile, aggressive, deceitful; in short, they must learn to act
like adults. Teachers share this responsibility with parents, often
having to take over where parents fail or abdicate, although,
again, parents are held accountable for not producing polite
children. Because a child's progress through the school's social
structure is contingent on how his or her self is formally defined,
parents stand to lose much if their children do not conform to
the school's version of good conduct. When teachers and parents
both fail, an explanation will be sought to relieve each party of
responsibility. The child may be diagnosed as hyperactive, or his
culture may have been so repressive in its effects that nothing
better can be accomplished. Career tracks for these students
often lead to the trade school or to the reformatory.

Another function of the schools is socialization into age
and sex roles. Girls must be taught how to be girls, and boys
must learn what a boy is. In preschool and daycare centers, this
is often difficult to accomplish, because bathrooms are not sex
segregated. But while there are open territories, many preschools
make an effort to hire at least one male instructor who can serve
as male caretaker and entertainer of boys. He handles their toilet
problems, among other things. Preschool instructors can often be
observed to reinterpret stories to fit their conception of the male
or female role, usually attempting to place the female on an
equal footing with the male. In these ways, the sexual component
of self-indentity is transmitted and presented to the young child.
Problem children become those who switch sex roles or accen-
tuate to an unacceptable degree maleness or femaleness.

Age grading is accomplished through the organization of
classes on a biological age basis. Three-year-olds quickly learn
that they cannot do the same things as four-year-olds do, and so
on. High schools are deliberately organized so as to convey to
freshmen and sophomores how important it is to be a junior or
senior. Homecoming queens, student body presidents, and athletic leaders come from the top classes. The message is direct:
Work hard, be a good student, and you too can be a leader and
enjoy the fruits of age.

It has been suggested by many that most schools centrally function to socialize children into racial roles, stressing skin color as the dominant variable in social relationships. Depictions of American history and favored symbolic leaders stress the three variables of age, sex, and race. The favored role model becomes the twenty- to twenty-five-year-old, white, university-educated male who has had an outstanding career in athletics. Implicitly and explicitly, students are taught that Western culture is a male-oriented, white-based enterprise.

Shifting from the school as a collectivity to the classroom, we find that teachers attempt to construct their own versions of appropriate conduct. Students are likely to find great discrepancies between a school's formal codes of conduct and the specific rules they encounter in each of their courses and classes. They will find some teachers who are openly critical of the school's formal policies, while at the same time they are forced to interact with teachers who take harsh lines toward misconduct. They will encounter some teachers who enforce dress standards and some who do not. Some teachers use first names, others do not, and so on. The variations are endless.

The importance of these variations for the student's career and self-conception should be clear. It is difficult to manage self in a social world that continually changes its demands, rewards, and rules of conduct. But students are obliged to do just that. Consequently, the self-conception of the student emerges as a complex and variegated object. He or she is tied into competing and complementary worlds of influence and experience. Depending on where students stand with respect to the school's dominant moral order, they will find their self-conceptions complemented or derogated and sometimes both. But for the most part schools are organized so as to complement the self-conception of the child most like the teacher and to derogate those most unlike him or her. And, needless to say, the moral career of the nonwhite, low-income student is quite different from the career of his white peer.

I have spelled out the dimensions around which a student comes to evaluate himself in school. Classrooms, however, are the most vivid stage on which students confront the school, and it is here that the teacher at some level must emerge as a negative or positive force on the student's career. While the underlife of schools reflects attempts to "beat" or "make out" in the school, in large degree the student learns to submit to the system. The ultimate fact of life is that unless he gets through school with some diploma he is doomed to failure. Not only is he doomed to failure, but he is also socially defined as a failure. His career opportunities and self-conceptions are immediately tied to his success in school.

Schools, then, inevitably turn some amount of their attention to the problem of socializing students for failure. Indeed, the school's success as a socializing agent in part depends on its ability to teach students to accept failure. A complex rhetoric and set of beliefs must be instilled in the students. Children must come to see themselves as the school defines them. They are taught that certain classes of selves do better than other classes; but the classes referred to are not sociological but moral. A variation of the Protestant ethic is communicated, and the fiction of equality in education and politics is stressed. Students must grasp the fact that all that separates them from a classmate who goes to Harvard (when they are admitted to a junior college) are grades and hard work, not class, race, money, or prestige. Schools, then, function as complex, cooling-out agencies.

Two problems are created. First, school officials must communicate their judgments—usually cast as diagnoses, prescriptions, treatments, and prognoses—to students and parents. And, second, they must establish social arrangements that maximize the likelihood that their judgments will be accepted; that is, submission to fate control is maximized, and scenes between parents and students are minimized.

Fate Control

The most obvious cooling-out agents in schools are teachers and counselors. It is they who administer and evaluate tests. It is they who see the student most frequently. In concert, these two classes of functionaries fulfill the schools' functions of sorting out and cooling out children. Their basic assignment is to take imperfect selves and fit those selves to the best possible moral career. They are, then, moral entrepreneurs. They design career programs and define the basic contours around which a student's self will be shaped (Goffman, 1963).

A basic strategy of the moral entrepreneur in schools is co-option. He attempts to win a child's peers and parents over to his side. If this can be accomplished, the job is relatively easy. For now everyone significant in the child's world agrees that he is a failure or a partial success. They agree that a trade school or a junior college is the best career track to be followed.

Another strategy is to select exemplary students who epitomize the various tracks open to a student. Former graduates may be brought back and asked to reflect on their careers. In selecting types of students to follow these various paths, schools conduct talent searches and develop operating perspectives that classify good and bad prospects. Like the academic theorist of social stratification, these officials work with an implicit image of qualified beings. They know that students from middle- and upper-income groups perform better than those from lesser backgrounds. They know that students who have college-educated parents do better than those whose parents dropped out of high school. They learn to mistrust nonwhites. In these respects, schools differ only slightly from medical practitioners, especially the psychiatrist who has learned that his trade works best on persons who are like him in background. Teachers, too, perpetuate the system of stratification found in the outside world.

Student Types

Schools can cool out the failures in their midst. They have more difficulty with another type of student, the troublemakers or militants. Troublemakers, as would be predicted, typically come from low-income white and nonwhite ethnic groups. Forced to process these children, school systems developed their own system of stratification, making low-status schools teach troublemakers. This has become the fate of the trade school or the continuation high school. Here those who have high truancy or arrest records, are pregnant, hyperactive, or on probation are thrown together. And here they are presented with white middle-class curricula.

Militants and troublemakers refuse to accept the school's operating perspective. To the extent that they can band together and form a common world view, they challenge the school's legitimacy as a socializing agent. They make trouble. They represent, from the middle-class point of view, failures of the socializing system.

In response to this, schools tend to adopt a strategy of denial. Denial can take several forms, each revealing a separate attempt to avoid accountability. Denial of responsibility takes the form of a claim that "We recognize your problem, but the solution is outside our province." The need for alternative educational arrangements is recognized, but denied because of reasons beyond control. Private and public guilt is neutralized by denying responsibility and placing blame on some external force or variable such as the state of the economy.

When some resource is denied to a social group, explanations will be developed to justify that denial. My earlier discussion has suggested that one explanation places blame on the shoulders of the denied victim. Thus, the theory of cultural deprivation removes blame by blaming the victim. Scientific theory thus operates as one paradigm of responsibility.

Another form of the strategy is to deny the challengers' essential moral worth. Here the victim is shown to be socially unworthy and thereby not deserving of special attention. This has been the classic argument for segregation in the South, but it works only so long as the victim can be kept in place, which lately, in that part of the world, has involved ensuring that the challenger or victim is not presented with alternative self-models. Shipping black instructors out of the South into northern urban ghettos represents an attempt to remove alternative self-models for the southern black child.

The Victim's Response

Insofar as they can organize themselves socially, victims and challengers may assume one of three interrelated stances. They may condemn the condemner, make appeals to higher authorities, or deny the perspective that has brought injury. In so doing, they will seek and develop alternative scientific doctrines that support their stance.

Condemning the condemner reverses the condemner's denial of moral worth. Here the school or political and economic system is judged hypocritical, corrupt, stupid, brutal, and racist. These evaluations attempt to reveal the underlying moral vulnerability of the institution in question. The victim and his cohort reverse the victimizer's vocabulary and hold him accountable for the failures they were originally charged with (for example, poor grades or attendance records).

These condemnations reveal a basic commitment to the present system. They are claims for a just place. They are a petition to a higher authority. Democratic ideology is proclaimed as a worthy pursuit. The school is charged with failure to offer proper and acceptable means to reach those goals. Here the victim's perspective corresponds with dominant cultural ideologies.

Denial of perspective is another stance. Best seen in the Nation of Islam schools, the victim now states that he wants nothing the larger system can offer. He leaves the system and constructs his own educational arrangements. He develops his own standards of evaluation. He paints his own version of right and proper conduct. (Private educational academies in the South, the establishment of which is partly a function of the Nixon administration, serve a similar function for whites.)

Denials of perspective thus lead to the substitution of a new point of view. If successfully executed, as in the case of the Nation of Islam, the victims build their own walls of protection and shut off the outside world. In such a setting, one's self-conception is neither daily denied nor derided. It is affirmed and defined in positive terms.

Lower self-conceptions would be predicted in those settings where the black or brown child is taught to normalize his deficiencies and to compensate for them. This is the setting offered by Head Start and Follow-Through. The victim accepts the victimizers' judgments and attempts to compensate for socially defined flaws.

Americans of all income levels and from all racial groups, including white, are troubled over the current educational sys-

tem. They are demanding a greater say in the social organization
of schools; they are challenging the tenure system now given
teachers; they feel that schools should accept greater responsibilities for the failures of the system. Accordingly, it is necessary to
consider a series of proposals that would bring education more
in line with cultural and social expectations.

From this perspective, education must be grounded in
principles that recognize the role of the self in everyday conduct. The child possesses multiple selves, each grounded in special situations and special circles of significant others. Possessing
a self, the child is an active organism, not a passive object into
which learning can be poured.

Conventional theories of learning define the child as a
passive organism. An alternative view of the social act of learning must be developed. George Herbert Mead's analysis provides
a good beginning. Creativity or learning occurred, Mead argued,
when the individual was forced to act in a situation where conventional lines of conduct were no longer relevant. Following
Dewey's discussion of the blocked act, Mead contended that
schools and curricula must be organized in ways that challenge
the child's view of the world. Standard curricula are based on an
opposite view of the human. Redundancy, constant rewards and
punishments, piecemeal presentation of materials, and defining
the child as incompetent or unable to provoke his own acts best
characterizes these programs. Course work is planned carefully
in advance and study programs are assiduously followed. The
teacher, not the child, is defined as the ultimate educational resource. Parents and local community groups, because they tend
to challenge the school's operating perspective, are treated only
ritualistically at PTA meetings, open houses, school plays, and
athletic contests. Their point of view, like the child's, is seldom
taken seriously. They are too incompetent. Taking them seriously
would force a shift in existing power arrangements in the school.

Mead's perspective proposes just the opposite view of
parents, children, and education. Education, he argued, is an
unfolding, social process wherein the child comes to see himself
in increasingly more complex ways. Education leads to self-

understanding and to the acquisition of the basic skills. This principle suggests that schools must be socially relevant. They must incorporate the social world of child and community into curriculum arrangements. Cultural diversity must be stressed. Alternative symbolic leaders must be presented, and these must come from realistic worlds of experience. (Setting an astronaut as a preferred "self-model" for seven-year-old males, as a current textbook does, can hardly be defined as realistic.) Problematic situations from the child's everyday world must be brought into the classroom. For example, Mead proposed in lectures, as early as 1908, that schools teach sex education to children.

Children and parents, then, must be seen as resources around which education is developed and presented. They must be taken seriously. This presupposes a close working relationship between home and school. Parents must take responsibility for their children's education. They can no longer afford to shift accountability to the schools. This simple principle suggests that ethnic studies programs should have been central features of schools at least fifty years ago. Schools exist to serve their surrounding communities, not bend those communities to their perspective.

Redefining Schools

If this reciprocal service function is stressed, an important implication follows. Schools should educate children in ways that permit them to be contributing members in their chosen worlds. Such basics as reading, writing, and counting will never be avoided. But their instruction can be made relevant within the worlds the child most directly experiences. This suggests, initially at least, that black and brown children be taught to respect their separate cultural heritages. Second, it suggests that they will probably learn best with materials drawn from those cultures. Third, it suggests that they must be presented with self-models who know, respect, and come from those cultures.

To the extent that schools and teachers serve as referent points for the child's self-conception, it can be argued that it is not the minority student who must change but, instead, that it is the white middle-class child who must be exposed to alternative cultural perspectives. Minority teachers must be made integral components of all phases of the educational act.

Mead's perspective suggests, as I have attempted to elaborate, that the classroom is an interactive world. Research by Roger G. Barker and Paul V. Gump on big schools and little schools supports this position, and findings suggest an additional set of proposals. Briefly, they learned that as class and school size increases, student satisfaction decreases. Teaching becomes more mechanized, students become more irrelevant, and activities not related to learning attain greater importance—social clubs, for example. In short, in big schools students are redundant.

Classroom size and school size must be evaluated from this perspective. If schools exist to serve children and their parents, then large schools are dysfunctional. They are knowledge factories, not places of learning or self-development. Culturally heterogeneous, small-sized classes must be experimented with. Students must have opportunities to know their teachers in personal, not institutional, terms. Students must be taught to take one another seriously, not competitively. Small, ecologically intimate surroundings have a greater likelihood of promoting these arrangements than do large-scale, bureaucratically organized classes.

At present, standardized, state- and nation-certified tests are given students to assess their psychological, emotional, intellectual, and social development. Two problems restrict the effectiveness of these methods, however. With few exceptions, they have been standardized on white middle-class populations. Second, they are the only measurement techniques routinely employed.

A number of proposals follow from these problems. First, open-ended tests that permit the child to express his or her perspective must be developed. These tests, such as the "Who Am I?" question, would be given to students to determine the major contours of their self-conceptions. With this information in hand, teachers would be in a better position to tailor teaching programs to a child's specific needs, definitions, intentions, and goals.

Second, tests such as "Who Is Important to You?" could be given students on a regular basis to determine who their significant others are. It is near axiomatic that derogation of the people most important to one leads to alienation from the setting and spokesman doing the derogation. Teachers must learn to respect and present in respectful terms those persons most important to the child.

A third methodological proposal directs observers to link a student's utterances, wishes, and self-images to his or her day-to-day conduct. Written test scores often fail to reflect what persons really take into account and value. In many social settings, verbal ability, athletic skills, hustling aptitudes, money, and even physical attractiveness serve as significant status locators. IQ tests often do not. Furthermore, a person's score on a test may not accurately reflect his ability to handle problematic situations, which is surely a goal of education. Observations of conduct (behavior) in concrete settings can provide the needed leads in this direction.

Methodological Implications

A critic of these proposals might remark that such measures are not standardized, that their validity is questionable, that they cannot be administered nationally, and that they have questionable degrees of reliability. In response, I would cite the ability of Roger Barker (1968) and colleagues to execute such observations over time with high reliability (.80 to .98 for many measures). But, more to the point, I would argue that conventional tests are simply not working and that it is time to experiment with alternative techniques, perspectives, and theories.

This defense suggests that schools of education must begin to consider teaching their students the methodologies of participant observation, unobtrusive analysis, and life history construction. These softer methods have been the traditional province of sociologists and anthropologists. Members of these disciplines must consider offering cross-disciplinary courses in methodology, especially aimed for everyday practitioners in school settings. Graduate requirements for teaching credentials must also be reexamined, and greater efforts must be made to recruit and train minority students in these different approaches.

These proposals reflect a basic commitment. Schools should be organized so as to maximize a child's self-development, and they should permit maximum child-parent participation (see Joffe, 1977). It is evident that my discussion has not been limited to an analysis of compensatory education programs. This has been deliberate. It is my conviction that education, wherever it occurs, involves interactions between social selves. Taking the self as a point of departure, I have attempted to show that what happens to a preschool child is not unlike the moral experiences of a black or brown seventeen-year-old senior in high school. But most importantly, both should find themselves in schools that take them seriously and treat them with respect. Schools exist to serve children and the public. This charge must be taken seriously.

Bibliography

ABRAMSON, P. *Schools for Early Childhood*. New York: Educational Facilities Laboratories, 1970.

ALLPORT, G. *Pattern and Growth in Personality*. New York: Holt, Rinehart and Winston, 1961.

ANDERSON, J. E. *"The Theory of Early Childhood Education."* In N. B. Henry (Ed.), *46th Yearbook of the National Society for the Study of Education*. Chicago: University of Chicago Press, 1947.

ARIÈS, P. *Centuries of Childhood*. New York: Knopf, 1962.

AVEDON, E. M., and SUTTON-SMITH, B. (Eds.). *The Study of Games*. New York: Wiley, 1971.

BACK, K. W. "The Will-Informed Informant." In R. N. Adams and J. D. Preiss (Eds.), *Human Organization Research*. Homewood, Ill.: Dorsey, 1960.

BAIN, R. "The Self-and-Other Words of a Child." *American Journal of Sociology*, 1936, *41*, 767–775.

BALDWIN, B. T. "Administration and Scope of the Iowa Child Welfare Research Station." Bulletin No. 10. Iowa City: University of Iowa, 1920.

BALDWIN, J. M. *Mental Development and the Child and the Race*. New York: Macmillan, 1895.

BALDWIN, J. M. *Social and Ethical Interpretations in Mental Development*. New York: Macmillan, 1897.

BALDWIN, J. M. *History of Psychology*. New York: Putnam, 1913.

BALL, D. "Toward a Sociology of Toys: Inanimate Objects, Socialization, and the Demography of the Doll World." *Sociological Quarterly*, 1967, *8*, 447–458.

BANDURA, A. "Social-Learning Theory of Identificatory Processes." In D. A. Goslin (Ed.), *Handbook of Socialization Theory and Research*. Chicago: Rand McNally, 1969.

BARKER, R. G. *Ecological Psychology*. Stanford, Calif.: Stanford University Press, 1968.

BARKER, R. G., and GUMP, P. V. *Big School, Small School*. Stanford, Calif.: Stanford University Press, 1964.

BECKER, H. S. "Whose Side Are We On?" *Social Problems*, 1967, *14*, 239–248.

BECKER, H. S. "Practitioners of Vice and Crime." In R. W. Habenstein (Ed.), *Pathways to Data*. Chicago: Aldine, 1970a.

BECKER, H. S. *Sociological Work*. Chicago: Aldine, 1970b.

BECKER, H. S. and OTHERS. *Boys in White: Student Culture in Medical School*. Chicago: University of Chicago Press, 1961.

BERLYNE, D. E. *Conflict, Arousal and Curiosity*. New York: McGraw-Hill, 1960.

BERLYNE, D. E. "Laughter, Humor, and Play." In G. Lindzey and E. Aronson (Eds.), *The Handbook of Social Psychology*. (2nd ed.) Reading, Mass.: Addison-Wesley, 1969.

BERNARD, L. L. *An Introduction to Social Psychology*. New York: Holt, Rinehart and Winston, 1926.

BERNSTEIN, B. "Elaborated and Restricted Codes: Their Social Origins and Some Consequences." *American Anthropologist*, 1964, *66*, 55–69.

BERNSTEIN, B. "Class and Pedagogies: Visible and Invisible." In

B. Bernstein, *Class, Codes, and Control*. Vol. 3. London: Routledge & Kegan Paul, 1973.

BIRDWHISTELL, R. L. *Kinesics and Context*. Philadelphia: University of Pennsylvania Press, 1970.

BLUMENTHAL, A. L. (Ed.). *Language and Psychology: Historical Aspects of Psycholinguistics*. New York: Wiley, 1970.

BLUMER, H. "Society as Symbolic Interaction." In A. M. Rose (Ed.), *Human Behavior and Social Process*. Boston: Houghton Mifflin, 1962.

BLUMER, H. *Symbolic Interactionism*. Englewood Cliffs, N. J.: Prentice-Hall, 1969.

BOSSARD, J. H. S., and BOLL, E. S. *The Sociology of Child Development*. New York: Harper & Row, 1948.

BOWLBY, J. *Child Care and the Growth of Love*. Baltimore, Md.: Penguin Books, 1953.

BREDE, R. "The Policing of Juveniles in Chicago." Unpublished doctoral dissertation, University of Illinois, 1971.

BRETT, G. S. *A History of Psychology*. New York: Norton, 1912.

BRONFENBRENNER, U. *Two Worlds of Childhood: US and USSR*. New York: Russell Sage, 1970.

BROWN, R. *Words and Things*. New York: Free Press, 1958.

BROWN, R. "The Acquisition of Language." In D. M. Rioch and E. A. Weinstein (Eds.), *Disorders of Communication: Proceedings of the Association for Research in Nervous and Mental Disease*. Vol. 42. Baltimore, Md.: Williams and Wilkins, 1964.

BROWN, R. *Social Psychology*. New York: Free Press, 1965.

BROWN, R. *Psycholinguistics: Selected Papers by Roger Brown*. New York: Free Press, 1970.

BROWN, R. *A First Language*. New York: Free Press, 1971.

BROWN, R., and BELLUGI, U. "Three Processes in the Child's Acquision of Syntax." *Harvard Educational Review*, 1964, *34*, 133–151.

BROWN, R., and FORD, M. "Address and American English." *Journal of Abnormal and Social Psychology*, 1961, *62*, 375–385.

BROWN, R., and FRASER, C. "The Acquisition of Syntax." In C. N.

Cofer and B. S. Musgrave (Eds.), *Verbal Behavior and Learning*. New York: McGraw-Hill, 1963.

BROWN, R., FRASER, C., and BELLUGI, U. "Explorations in Grammar Evaluation." In U. Bellugi and R. Brown (Eds.), *The Acquisition of Language: Monographs of the Society for Research in Child Development, 29,* 1. Chicago: University of Chicago Press, 1964.

CAILLOIS, R. *Man, Play, and Games.* (M. Barash, Trans.) New York: Free Press, 1961. (French edition, *Les Jeux et les Hommes.* Paris: Librairie Gallimard, 1958.)

CAMPBELL, D. T. "A Phenomenology of the Other One: Corrigible, Hypothetical and Critical." In T. Mischel (Ed.), *Human Action: Conceptual and Empirical Issues.* New York: Academic Press, 1969.

CATTON, W. R., JR. *From Animistic to Naturalistic Sociology.* New York: McGraw-Hill, 1966.

CAVAN, S. *Liquor License: An Ethnography of Bar Behavior.* Chicago: Aldine, 1966.

CHOMSKY, N. "A Review of *Verbal Behavior* by B. F. Skinner." *Language,* 1959, *35,* 26–58.

CHOMSKY, N. *Current Issues in Linguistic Theory.* The Hague: Moulton, 1964.

CHOMSKY, N. *Aspects of the Theory of Syntax.* Cambridge, Mass.: M.I.T. Press, 1965.

CHOMSKY, N. *Cartesian Linguistics: A Chapter in the History of Rationalistic Thought.* New York: Harper & Row, 1966.

CHOMSKY, N. *Language and Mind.* New York: Harcourt Brace Jovanovich, 1968.

CHOMSKY, N. *Syntactic Structures.* The Hague: Mouton, 1975.

CICOUREL, A. V. "The Acquisition of Social Structure: Toward a Developmental Sociology of Language and Meaning." In J. D. Douglas (Ed.), *Understanding Everyday Life.* Chicago: Aldine, 1970.

CICOUREL, A. V. *Cognitive Sociology.* New York: Free Press, 1974.

CICOUREL, A. V., and BOESE, R. "Sign Language Acquisition and the Teaching of Deaf Children." In D. Hymes, C. Cazden, and V. Johns (Eds.), *The Functions of Language:*

An Anthropological and Psychological Approach. New York: Teachers College Press, 1975.

CLAUSEN, J. (Ed.). *Socialization and Society.* Boston: Little, Brown, 1968.

COOK, K. M., and REYNOLDS, F. E. *The Education of Native and Minority Groups: A Bibliography, 1932–1934.* Pamphlet No. 63. Washington, D.C.: U.S. Government Printing Office, 1935.

COOLEY, C. H. "A Study of the Early Use of Self-Words by a Child." *Psychological Review,* 1908, *15,* 339–357.

COOLEY, C. H. *Human Nature and the Social Order.* New York: Scribner's, 1922.

COOLEY, C. H. "The Roots of Social Knowledge." *American Journal of Sociology,* 1926, *32,* 59–79.

COTTRELL, L. S. "Interpersonal Interaction and the Development of Self." In D. A. Goslin (Ed.), *Handbook of Socialization Theory and Research.* Chicago: Rand McNally, 1969.

COTTRELL, L. S., and DYMOND, R. F. "The Empathetic Responses: A Neglected Field for Research." *Psychiatry,* 1949, *12,* 355–359.

COUCH, C. J. "Dimensions of Association in Collective Behavior Episodes." *Sociometry,* 1970, *33,* 457–471.

COUTU, W. "Role Playing versus Role Taking: An Appeal for Clarification." *American Sociological Review,* 1951, *16,* 180–187.

DALTON, M. "Preconceptions and Methods in Men Who Manage." In P. E. Hammond (Ed.), *Sociologists at Work.* New York: Basic Books, 1964.

DARWIN, C. R. "Biographical Sketch of an Infant." *Mind,* 1877, *7,* 285–294.

DAVIS, F. "Deviance Disavowal: The Management of Strained Interaction by the Visibly Handicapped." *Social Problems,* 1961, *9,* 120–132.

DAVIS, M. *Intimate Relations.* New York: Free Press, 1973.

DEALEY, J. Q. and OTHERS. "Symposium on the Purposes of Historical Instruction in the 7th and 8th Grades." In G. M. Whipple (Ed.), *17th Yearbook of the National Society* for the Scientific Study of Education. Bloomington, Ill.: Public School Publishing, 1918.

DENZIN, N. K. The Research Act. Chicago: Aldine, 1970a.

DENZIN, N. K. "Rules of Conduct and the Study of Deviant Behavior: Some Notes on the Social Relationship." In G. J. McCall and others, Social Relationships. Chicago: Aldine, 1970b.

DENZIN, N. K. "Socialization as Interaction." Address given as the annual W. I. Thomas Lecture, Department of Sociology, University of Tennessee, Knoxville, April 6, 1971.

DEUTSCHER, I. "Words and Deeds." Social Problems, 1966, 13, 235–254.

DEUTSCHER, I. "Language, Methodology, and the Sociologist." Sociological Focus, 1969–1970, 3, 1–12.

DEVRIES, R. "The Development of Role Taking as Reflected by Behavior of Bright, Average, and Retarded Children in a Social Guessing Game." Child Development, 1970, 41, 759–770.

DEWEY, J. "The Relation of Theory to Practice in Education." In C. A. McMurry (Ed.), 3rd Yearbook of the National Society for the Scientific Study of Education. Bloomington, Ill.: Public School Publishing, 1904.

DEWEY, J. The Child and the Curricula. Chicago: University of Chicago Press, 1906.

DOBY, J. T. "Man, the Species and the Individual: A Sociological Perspective." Social Forces, 1970, 49, 1–15.

DOUGLAS, J. D. (Ed.). Understanding Everyday Life. Chicago: Aldine, 1970.

DRIETZEL, H. P. "Introduction: Childhood and Socialization." In H. P. Dreitzel (Ed.), Sociology No. 5: Childhood and Socialization. Vol. 5. New York: Macmillan, 1973.

ELKIND, D. "Children's Conceptualization of Brother and Sister: Piaget Replication Study V." Journal of Genetic Psychology, 1962, 100, 129–136.

ELKINS, S. The Child and Society. New York: Random House, 1960.

ELLIS, M. J. Why People Play. Englewood Cliffs, N.J.: Prentice-Hall, 1973.

ERIKSON, E. H. *Childhood and Society.* New York: Norton, 1950.

ERVIN-TRIPP, S. "An Analysis of the Interaction of Language, Topic and Listener." *American Anthropologist,* 1964, *66,* 86–102.

ERVIN-TRIPP, S. "Research on Children's Acquistion of Communicative Competence." Social Science Research Council Items, 1969a, *23,* 22–26.

ERVIN-TRIPP, S. "Social Dialects in Developmental Sociolinguistics." Washington, D.C.: Center for Applied Linguistics, 1969b.

ESCALONA, S. "Play and Substitute Satisfaction." In R. G. Baker and others (Eds.), *Child Behavior and Development.* New York: McGraw-Hill, 1943.

FARIS, E. "The Retrospective Act and Education." *Journal of Educational Sociology,* 1940, *14,* 79–91.

FIRTH, R. "On Sociological Linguistics." In D. Hymes (Ed.), *Language in Culture and Society.* New York: Harper & Row, 1964.

FISHMAN, J. A. "A Systemization of the Whorfian Hypothesis." *Behavioral Science,* 1960, *5,* 323–339.

FLAVELL, J. H. *The Developmental Psychology of Jean Piaget.* Princeton, N.J.: Van Nostrand Reinhold, 1963.

FLAVELL, J. H., and OTHERS. *The Development of Role Taking and Communication Skills in Children.* New York: Wiley, 1968.

FRASER, C., BELLUGI, U., and BROWN, R. "Control of Grammar in Imitation, Comprehension and Production." *Journal of Verbal Learning and Verbal Behavior,* 1963, *2,* 121–135.

FREUD, S. "Beyond the Pleasure Principle." (J. Strachey, Trans.) In J. Strachey (Ed.), *The Standard Edition of the Complete Psychological Works of S. Freud, 1920–1922.* Vol. 18. London: Hogarth Press and the Institute of Psychoanalysis, 1959. (Originally published 1920–1922.)

FROEBEL, F. *Autobiography of Friedrich Froebel.* (E. Michaelis and H. K. Moore, Trans. and Annotations) Syracuse, N.Y.: Bardeen, 1889.

GARFINKEL, H. *Studies in Ethnomethodology*. Englewood Cliffs, N.J.: Prentice-Hall, 1967.

GESELL, A. *The Pre-School Child*. Boston: Houghton Mifflin, 1923.

GILMORE, J. B. "Play: A Special Behavior." In R. E. Herron and B. Sutton-Smith (Eds.), *Child's Play*. New York: Wiley, 1971.

GLASER, B. G., and STRAUSS, A. "Awareness Contexts and Social Interaction." *American Sociological Review*, 1964, *29*, 669–679.

GLASER, B. G., and STRAUSS, A. *The Discovery of Grounded Theory*. Chicago: Aldine, 1967.

GLASER, B. G., and STRAUSS, A. *Status Passage*. Chicago: Aldine, 1970.

GOFFMAN, E. "The Nature of Deference and Demeanor." *American Anthropologist*, 1956, *58*, 473–502.

GOFFMAN, E. *Encounters*. Indianapolis: Bobbs-Merrill, 1961a.

GOFFMAN, E. *Asylums*. New York, Doubleday, 1961b.

GOFFMAN, E. *Behavior in Public Places*. New York: Free Press, 1963.

GOFFMAN, E. "The Neglected Situation." *American Anthropologist*, 1964, *66*, 133–136.

GOFFMAN, E. *Interaction Ritual*. Chicago: Aldine, 1967.

GOFFMAN, E. *Relations in Public*. New York: Basic Books, 1971.

GOFFMAN, E. *Frame Analysis*. New York. Harper & Row, 1974.

GOODMAN, M. E. *The Culture of Childhood*. New York: Teachers College Press, 1970.

GOODY, J., and WATT, I. "The Consequences of Literacy." *Comparative Studies in Society and History*, 1962–1963, *5*, 304–326, 332–345.

GREENFIELD, P. M., and BRUNER, J. S. "Culture and Cognitive Growth." In D. A. Goslin (Ed.), *Handbook of Socialization Theory and Research*. Chicago: Rand McNally, 1969.

GRIMSHAW, A. "Language as Obstacle and as Data in Sociological Research." *Social Science Research Council Items*, 1969a, *23*, 17–21.

GRIMSHAW, A. "Sociolinguistics and the Sociologist." *American Sociologist*, 1969b, *4*, 312–321.

GROOS, K. *The Play of Man*. (E. L. Baldwin, Trans.) New York: Appleton-Century-Crofts, 1901.

GROSS, E., and STONE, G. "Embarrassment and the Analysis of Role Requirements." *American Journal of Sociology*, 1963, *70*, 1–15.

GUDSCHINSKY, S. C. *How to Learn an Unwritten Language*. New York: Holt, Rinehart and Winston, 1967.

GULICK, L. "Interest in Relation to Muscular Exercise." *American Physical Education Review*, 1902, *7*, 57–65.

GUMPERZ, "Language and Communication." *The Annals of the American Academy of Political and Social Sciences*, 1967, *373*, 219–231.

HABENSTEIN, R. W. "Introduction: The Pathways to Data." In R. W. Habenstein (Ed.), *Pathways to Data*. Chicago: Aldine, 1970.

HALL, G. S. *Adolescence*. New York: Appleton-Century-Crofts, 1904.

HALL, G. S. *Life and Confessions of a Psychologist*. New York: Appleton-Century-Crofts, 1923.

HERRON, R. E., and SUTTON-SMITH, B. (Eds.). *Child's Play*. New York: Wiley, 1971.

HERTZLER, J. O. *A Sociology of Language*. New York: Random House, 1965.

HOLT, J. *How Children Fail*. New York: Dell, 1970.

HUIZINGA, J. *Homo Ludens: A Study of the Play Element in Culture*. New York: Pantheon, 1939.

HUTT, S. J., and HUTT, C. *Direct Observation and Measurement of Behavior*. Springfield, Ill.: Thomas, 1970.

HYMES, D. (Ed.). *Language in Culture and Society*. New York: Harper & Row, 1964.

ISAACS, S. *Social Development in Young Children: A Study of Beginnings*. London: Routledge & Kegan Paul, 1933.

JAMES, W. *Psychology: The Briefer Course*. New York: Holt, Rinehart and Winston, 1910.

JENKINS, J. J. "The Acquisition of Language." In D. A. Goslin

(Ed.), *Handbook of Socialization Theory and Research*. Chicago: Rand McNally, 1969.

JOFFE, C. "Taking Little Children Seriously." In N. K. Denzin (Ed.), *Children and Their Caretakers*. New York: Dutton, 1973.

JOFFE, C. *The Friendly Intruders*. Berkeley: University of California Press, 1977.

JOHNSON, H. M. "The Education of the Nursery School Child." In *Proceedings of the 64th Annual Meeting of the National Education Association of the U.S.* Washington, D.C.: National Education Association, 1926.

KAPLAN, A. *The Conduct of Inquiry*. San Francisco: Chandler, 1964.

KARPF, F. B. *American Social Psychology*. New York: McGraw-Hill, 1932.

KENDON, F. *The Small Years*. London: Cambridge University Press, 1930.

KOHLBERG, L. "Early Education: A Cognitive-Developmental View." *Child Development*, 1968, *39*, 1013–1062.

KOHLBERG, L. "Stage and Sequence: The Cognitive-Developmental Approach to Socialization." In D. A. Goslin (Ed.), *Handbook of Socialization Research and Theory*. Chicago: Rand McNally, 1969.

KUHN, M. H. "Factors in Personality: Sociocultural Determinants as Seen Through the Amish." In F. L. K. Hsu (Ed.), *Aspects of Culture and Personality*. New York: Abelard-Schuman, 1954.

KUHN, M. H. "The Interview and the Professional Relationship." In A. M. Rose (Ed.), *Human Behavior and Social Processes*. Boston: Houghton Mifflin, 1962.

KUHN, M. H. "The Reference Group Reconsidered." *Sociological Quarterly*, 1964, *5*, 5–21.

LADNER, J. A. *Tomorrow's Tomorrow*. New York: Doubleday, 1971.

LASHLEY, K. S. "The Problem of Serial Order in Behavior." In L. A. Jeffress (Ed.), *Cerebral Mechanisms in Behavior*. New York: Wiley, 1961.

LAZERSON, M. "The Historical Antecedents of Early Childhood Education." In I. J. Gordon (Ed.), *The 71st Yearbook of the National Society for the Study of Education, Part 2.* Chicago: University of Chicago Press, 1972.

LEOPOLD, R. W., and LINK, A. S. (Eds.). *Problems in American History.* Englewood Cliffs, N.J.: Prentice-Hall, 1952.

LEWIS, M. M. *Language, Thought, and Personality in Infancy and Childhood.* London: Harrap, 1963.

LIEBERSON, S. (Ed.). "Exploration of Sociolinguistics." *Sociological Inquiry,* 1966, *36,* entire issue.

LIEBERSON, S. *Language and Ethnic Relations in Canada.* New York: Wiley, 1970.

LINDESMITH, A. R. *Opiate Addiction.* Bloomington, Ind.: Principia, 1947.

LINDESMITH, A. R., STRAUSS, A., and DENZIN, N. K. *Social Psychology.* (5th ed.) New York: Praeger, 1978.

LOFLAND, J. *Analyzing Social Settings.* Belmont, Calif.: Wadsworth, 1971.

LUESCHEN, G. (Ed.). *The Cross-Cultural Analysis of Sport and Games.* Champaign, Ill.: Stipes, 1970.

LUESCHEN, G., and OTHERS. "Family Organization, Interaction and Ritual: A Cross-Cultural Study in Bulgaria, Finland, Germany, and Ireland." *Journal of Marriage and the Family,* 1971, *33,* 228–234.

LURIA, A. R. *Higher Cortical Functions in Man.* (B. Haigh, Trans.) New York: Basic Books, 1966.

MC CANDLESS, B. R. "Childhood Socialization." In D. A. Goslin (Ed.), *Handbook of Socialization Theory and Research.* Chicago: Rand McNally, 1969.

MC DOUGALL, W. *Introduction to Social Psychology.* Boston: Luce, 1908.

MC DOUGALL, W. *Outline of Psychology.* New York: Scribner's, 1923.

MC NEILL, D. "The Creation of Language." *Discovery,* 1966a, *27,* 34–38.

MC NEILL, D. "The Development of Language." In F. Smith and G. A. Miller (Eds.), *The Genesis of Language: A Psy-*

cholinguistic Approach. Cambridge, Mass.: M.I.T. Press, 1966b.

MC PHAIL, C., and TUCKER, C. W. "The Classification and Ordering of Responses to the Question 'Who Am I?' " *Sociological Quarterly*, 1972.

MANNING, P. K. "Talking and Becoming: A View of Organizational Socialization." In J. D. Douglas (Ed.), *Understanding Everyday Life*. Chicago: Aldine, 1970.

MARKEY, J. F. *The Symbolic Process and Its Integration in Children*. New York: Harcourt Brace Jovanovich, 1928.

MATZA, D. *Becoming Deviant*. Englewood Cliffs, N.J.: Prentice-Hall, 1969.

MEAD, G. H. "A Behavioristic Account of the Significant Symbol." *Journal of Philosophy*, 1922, *19*, 157–163.

MEAD, G. H. "The Genesis of the Self and Social Control." *International Journal of Ethics*, 1924–1925, *35*, 251–277.

MEAD, G. H. *Mind, Self, and Society*. Chicago: University of Chicago Press, 1934.

MEAD, G. H. *The Philosophy of the Act*. Chicago: University of Chicago Press, 1938.

MEAD, M., and WOLFENSTEIN, M. (Eds.). *Childhood in Contemporary Cultures*. Chicago: University of Chicago Press, 1955.

MENNINGER, W. C. "Recreation and Mental Health." In B. Hill (Ed.), *Recreation and Psychiatry*. New York: National Recreation Association, 1960.

MERTON, R. K. *Social Theory and Social Structure*. (2nd ed.) New York: Free Press, 1957.

MICOSSI, A. L. "Conversion to Women's Lib." *Trans-Action*, 1970, *8*, 82–90.

MILLER, G. A., and MC NEILL, D. "Psycholinguistics." In G. Lindsey and E. Aronson (Eds.), *The Handbook of Social Psychology*. (2nd ed.) Vol. 3. Reading, Mass.: Addison-Wesley, 1969.

MILLER, P. H., KESSEL, F. S., and FLAVELL, J. H. "Thinking About People Thinking About People Thinking About . . . : A Study of Social Cognitive Development." *Child Development*, 1970, *41*, 613–623.

MILLER, S. A., SHELTON, J., and FLAVELL, J. H. "A Test of Luria's Hypotheses Concerning the Development of Verbal Self-Regulation." *Child Development*, 1970, *41*, 651–665.

MILLS, C. W. *The Sociological Imagination*. New York: Oxford University Press, 1959.

MILNE, A. A. *It's Too Late Now: The Autobiography of a Writer*. London: Methuen, 1939.

MILNE, A. A. *Now We Are Six*. New York: Dell, 1974.

MOOREHEAD, A. H., and MOTT-SMITH, G. *Hoyle's Rules of Games: Descriptions of Indoor Games of Skill and Chance with Advice on Skillful Play*. New York: New American Library of World Literature, 1958.

MURPHY, L. *Social Behavior and Child Personality*. New York: Columbia University Press, 1937.

NICE, M. M. "A Child Who Would Not Talk." *Journal of Genetic Psychology*, 1925, *32*, 105–142.

NIMKOFF, M. F. *The Child*. Philadelphia: Lippincott, 1934.

OGG, F. A. *Research in the Humanistic and Social Sciences*. New York: Appleton-Century-Crofts, 1928.

OPIE, I., and OPIE, P. *The Lore and Language of Schoolchildren*. New York: Oxford University Press, 1959.

OPIE, I., and OPIE, P. *Children's Games in Street and Playground*. New York: Oxford University Press, 1969.

PARSONS, T. "The Position of Identity in the General Theory of Action." In C. Gordon and K. J. Gergen (Eds.), *The Self in Social Interaction*. New York: Wiley, 1968.

PARSONS, T., and BALES, R. F., in collaboration with J. Olds, M. Zelditch, Jr., and P. E. Slater. *Family, Socialization and Interaction Process*. New York: Free Press, 1955.

PARSONS, T., and SHILLS, E. (Ed.). *Toward a General Theory of Action*. Cambridge, Mass.: Harvard University Press, 1959.

PIAGET, J. *The Language and Thought of the Child*. New York: Harcourt Brace Jovanovich, 1926.

PIAGET, J. "Autobiography." In E. G. Boring (Ed.), *History of Psychology in Autobiography*. Vol. 4. Worcester, Mass.: Clark University Press, 1952.

PIAGET, J. *Play, Dreams and Imitation in Childhood.* New York: Norton, 1962.

PIAGET, J. *Six Psychological Studies.* (D. Elkind, Ed.) New York: Knopf, 1968.

PIAGET, J. *Structuralism.* (C. Maschler, Trans.) New York: Basic Books, 1970.

PIAGET, J., and INHELDER, B. *The Psychology of the Child.* (H. Weaver, Trans.) New York: Basic Books, 1969.

RAINWATER, L. *Behind Ghetto Walls.* Chicago: Aldine, 1971.

RHEINGOLD, H. L. "The Social and Socializing Infant." In D. Goslin (Ed.), *Handbook of Socialization Theory and Research.* Chicago: Rand McNally, 1969.

ROSSI, A. S. "Naming Children in Middle-Class Families." *American Sociological Review,* 1965, *30,* 499–513.

SALMON, L. M., "Some Principles in the Teaching of History." In C. A. McMurry (Ed.), *1st Yearbook of the National Society for the Scientific Study of Education.* Chicago: University of Chicago Press, 1902.

SALTIEL, J. "Daydreaming: An Interactionist Approach." Mimeographed. Urbana: Department of Sociology, University of Illinois, 1969.

SAPORA, A. V., and MITCHELL, E. D. *The Theory of Play and Recreation.* (3rd ed.) New York: Ronald Press, 1961.

SCHATZMAN, L., and STRAUSS, A. *Field Research: Strategies for a Natural Sociology.* Englewood Cliffs, N.J.: Prentice-Hall, 1973.

SCHULZ, D. A. *Coming up Black.* Englewood Cliffs, N.J.: Prentice-Hall, 1969.

SHIBUTANI, T. *Society and Personality.* Englewood Cliffs, N.J.: Prentice-Hall, 1961.

SHINN, M. *Biography of a Baby.* Boston: Houghton Mifflin, 1900.

SIMMEL, G. "Social Interaction as the Definition of the Group in Time and Space." Pp. 348–356 in R. E. Park and E. W. Burgess (Eds.), *Introduction to the Science of Sociology.* Chicago: University of Chicago Press, 1921.

SIMMEL, G. S. *The Sociology of Georg Simmel.* (K. Wolff, Trans.) New York: Free Press, 1950.

SINGER, J. L. *The Child's World of Make-Believe.* New York: Academic Press, 1973.

SKINNER, B. F. *Verbal Behavior.* New York: Appleton-Century-Crofts, 1957.

SLOBIN, D. I. *Psycholinguistics.* Glenview, Ill.: Scott, Foresman, 1971.

SMITH, M. E. "An Investigation of the Development of the Sentence and the Extent of Vocabulary in Young Children." *Studies in Child Development* No. 3–5. Iowa City, Iowa: University of Iowa, 1926.

SPEIER, M. "The Everyday World of the Child." In J. D. Douglas (Ed.), *Understanding Everyday Life.* Chicago: Aldine, 1970.

SPOCK, B. *Baby and Child Care.* New York: Simon & Schuster, 1970.

STARK, R. *Police Riots.* Belmont, Calif.: Wadsworth, 1973.

STECHER, L. I. *The Psychology of the Preschool Child.* New York: Appleton-Century-Crofts, 1927.

STONE, G. P. "Appearance and the Self." In A. M. Rose (Ed.), *Human Behavior and Social Processes.* Boston: Houghton Mifflin, 1962.

STONE, G. P. "The Play of Little Children." *Quest,* 1965, *4,* 23–31.

STONE, G. P. and FARBERMAN, H. A. (Eds.). *Social Psychology Through Symbolic Interaction.* Waltham, Mass.: Ginn-Blaisdell, 1970.

STONE, L. J., SMITH, H. T., and MURPHY, L. B. (Eds.). *The Competent Infant: Research and Commentary.* New York: Basic Books, 1973.

STRAUSS, A. *Mirrors and Masks.* San Francisco: Sociology Press, 1969. (Originally published by Free Press, 1959.)

STRAUSS, A., and GLASER, B. G. *Anguish: A Case Study of a Dying Trajectory.* San Francisco: Sociology Press, 1970.

SUDNOW, D. "Normal Crimes: Sociological Features of the Penal Code in a Public Defender Office." *Social Problems,* 1965, *12,* 255–276.

SULLIVAN, H. S. *The Interpersonal Theory of Psychiatry.* New York: Norton, 1953.

SUNLEY, R. "Early Nineteenth-Century American Literature on Child Rearing." In M. Mead and M. Wolfenstein (Eds.), *Childhood in Contemporary Cultures*. Chicago: University of Chicago Press, 1963.

SUTTER, A. G. "The World of the Righteous Dope Fiend." *Issues in Criminology*, 1966, *2*, 177–222.

SUTTLES, G. *The Social Order of the Slum*. Chicago: University of Chicago Press, 1968.

SUTTON-SMITH, B. "Piaget on Play: A Critique." *Psychological Review*, 1966, *73*, 104–110.

SWANSON, G. E. "Mead and Freud: Their Relevance for Social Psychology." *Sociometry*, 1961, *24*, 319–339.

SYKES, G., and MATZA, D. "Techniques of Neutralization: A Theory of Delinquency." *American Sociological Review*, 1959, *22*, 664–670.

TAINE, M. "On the Acquisition of Language by Children." *Mind*, 1877, *6*, 252–259.

THOM, D. A. "Habit Clinics for the Child of Preschool Age." Publication No. 135. Washington, D.C.: U.S. Government Printing Office, 1924.

THOMAS, W. I., and THOMAS, D. S. *The Child in America*. New York: Knopf, 1928.

THORNDIKE, E. L. "Measurement in Education." In G. M. Whipple (Ed.), *21st Yearbook of the National Society for the Study of Education*. Bloomington, Ill.: Public School Publishing, 1922.

THRASHER, F. M. *The Gang*. Chicago: University of Chicago Press, 1963. (Originally published 1927.)

TURNER, R. "Words, Utterances, and Activities." In J. D. Douglas (Ed.), *Understanding Everyday Life*. Chicago: Aldine, 1970.

TURNER, R. H. "Role Taking, Role Standpoint, and Reference Group Behavior." *American Journal of Sociology*, 1956, *6*, 316–328.

TURNER, R. H. "The Self-Conception in Social Interaction." In G. Gordon and K. J. Gergen (Eds.), *The Self in Social Interaction*. New York: Wiley, 1968.

TURNER, R. H. *Family Interaction.* New York: Wiley, 1970.

VON RAFFLER-ENGLE, W. "The LAD, Our Underlying Unconscious, and More On 'Felt Sets.'" *Language Sciences,* 1970 (December), 15–18.

VYGOTSKY, L. *Thought and Language.* Cambridge, Mass.: M.I.T. Press, 1962. (Originally published 1934.)

WALLER, W. *The Sociology of Teaching.* New York: Wiley, 1965. (Originally published 1937.)

WEBB, E. J., and OTHERS. *Unobtrusive Measures: Non-Reactive Research in the Social Sciences.* Chicago: Rand McNally, 1964.

WHIPPLE, G. M. (Ed.). *28th Yearbook of the National Society for the Study of Education.* Bloomington, Ill.: Public School Publishing, 1929.

WHYTE, W. F. *Street Corner Society.* (2nd ed.) Chicago: University of Chicago Press, 1955.

WIEDER, D. L. "On Meaning by Rule." In J. D. Douglas (Ed.), *Understanding Everyday Life.* Chicago: Aldine, 1970.

WILLEMS, E. P., and RAUSCH, H. L. (Eds.). *Naturalistic Viewpoints in Psychological Research.* New York: Holt, Rinehart and Winston, 1969.

WOLFENSTEIN, M. *Children's Humor.* New York: Free Press, 1954.

WOLFENSTEIN, M. "Children's Humor: Sex, Names, and Double Meanings." In T. Talbot (Ed.), *The World of the Child.* New York: Anchor Books, 1968.

WRIGHT, H. F. *Recording and Analyzing Child Behavior.* New York: Harper & Row, 1962.

ZIGLER, E., and CHILD, I. L. "Socialization." In G. Lindzey and E. Aronson (Eds.), *The Handbook of Social Psychology.* (2nd ed.) Vol. 3. Reading, Mass.: Addison-Wesley, 1969.

ZIMMERMAN, D. H. "The Practicalities of Rule Use." In J. D. Douglas (Ed.), *Understanding Everyday Life.* Chicago: Aldine, 1970.

Index